K.I.S.S.

The Only Guides You'll Ever Need!

THIS SERIES IS YOUR TRUSTED GUIDE through all of life's stages and situations. Want to learn how to surf the Internet or care for your new dog? Or maybe you'd like to become a wine connoisseur or an expert gardener? The solution is simple: just pick up a K.I.S.S. Guide and turn to the first page.

Expert authors will walk you through the subject from start to finish, using simple blocks of knowledge to build your skills one step at a time. Build upon these learning blocks and, by the end of the book, you'll be an expert yourself! Or, if you are familiar with the topic but want to learn more, it's easy to dive in and pick up where you left off.

The K.I.S.S. Guides deliver what they promise: simple access to all the information you'll need on one subject. Other titles you might want to check out include: Gardening, the Internet, Pregnancy, Astrology, Weight Loss, and many more to come.

GUIDE TO

Selling

KEN LLOYD, Ph.D.

Foreword by Robert Heller

A Dorling Kindersley Book

Dorling Kindersley

LONDON, NEW YORK, SYDNEY, DELHI, PARIS,
MUNICH, AND JOHANNESBURG

Dorling Kindersley Limited

Project Editor David Tombesi-Walton
Project Art Editor Simon Murrell

Managing Editor Maxine Lewis
Managing Art Editor Heather McCarry
Category Publisher Mary Thompson

Jacket Designer Neal Cobourne
Picture Researchers Melanie Simmonds, Marcus Scott
Production Heather Hughes

Dorling Kindersley Publishing, Inc.

Category Publisher LaVonne Carlson
Senior Editor Jennifer Williams
Editor Ruth Strother

Produced for Dorling Kindersley by **Cooling Brown**
9–11 High Street, Hampton,
Middlesex TW12 2SA

Creative Director Arthur Brown
Art Editor Pauline Clarke
Senior Editor Amanda Lebentz
Editor Helen Ridge

First published in Great Britain in 2001 by
Dorling Kindersley Limited,
9 Henrietta Street,
Covent Garden, London WC2E 8PS

2 4 6 8 10 9 7 5 3 1

A CIP catalogue record for this book is available from the British Library

ISBN 0 7513 1244 4

Colour reproduction by ColourScan, Singapore
Printed and bound by Printer Industria Grafica, S.A., Barcelona, Spain

For our complete catalogue visit

www.dk.com

Contents at a Glance

CONTENTS

PART ONE *The World of Selling*

CHAPTER 1   *Is Selling Right for You?*   22

CHAPTER 2   *Getting the Right Sales Job*   36

PART TWO Successful Sales Relationships

PART THREE The Key Components

PART FOUR Looking Back

PART FIVE Looking Forward

APPENDICES

Foreword

THE ABILITY TO SELL is one of those talents that people believe to be innate, like having red hair. They are wrong. You can teach anyone to sell, and sell brilliantly. Even instinctive salespeople can greatly improve their selling by learning and practice. That's why sales managers easily lead other categories of management in time and trouble spent training their front-line staff. That's also why Ken Lloyd's excellent guide is so obviously powerful and valuable to anybody who ever has to sell – and that means everybody.

The idea that salesmen and saleswomen are born, not made, is attractive for very negative reasons. Selling has some long-lasting unfavourable associations. It's not just a question of high pressure and low ethics, feet in the door, and dud offers. The deeper reason is that people are frightened of selling and avoid it, largely because they shy away from being rejected, and they jump at the handy excuse of being "no good at selling". Also, many consider selling to be socially inferior. "Marketing" sounds much better to management ears – even though marketing without selling is worse than eggs without bacon.

The marketing myth is that if you supply the right goods to the right customers at the right time, in the right way, and at the right price, the goods or services will sell themselves. Business is seldom that easy. In a competitive world – and competition is getting tougher by the minute – the customer faces many "right" alternatives. The choice will be swayed in your company's favour by effective selling that arouses the customer's interest, creates desire for what you are selling, and persuades the good prospect to become a happy purchaser.

One of Ken Lloyd's many strengths is his prime emphasis on the selling that must be done before a client is ever faced. Salespeople must sell their talents to the best available employer – that is a sales job like any other. Even before this sale, they must sell the job to themselves, developing the conviction that the work involved will meet their carefully defined and ambitious goals, laying down what they must learn and practise for that conviction to be translated into success, and planning how to set about the task.

Selling plays a fundamental role throughout your business life, from selling yourself as the best candidate to selling your projects and ideas – and the self-development and other training described in this guide are indispensable to putting yourself across to any audience. The manager must also be a convincing salesperson for the company, good at making the case for its strengths, and expert at building and sustaining really strong customer relationships. Any line drawn between being good at selling and effective as a manager is thus entirely artificial.

The customer is becoming more and more powerful in relation to the supplier. This explains the strenuous efforts of companies to achieve genuine customer focus – starting with what the customers want and working back through their own processes to satisfy those wants with the greatest possible speed, quality, and efficiency. Companies will never achieve this ideal unless they listen to their frontline experts on the customer – the sales teams.

Selling embodies the key tasks that companies must execute to succeed in modern conditions. Ken Lloyd vividly and practically sets out the essentials: putting the customers truly first, building trust in the company and what it sells, communicating inside and outside the business, and using developed skills of analysis and feedback to win continuous improvement in performance. More than any other group, salespeople are judged on measurable achievements. That's why effective selling, as taught so well in these pages, is so satisfying. You not only do well, but you can prove it, to yourself and others – which includes those satisfied customers.

Robert Heller

ROBERT HELLER

Introduction

IT WAS A COLD AND FOGGY December day in the Richmond District of San Francisco when Bobby Simon and I, two ambitious 11-year-olds, embarked on our first sales venture. We gathered pine branches from nearby Lincoln Park, borrowed some red ribbon and string from our mothers, and set out to create and sell Christmas wreaths. The weather was brisk, but sales were not. We could hardly get anyone even to open the door, and this meant that there was no way to live up to the old sales adage of getting one's foot in the door.

We decided to get some expert advice, so we went to my father, L.K. Lloyd, a pioneer in group insurance sales. He heard our woes and asked to see our sales presentation, starting with the ring of the doorbell. When we finished, he had one suggestion: "After you ring the doorbell, don't hover by the door. Take two steps back and watch what happens." Later that day, we did just that. It was a Christmas miracle. People opened their doors, and many opened their wallets as well.

That was the precise point when I realized that there is more to selling than ringing a doorbell and making a pitch. Some clear and simple sales advice can make all the difference in the world.

And that's exactly what I hope this book will do for you. Here is a step-by-step look at the sales process, starting at the very beginning. At each step along the way, I will be giving you some simple pointers, tips, and strategies to help you achieve sales success and the personal satisfaction that goes with it. Just as my father's advice opened many doors during that cold Christmas season, I hope that this book will literally and figuratively open many doors for you.

KEN LLOYD, PH.D.

Dedication
This book is dedicated to L.K. Lloyd
A great father, friend, businessman, and salesman
Thanks for the memory.

What's Inside?

THE INFORMATION IN the K.I.S.S. Guide to Selling *is arranged so you can grasp the basics of selling and successful sales relationships before moving on to perfecting your technique and advancing your career.*

PART ONE

In Part One, you're going to see that you already have more sales skills than you might have imagined. You'll learn about the different kinds of sales jobs that are available and how to land the one that's right for you. You'll also find out how to manage your time and set some plans and goals so that all of your sales activities are well organized.

PART TWO

It's hard to sell if you don't have customers, so Part Two is where you'll learn how to find them. You'll also see the best way to screen prospective customers and prepare yourself for a successful sales presentation. Since it is so important to build trust and rapport quickly, you'll be getting some step-by-step tips in this area, too.

PART THREE

In Part Three you'll be face-to-face with a prospect. To make a sale, you will need to understand what this potential customer really needs. This is where you will be provided with some powerful questioning strategies, along with some of the techniques that the great salespeople use to persuade, handle objections, and close a sale.

PART FOUR

With the sales presentation behind you, Part Four looks at what happened. This is where you review the session and prepare for your next one, which may call for more negotiating, a written proposal, or a presentation to a group. None of this will present a problem for you, because this part of the book gives you hands-on tools.

PART FIVE

In Part Five you'll be looking to the future. We go over the ways you can benefit from training, as well as the ways you can increase your chances of having safe, hassle-free, and successful business trips. We also enter the world of sales ethics, and then focus on how your sales experience and expertise can help you advance your career.

The Extras

TO KEEP THE PROCESS SIMPLE, *you'll find a number of boxes and symbols throughout the book. Check them out carefully, because they contain all sorts of information that can drive your sales skills to higher and higher levels. Here they are:*

Very Important Point

This symbol is used to emphasize extremely important sales information that you will need to know before you move to the next section.

Complete No-No

This is a loud and clear warning about something that you should not do in sales.

Getting Technical

There are some technical aspects to selling, and this is where I will spell out and clarify the details for you.

Inside Scoop

Here are some powerful suggestions and nuggets of sales information that are the result of years of experience in selling and sales research.

You are also going to find some little boxes with information that is interesting, useful, and very informative. And they can be plenty of fun, too.

Trivia...
Here are some fun facts and stories that will give you some slightly different insights into the world of selling.

DEFINITION
There is a unique language in selling, so when sales words and terms are used within the text, you'll find a clear explanation in a box on the same page.

INTERNET
www.dk.com

There is a tremendous amount of sales-related information and support available on the Internet, and I have listed some of the key sites that can help you in all of your sales-related activities. These sites are also listed at the back of the book.

PART ONE

SALES ACHIEVEMENT IS BUILT ON SOLID FOUNDATION

THE WORLD OF SELLING

THINK BACK TO THE GREATEST SALES presentation you have ever heard. Do you wonder if you could ever sell like that? Well, the fact is you can. But to build yourself into an outstanding salesperson, the first step is to get the foundation in place, and that's exactly where we'll start.

You're going to see that you've already had some *solid sales* experiences in your life, even if you weren't aware of them, so you simply need to transfer these skills into a real sales job. Of course, you'll need to know about the *different* kinds of sales jobs that are available and the best ways to land one that meets your needs. And when you get that job, you'll be *setting goals, planning,* and *managing time,* but there are simple ways to do this, particularly when you use some of the new high-tech options.

Chapter 1

Is Selling Right for You?

FOR MOST OF US, selling has a familiar ring because we have all sold something at one point or another. We also deal with salespeople practically every day, in our jobs, in shops, and in countless other settings. Can you remember your first sales experience? Perhaps it was working on a lemonade stand or selling biscuits. For most people, that first sales experience boiled down to being cute and asking for orders. However, over the years, as you will soon see, you have already done some major selling in several key areas of your life. Now you are about to take your selling skills to an entirely new level.

In this chapter...

✓ You are a salesperson

✓ Sales jobs galore

✓ The hits and myths of selling

✓ Something old, something new

THERE ARE ALL KINDS OF SALES JOBS, ANY NUMBER OF WHICH CAN BE JUST RIGHT FOR YOU

You are a salesperson

MANY PEOPLE WHO ARE ABOUT TO ENTER the sales field look at themselves and wonder if they have what it takes to be successful. They may not have sold much of anything in the past, or they may fear that they lack the necessary personality and people skills to be successful in selling. The problem is that many of these beliefs are based on major misconceptions.

The first steps in sales

Even if you have never held a sales job in your life, you have had sales experience. In fact, you sold the most important item that you possess. This may sound like some sort of sales trick, but it is not. If you want to see how you operated as a salesperson in the past, just think back to your most recent job interview. No matter what the position was, you were the salesperson and the interviewer was the *prospect*. The prospect needed labour, and that is precisely what you were selling.

> **DEFINITION**
>
> *A **prospect** is a potential customer. Prospects are prospective buyers of what you are selling, hence the name. Once the sale is consummated, they move from the realm of prospect to the realm of customer. Prospects are also referred to as leads or sales leads.*

When you were offered a job, it meant you had a successful sales transaction. You met with a prospect, helped the prospect understand why he or she needed what you had to offer, developed enough trust for the prospect to commit to paying for your product, and then you closed the sale and began delivering the goods and services as promised.

■ **Think back** *to your very first job. Perhaps you delivered newspapers or babysat for the neighbours' children? In getting that job, you clinched your first sale.*

Selling yourself

Having obtained a job, any job at all, you now know that you can sell. Whether you are going to be *selling* alligators or zebras in that job is incidental. You have already been successful in selling the most important part of any sales package: yourself. If a prospect is not buying you, he or she will not buy whatever else you may be selling.

The essence of selling is trust, and if you can build trust with a prospect, you can build a successful career in sales.

■ **Being offered a job** *means that you have successfully sold yourself and your skills. The next step as an employee is to build your sales skills to the highest level possible.*

Sales jobs galore

IT IS IMPORTANT TO UNDERSTAND that there is a broad range of sales jobs, from the most basic and structured of jobs all the way to high-level, fully autonomous, professional positions. A salesperson is the individual behind the counter who asks if you would like chips with your order. A salesperson is also the individual who tries to convince you that 10,000 acres of undeveloped desert will be the next property mecca. On the other hand, a salesperson might be the individual who successfully demonstrates to a team of endocrinologists how a new pump can greatly improve the quality of life for people with diabetes.

To find a place on the sales continuum that is the best for you, there are three places to look: the company, the position, and the mirror.

■ **A job in sales** *can be anything from a grocer selling produce in the local shop to a high-powered computer expert selling technology around the world. What's important is finding the right job for you.*

Checking out the company

Before you apply for any sales job, and definitely before an interview, you can take several steps to learn about a company and its products. For example, you can look in newspapers, magazines, and trade journals for articles on the company. It is also helpful to talk to friends and associates who have either worked for the company or had dealings with it.

You can also learn a good deal about a company on the Internet. You can go to a company's own web site, and you may also find web sites that some of the employees or former employees have established. Bear in mind, however, that many of these web sites should be viewed with a grain of salt.

You should have a clear idea of the company's reputation before accepting any sales job. A company's credibility can build a great deal of trust for you before you even meet a prospect. When a company has a tarnished reputation, your sales presentation will go nowhere until the prospect's concerns about the company have been allayed. You can certainly sell under these circumstances, but it is going to be more difficult. Even though a company may have instituted major positive changes in order to put its problems behind it, you need to have a clear understanding of this before accepting a job offer.

If a company has a dubious reputation, you are going to have a doubly difficult time in sales.

INTERNET

www.google.com

This search engine will rapidly take you to a company's site, if there is one, as well as to a broad array of sites that merely mention the company.

■ **Newspaper articles** *can be a good source of information when you are checking out prospective companies, particularly larger organizations.*

Checking out the job

You may be looking at a sales job, but prior to making any commitments you need to remember that there are sales jobs and there are sales jobs. For example, some are straight order-taking jobs, while others offer great variety and challenge. Some will pay you on straight commission, which means that you will be paid only when sales are consummated. In fact, some commission jobs will pay you only after the actual product that you sold has been installed and paid for by the customer.

All sorts of pay configurations are offered to salespeople, and too many salespeople take jobs without fully knowing how they are actually going to be paid. In spite of great pronouncements of six-figure incomes, never accept any sales job until you have a complete understanding of the pay system.

Another key area to check out before going to work for any company is the level of support it provides for the employees. Take a look at such elements as the training programme, size and potential of the territory, managerial guidance and coaching, travel reimbursement, and promotion opportunities.

■ **Investing in staff training** *is a sign that a company is committed to its employees. It also suggests that it actively encourages internal promotion.*

Sometimes companies provide salespeople with high potential territories, only to split the territory after the salesperson has developed it. This results in a cut in territory and earnings. To avoid this unkind cut, be sure to find out about the company's policies in this area before you get on board.

A look in the mirror

There may be any number of outstanding sales jobs out there, but this does not mean they are outstanding for you. For example, a job might be available at a well-established company that offers excellent stability, security, and a reliable customer base. For some salespeople, this job description might sound like nirvana, but for others it might not.

Having checked out a company and the sales job carefully, you should take a look at the kinds of factors you enjoy in a job and try to determine how close the match would be between your motivation and the sales position in question.

The best way to determine your work motivation is to make a list of the most satisfying work experiences you've had, and then look for themes that connect them. For some people, themes might point to independence, achievement, risk, and challenge, while for others camaraderie, security, and a laid-back atmosphere might be more satisfying. Don't simply list your work motivations, because you're likely to end up with little more than a wish list.

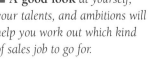

■ **A good look** *at yourself, your talents, and ambitions will help you work out which kind of sales job to go for.*

Is there an overlap?

The next step is to take what you know about yourself and the company and see how much of an overlap there is. For example, themes that point to satisfaction associated with risk taking, autonomy, and ambiguous assignments may indicate that a straight commission job is right for you.

Although often maligned, one of the best barometers to use in this situation is "gut feeling", which is formed through the knowledge you've accumulated from previous experiences. Although much of this knowledge may be on a subconscious level now, it still serves as a filter that can be helpful in the decision-making process.

Trivia...

A study of successful entrepreneurs found that although many used sophisticated methods to aid them when making decisions, large numbers still relied heavily on "gut feeling". If a decision turns your stomach, perhaps you should turn the opportunity down.

The hits and myths of selling

ANY NUMBER OF MYTHS *about selling have resulted in deterring people from entering a field that might otherwise give them a high degree of personal and financial satisfaction. As you approach the field, you need to be able to separate fact from fiction.*

The gift of the gab

How many times have you heard someone described as a natural salesperson because he or she has the so-called gift of the gab? No doubt you have encountered salespeople with the gift of the gab in your work and personal life. This is one of the most prevalent sales myths. The best salespeople certainly have solid verbal skills, but more important than the gift of the gab is the gift of listening.

■ **Purported sales pros**, *who are always trying to sell, typically talk non-stop, but often the gift of the gab is little more than the gift of blab, and it does not sell.*

The best salespeople are also the best listeners. It is by listening that they learn the prospects' needs and then help to satisfy them.

The best salespeople are born salespeople

This myth is right up there with the gift of the gab. There is no doubt that some people show precocious persuasive skills quite early in life, but there is no data to prove that they enter adulthood as polished sales professionals. And, more important, there are countless highly successful salespeople today who would have been described as nothing short of sales-challenged when young.

WHEN LESS IS MORE

Once, many years ago, in a small village, there were three tailors whose shops were next door to each other. At great expense, one of the tailors bought a huge sign that read, "The Best Tailor in Britain".

The second tailor, not to be outdone, bought an even bigger, grander, and more ornate sign that read, "The Best Tailor in the World".

The third tailor looked at the grand pronouncements of the competition and returned to his desk. He took out a small sheet of paper and his trusty pen and wrote the sign, "The Best Tailor in the Village". His message was clear and simple, for he knew that he could say far more by saying less.

■ **A simple window display** *reinforces the sales maxim that sometimes the classic undersell is the best sell of all.*

A SHOW OF HANDS

A professor at a prominent business school asked his students how many would like to work in sales. A few reluctantly raised their hands. Then the professor asked the students how many would like to have jobs that offered a high degree of independence, variety, challenge, and people contact, with rewards based upon their performance. Practically all of the students raised their hands. The professor then told the students that they had just indicated that they would like to work in sales. The myths about sales jobs initially kept the students' hands down, while the reality of sales work hit the spot for more than a few of them.

Many of today's greatest salespeople went through years of struggle, strife, and failure when they entered this field. With practice, experience, education, mentoring, and tremendous drive, persistence, and work, they developed into polished sales professionals. The reality is that great salespeople are made, not born.

Extroverts make the best salespeople

Many excellent salespeople are extroverts, but there are many introverts who are excellent salespeople, too. In fact, the whole introversion–extroversion scale is highly questionable in predicting sales ability, aptitude, or potential.

It is far more realistic to focus upon factors such as persistence, drive, energy, independence, a strong need to achieve, and strong initiative.

Great salespeople have flair and panache

Many people have bought into the myth that salespeople are continuously on stage and need to put on a real show if they are to succeed. The misconception that great salespeople need to have dazzling, glitzy, glamorous presentations has no doubt turned many a promising individual away from sales. In reality, many highly effective salespeople make simple, clear, and concise presentations. In today's fast-paced business environment, most people appreciate this simplicity.

As soon as the sales myths, legends, and caricatures that make fun of salespeople have been dispelled, you can focus on the simple truths of sales jobs.

Something old, something new

THE BIGGEST CHANGE in the selling process is a movement away from the salesperson-centred approach and towards the customer-centred approach. This change is a work in progress, so it can be easy to fall back into the old sales methods.

The old sales traps

There are still plenty of salespeople who adhere to the maxim that they must be in total control of the sales process. Typically, they follow a structured sales format – often linked to a catchy acronym – to propel them from one step to the next from beginning to end. The only problem is that a salesperson using this approach can totally miss what the customer really needs, and, as a result, totally miss a sale.

Although it is essential for the salesperson to have a high degree of product knowledge, the customer does not need to hear every last bit and byte of knowledge that the salesperson possesses. Some salespeople try to use their expertise to overpower a customer's objections, but salespeople with any expertise about selling use a far simpler approach.

■ **The overpowering salesman** *who bombards prospects with facts and figures will succeed only in confusing and boring them, thereby losing sales.*

Selling techniques that once were tried-and-true are now tired and blue.

If you approach a prospect with the belief that you have all the answers, the one answer you are most likely to hear is "No!" Sales professionals today are the ones with the questions, and the prospects are the ones with the answers.

The new sales trappings

Successful selling today is based on partnering with the prospect, asking questions to learn more about his or her needs, listening carefully, and jointly developing solutions. This means moving away from the "me vs. you" sales situation, where one side wins and one side loses, and moving towards a "win-win" sales situation, where salesperson and customer both win.

Today's partnering approach has transformed the "me vs. you" sales approach into one that is based upon "us". This type of approach gives your prospect a far more positive feeling about the entire sales process and his or her role in it.

Trivia...

You can easily get a clear picture of the "me vs. you" relationship between buyer and seller by looking at the old techniques of closing a sale. One of the popular approaches was called the "silent close". With this approach, the salesperson asks a closing question, such as, "Can we sign you up today?" and then says nothing until the prospect talks. The accompanying adage was, "Whoever talks first loses."

■ **The role of a salesperson** *today is based on partnership, which means helping the prospect to understand his or her needs and then solving any problems.*

People would much rather feel that they bought, rather than were sold, something.

It's not that there are no longer any simple steps to follow to be an effective salesperson. Quite the contrary is true; you are about to learn a full range of simple steps. The difference is that these steps will build trust, value, and relationships, along with sales. You will be able to apply proven techniques of planning, managing time, prospecting, qualifying, asking the best questions, providing the most productive answers, and generating a commitment to action from your prospects.

The big difference in selling today goes back to the old Latin expression "caveat emptor", or "let the buyer beware". In today's business environment, the emphasis is on meeting the customer's needs, fulfilling sales commitments, providing excellent service and support, and adhering to the highest ethical standards. Customers have many choices, and they do not need to buy from you. We are now in the era of what can be called "caveat venditor", or "let the seller beware".

A simple summary

✔ Selling is not a foreign activity for you. You have built trust and sold yourself in the past, and there are simple steps that can help you to become a highly productive and successful salesperson in the near future.

✔ A broad range of sales jobs with various expectations, challenges, responsibilities, and reward systems are available. Carefully screen any potential sales job, and match the job content with your own work-related needs, interests, and objectives.

✔ Be on the lookout for the myths about selling, and do not be fooled, discouraged, or dissuaded by them. Great salespeople are made, not born.

✔ To be successful in sales you do not need the gift of the gab, but you do need the gift of listening.

✔ Selling today is based on the customer's needs rather than on the salesperson's needs. Listen carefully to what the customers have to say and treat them with trust and respect.

Chapter 2

Getting the Right Sales Job

THE FIRST POINT TO KEEP IN MIND when seeking a sales job is that you do not want just any old sales job! If you wanted any sales job, you could go out tomorrow with no planning or preparation and get ten job offers. Salespeople are always in demand, and there are plenty of sales-oriented companies that subscribe to the warm body theory of employment: if a warm body shows up, employ it. However, companies that do this are typically not the kind that professional salespeople seek. The products are often quite iffy, and the sales tactics, including boiler room operations, payment practices, leadership, and support, often raise eyebrows. Besides, any job that is so easy to get is just as easy to lose.

In this chapter...

✓ Finding the best jobs

✓ Getting the interview

✓ Interview etiquette

✓ After the interview

MAKING A GOOD INITIAL IMPRESSION IS IMPORTANT

Finding the best jobs

THERE IS NO ONE BEST WAY to find the job that's right for you. The best strategy is to be as open-minded and creative as possible. You can choose from a broad array of traditional and high-tech options, along with orthodox and unorthodox options, any of which can land you directly in workplace nirvana.

Print media

One popular way to find a job is to scour the classified and display ads in newspapers and industry magazines and journals. Countless companies advertise for salespeople not only in local but in national newspapers and magazines as well. When you are selling on the road, complimentary copies of various local newspapers can help you become familiar with the local job market.

While scanning the print media, you may also locate information regarding recruitment drives at companies that interest you, along with job fairs that bring numerous companies together to provide applicants with "one-stop shopping".

■ **Going through** *the classified ads is a valuable approach to finding a job in sales.*

Traditional networking

Another powerful technique to help you find the right sales job is through good old-fashioned *networking*. You have been involved in networks from the very first day you left your house. You started with a network of family, friends, and neighbours, and now your network is composed of countless individuals whom you may have met through school, university, work, hobbies, social gatherings, community activities, religious organizations, recreational outings, and the like.

Of course, the question is whether your network is dormant or active. If you have not maintained these relationships, you have done yourself a disservice, not only from the job referral standpoint but also from the standpoint of surrounding yourself with diverse and interesting people. You have also lost some opportunities to help others, which most people find highly gratifying.

> **DEFINITION**
>
> Networking *means maintaining contact and communication with fellow professionals, associates, and friends, in order to form a wide social base that can provide mutual support, guidance, and job referrals.*

INCREASING YOUR CHANCES

An e-mail arrived for my syndicated workplace advice column from a salesperson who said that he was having difficulty finding a sales job because he did not finish college. I gave him information on a number of steps he could take to widen his search and market himself more effectively. A few days after the column ran, I received an e-mail from a sales manager with a solid company indicating that his company did not require salespeople to have university degrees, and that he would like to get in touch with the letter-writer. This certainly was not the most conventional way for a salesperson to get a job interview, but it illustrates what can happen if a salesperson continually looks for ways to increase his or her chances of finding a job.

If you have let your network collapse, the simplest way to revive it is to pick up the phone, set up some meetings, and get your network rolling again.

If you have an active job network, there will be a core of people out there who are trying to help you find the right opportunity or the key people to access. And, as they tap into their other networks, you may suddenly have hundreds of people energized on your behalf.

■ **Meeting up** *with ex-colleagues socially is an excellent way of maintaining an active job network.*

Jobs on the Internet

The most rapidly expanding arena for job listings and opportunities is on the Internet, and there are a number of ways in which you can access them.

You can go to various job database web sites and check out the sales jobs. You can make the search as narrow or broad as you like in terms of factors such as industry, geographical area, company size, and earnings potential.

These sites can also link you directly to the companies that are listed, and from that point you can learn all about the company itself and apply online for the job.

Typically, when you get to a particular company's web site, there is a broad range of information on its products, history, and employees, along with press releases. And there is usually a button that reads "Employment" or "Opportunities" or "Join Us" that you can click on to learn about current job opportunities. You can complete and submit an online work history, or you may be able to submit an *electronic CV*.

> **INTERNET**
>
> www.stepstone.co.uk
> www.totaljobs.com
> www.gisajob.com
>
> *These are a few of the many web sites that provide a listing of sales positions, which can be narrowed down to fit your needs.*

> **DEFINITION**
>
> *An electronic CV is prepared specifically for online submission. Once it is forwarded to a company, it is scanned electronically for key words that are relevant to the specific position. For a sales position, sample key words include industry jargon along with terms such as* increased sales, built territory, profit, tenacious, persistent, *and* travel. *Depending upon the number of hits on these and numerous other key words, the applicant typically receives an electronic rejection letter or invitation for an interview.*

■ **Check out** *specific companies on the Internet. The first step is to use a search engine and go to the company's web site.*

The Internet can also be helpful in your networking activities through the job networking and career networking web sites. In these sites, you can interact with other professionals in your field regarding jobs and job opportunities. From time to time, recruiters from various companies come to these sites and join in the discussions.

INTERNET

www.monster.co.uk

This key site provides an opportunity for sales people to interact with other sales professionals and potential employers.

The Internet also provides you with an opportunity to use more of a mixed-media approach. You can access a large number of newspapers on the Internet. By clicking on the "Classifieds" button, found on many of their sites, you can look at current sales job listings.

INTERNET

www.yahoo.co.uk
www.excite.com

When looking for a company's web site, you can go to search engines such as these. Just enter the company's name, and you will be provided with a direct link to the company (if it has a web site).

Employment agencies

One source of sales jobs is employment agencies. Typically, they have listed jobs from client companies, and they then set out to fill them. They are sales organizations themselves, in effect. The "counsellors" typically work on commission. Their pay is based on the pay for the position being filled. Agencies generally get paid when an applicant takes a job and stays on for a specified period of time.

If an employment agency asks you for a fee, head for the door. Any fees should be paid by the potential employer, not by the applicant.

■ **Employment agencies** *are in the business of matching people and jobs. They can be quite helpful in finding sales positions.*

Search firms and careers offices

Executive search firms ("head hunters") operate a little differently from employment agencies since they are generally retained by a client organization to fill a specific position. They are usually paid as consultants, and their job is to produce two or three viable candidates for the open job. The search firm is then paid for this consultation, whether a candidate is hired or not.

As part of the broad sweep you should make in your search for a job, check with the careers offices at the school, college, or university you attended. They may have strong network systems in place. In addition, local job centres occasionally list intriguing sales jobs that may be worth pursuing.

When you are looking for a job, that is your job. In the job-hunt process, remember the old adage, "The harder I work, the luckier I get".

■ **Looking for a new job** *is a full-time pursuit. Get up early each day as if you were going to work, get dressed for work, and then get to work. Make your phone calls, plan your activities, set your meetings, and then get out and get going.*

Getting the interview

ONCE YOU HAVE IDENTIFIED *a company that appears to be a good match for your skills, interests, and objectives, there are a few simple steps to take that can help you get an interview and handle it well.*

A simple CV

Typically, the first step in responding to a job listing is to send a traditional or electronic CV, depending upon the way in which the job is advertised or posted. With either type of CV, the most important point to remember is that your CV is a sales brochure. It should be neat, clear, succinct, accurate, and highly readable. The key topics to cover are the following:

- Your objectives
- Experience
- Awards
- Qualifications
- Education

Additional information should include such topics as relevant activities, interests, and hobbies.

Do not list references on your CV, as you do not want them to be bothered unless a serious job offer is close.

You can include the following at the end of your CV: "Excellent references available upon request." You should also keep all personal or demographic data, such as race, colour, religion, gender, national origin, and age, off your CV.

If you are applying for a job with a company whose system calls for hard-copy CVs, make sure that your CV is no longer than two pages. In fact, one-page CVs are clearly preferable. In addition, you should include a brief covering letter. This is not the place to write a long-winded dissertation about your sales skills. The letter should be a brief paragraph or two that basically indicates that you are interested in applying for the specified position and have enclosed your CV.

For companies that use an electronic CV system, you should also send a hard copy, just for some extra assurance and coverage.

Preparing for the interview

When your CV generates a positive reply from a company and you are invited for a job interview, there are some simple preparatory steps to set the stage for success.

Make sure that you have a solid understanding of yourself, the company, and the industry.

Looking first at yourself, be an expert on your work background. After all, if you are not interested in what you have been doing, why should an interviewer care? Have the following information at your fingertips:

- Your dates of employment
- Responsibilities
- Goals
- Job titles
- Accomplishments

In terms of your understanding of the company, you should have at least a basic comprehension of the position, along with information regarding the company's history, products, mission, and objectives. You should also be thinking about ways in which your experience and skills apply to the job.

It is helpful to have some knowledge about the industry itself. There are trends, developments, and significant changes in every industry, and having some insight into them demonstrates to an interviewer that you are not naively approaching a possible move into this company. You can access all such information through a combination of your network, the Internet, newspapers, and magazines.

■ **Familiarizing yourself** *with companies through brochures and annual reports will help you prepare for interviews.*

ANTICIPATING QUESTIONS

You can also prepare for the kinds of questions you will probably be asked, and do some practice interviews with a friend or family member. You can anticipate questions such as the following:

a) What were your responsibilities at your previous jobs?

b) What did you like about your previous jobs?

c) What did you dislike?

d) Why did you leave your previous jobs?

e) What are your short-term goals?

f) What are your long-term goals?

g) What were your main achievements?

h) Tell me about a failure; how did you handle it?

i) What is your greatest accomplishment?

j) What are your strengths?

k) What are your weaknesses?

l) Why do you want to work here?

One of the best ways to improve your interview skills is to videotape a practice session.

Videotaping a practice interview will show you where improvements need to be made in the way you present yourself. Listen carefully to your responses. Are they clear, precise, and succinct? Listen to your tone and volume, and notice your body language. Are you fidgeting, sitting with your arms crossed, looking everywhere but at the interviewer?

Be prepared for many interviewers to ask competence-based questions to check your understanding of some of the technical or content aspects of the position. You can also expect some work-sample questions that focus on what you would do in a particular situation. For example, you may be asked how you would handle the following scenario: you have just entered a prospect's office as she slams down the phone in disgust, glances at her watch, looks at you, and says, "All right, let's get this going."

During the interview, you will be given the opportunity to ask some questions of your own, so have them ready.

When it's your turn to ask questions, make sure they are substantive. If your questions are weak, the interviewer might conclude that you are rather weak too. Be ready to ask about such matters as:

- Sales training
- Opportunities to advance
- Support from marketing
- A typical day for a salesperson
- The sales software

- How leads are generated
- Travel
- New products
- Plans for growth and expansion

It is not appropriate to ask questions about the pay and benefits until you are much further along in the job process.

At the same time, there are some areas in which you should not be asking questions until later in the game. There is a great deal for you to learn about the company, and for the company to learn about you, before getting into the matter of pay. The time to talk about pay and benefits is when a job offer is about to be made. If you jump in early with questions about money, you will be perceived as a rather shallow candidate, whose major interests are in the company's coffers.

Be sure to bring a hard copy of your CV and your list of references to the interview. You should also have a notepad and pen or a palm organizer.

PALM ORGANIZER

By taking the steps outlined above, you will enter a job interview with confidence, clarity of purpose, and focus.

Interview etiquette

THE INTERVIEW SESSION USUALLY BEGINS *with social pleasantries about such benign matters as the weather, the view, or the parking. This icebreaking conversation seems innocuous enough until you realize that the average interviewer makes up his or her mind about an applicant within the first 5 to 15 minutes. It is important, therefore, to show your enthusiasm, passion, and positive attitude during this time.*

Many interviewers are trying to answer two simple questions: "Can this applicant do the job?" and "Will this applicant do the job?"

In determining whether you are up to the job, the interviewer will look at your experience, education, and expertise and try to assess if you actually have the basic skills to sell for the company. As for the "will do" issue, the interviewer is trying to determine if you have the energy, drive, motivation, and persistence for the job. The best way for interviewers to answer these questions is to ask about your work background. As you respond, ask yourself if you are clearly showing the interviewer that you can and will do the job.

Trivia...

Biases and stereotypes can be associated with one's handshake. For example, a weak handshake is thought to indicate a weak character, insecurity, shyness, lack of confidence, or hidden anxieties. There is not a shred of truth to any of this, but you should make sure that your handshake does not play into these prevalent beliefs.

■ **If an interviewer is** *going to make up his or her mind about you in the first 5 to 15 minutes, make sure that your initial handshake sends all the right messages.*

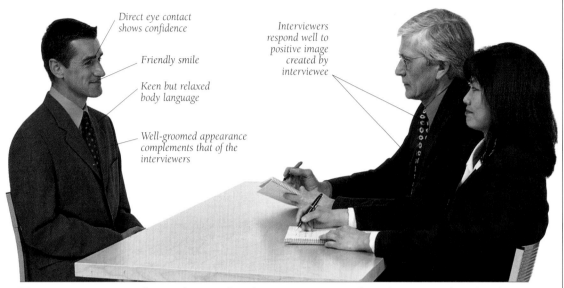

Direct eye contact shows confidence

Friendly smile

Keen but relaxed body language

Well-groomed appearance complements that of the interviewers

Interviewers respond well to positive image created by interviewee

■ **Your appearance and attitude** *count for a lot at interview. A smile, enthusiasm, and a relaxed, open manner all combine to create a favourable first impression.*

There are a few simple pointers that you can follow to help you make a positive initial impact at interview. These are:

1. Be on time

2. Dress the way that salespeople in this company dress, or be slightly more conservative

3. Be sure to smile when you meet the interviewer and maintain some eye contact without staring

4. When you shake hands with the interviewer, use a firm, but not knuckle-breaking, grip

Once the ice is broken, the formal interview begins. The first interview is usually a summary of the whos, whats, wheres, whens, whys, and hows of your work history. Keep your answers brief and to the point, and try to give some examples to demonstrate what you are saying. For example, if you say that you are persistent, give a quick example of a situation that illustrates that characteristic.

Avoid interrupting or criticizing the interviewer. Also avoid making negative comments about previous employers or co-workers, since most interviewers will conclude that you have problems dealing with others.

Just as there are key words in an electronic CV, so there are key words and expressions that you should try to include in an interview for a sales job. The following are some of them:

- Challenge
- Tenacity
- Productivity
- Autonomy
- Variety
- Success
- Independence
- Money
- Persistence
- Goals
- Growth
- Learning

You should also mention that you would like the opportunity to be paid based on your performance.

Describe your weaknesses or failures honestly when asked about them, while adding the specifics of how you learned, grew, and profited from them. Remember that people who have a good deal of confidence and self-assurance are more than willing to talk about their failures.

As the interview draws to a close, make sure that you have a clear idea of the next step. This may include another interview, a request for more information from you, or a list of your references.

> ## Trivia...
> One reason to avoid interrupting the interviewer and let him or her talk is that interviewers often tend to like the applicants in direct proportion to the amount of time that the interviewers have been talking.

Try to finish the session with a commitment from the interviewer to take some action to move you along in the hiring process. In wrapping up the session, briefly restate your interest in the position and then thank the interviewer for his or her time.

Before you leave the interview, make sure that you have the interviewer's business card.

If the interview went well, you can assume that at least there will be a second interview, and more likely a third and even a fourth before a job offer is made. These additional interviews may have more technical content or sales simulations. Either way, you should approach them in the same style as the initial interview, with one simple addition: as you answer questions, try to include information that you learned in the earlier interview or interviews. This will further demonstrate your interest in the company and your ability to listen.

After the interview

AS SOON AS POSSIBLE after the interview, you should sit down and make notes on as much as you can remember about the interview, particularly any company information that was shared with you. This will be a useful source of information as you prepare for the next interview with the company.

Stay in contact

No matter how the interview went, always write a thank-you note to the interviewer. Let him or her know how much you enjoyed the session, and express your positive thoughts about the company and your interest in being a part of it.

Close your thank-you letter by indicating that you look forward to hearing from the company.

REFUSING TO GIVE UP

A company manager interviewed a sales applicant, but felt that there were other individuals who were more qualified. When the applicant received the rejection letter, he immediately picked up the phone and called the individual who interviewed him.

When told that his experience just did not match up, the applicant then started making calls all over the organization, including a call to the company president. He was not obnoxious about it, but wanted to let the company see that he could truly help them meet their sales needs. He showed so much persistence that the sales manager brought him back in and ultimately hired him.

"He did exactly what we want our salespeople to do. When faced with a rejection, he didn't walk away."

The more you can illustrate or demonstrate your sales skills in the employment process, the more likely you are to be given a job.

Since you are seeking a sales job, it is important to let the company see that you are not a person who sits around and waits for things to happen.

■ **If you** *do not hear from the company within a week, contact the person who interviewed you.*

A simple summary

✔ To find the best sales job, treat the entire job search process as a job in itself, and use various resources, including print media, networking, the Internet, and agencies.

✔ Your CV, whether electronic or hard copy, is a sales and marketing tool and should be designed and constructed with that in mind.

✔ Make sure that you are prepared to talk not only about your work background, but also about the potential job, company, and industry.

✔ Be friendly, punctual, enthusiastic, and prepared with questions for the interviewer on such topics as training, promotion, opportunities, and plans for expansion.

✔ When trying to find a sales job, always remember that persistence pays.

Chapter 3

Go for the Goal

A HUSH FILLS THE AIR as the countdown at Cape Canaveral continues: "... five, four, three, two, one." Engines ignite and there's a deafening roar as the shuttle hurtles into space in another successful launch. Now, let's assume that the mission has no goals. A few minutes after lift-off, the captain speaks: "Let's make five or ten orbits of Earth, maybe try a space walk or study the impact of zero gravity on pizza. We'll be back in the next week or so." Without goals, and well-prepared plans for meeting those goals, this mission will be a waste of time and money. When salespeople go into the field without clearly defined goals, they are not going to reach new heights either. It is easy to establish sales goals, and easy to fail without them.

In this chapter...

✓ Working goals that really work

✓ Let's get personal goals

✓ Sales goals for sales gold

✓ What you expect is what you get

IF YOU WANT TO ACHIEVE GREAT GOALS, YOU NEED TO DO SOME GREAT PLANNING

Working goals that really work

MANY SALESPEOPLE STATE *that their goals are to close more sales, keep customers happy, get more business, and give better service. The problem is that these general statements are nothing more than wishes, hopes, and dreams. It is nice to have these positive thoughts, but they are not goals.*

Get specific

The first step in establishing real goals is to have a specific outcome in mind. For example, let's assume that you want to close more sales.

To turn your desire into a goal, you need to clarify what you are truly seeking. Do you have a specific number of additional closes in mind? In such a case, your objective would be to close X more sales. Or you may be seeking to increase the percentage of sales that you close, so your objective would be to increase the number of sales by Y per cent.

As simple as ABC

It's quite commendable to have specific work goals, but some are obviously more important than others. Without prioritizing, a salesperson could handle the minor goals beautifully, while the major goals are shoved aside. The best way to avoid this problem is to affix a ranking to each objective, such as an "A", "B", or "C", and then commit to focusing on the main events first.

■ **Think carefully** *about your working, personal, and sales goals. It's important to establish at the outset exactly what you are aiming for.*

Don't confuse a sales quota with your sales goals.

A sales quota is management's way of specifying a specific amount of production that is expected from you. That quota is a number for you to try to meet, while your sales goals comprise a broad programme for you to build revenue, goodwill, service, sales relationships, and the territory itself.

The plan's the thing

The next step is to have a detailed action plan that you can follow all the way to your goal. This plan should include clear dates and deadlines for each objective, as well as benchmark dates along the way to monitor your progress and provide for any necessary adjustments. The plan also includes any resources you may need, ranging from managerial support to physical equipment.

Unfortunately, not every plan goes according to plan. This means that although you have a thorough, detailed, and deadline-orientated plan, you also need to approach the entire process with flexibility.

■ **Once you know**
what kind of managerial support you need, you can approach the relevant people and enlist their help.

Dealing with obstacles

There can be any number of obstacles awaiting you, ranging from a minor blip on the radar screen to a fully fledged ambush. Each such obstacle will have to be analyzed based on its own merits and demerits, and some may call for a separate plan in and of themselves.

Sometimes the obstacles are good news, such as landing a time-consuming new major account that was unexpected when you had developed your plan. At other times the picture is not so bright, such as when your hard drive crashes – and does so again the following week. With a combination of flexibility, creativity, and tranquillity, along with some managerial support, you can often find a way to manage the obstacles and even turn some into opportunities.

■ **When things go wrong**, *try to stay calm and definitely don't panic. By keeping a level head, you can often resolve problems yourself, but if you can't, make sure you ask for help.*

EVERY CLOUD HAS A SILVER LINING

One of the leading salespeople at one of my dot com client companies all but consummated a sale that would have brought eyeballs and income to the site. Well past the eleventh hour, the prospect changed his mind. It appeared that the revenue and the plan were out of the window. The salesperson, however, asked the departing prospect for a referral, and the referred company ultimately became a major affiliate. Because the salesperson's plan included flexibility, she was able to turn an obstacle into an opportunity.

Time to commit

For any plan to work, there must be a real commitment from the players. In this case, the key player is you. One way to help build this commitment is for you to sign the plan, as a signature often has a strong psychological impact that compels people to act. In a word, you are the action in the action plan.

The plans and goals that you establish do not exist in a vacuum. They are intrinsic to the plans and goals of the company as a whole.

In many companies, the goals of the salespeople complement the goals of their sales manager, whose goals complement those of his or her manager, all the way up the organization to the very top. Many companies are held together by this linkage of goals, and a weak link along the way can create significant problems. Hence the importance of making a bona fide commitment to strive to meet one's objectives.

Will the failure of one employee bring down an entire company? It is possible, particularly if that person is a key leader. Rather than adhering to the philosophy that companies comprise a chain and that one weak link can break them, many companies today are trying to structure themselves more as ropes, perceiving individual employees as strands. If one strand fails, the entire rope still holds.

■ **If you are working** *as part of a team with shared goals, commitment from each individual, including you, is essential. A detailed action plan will help keep you committed and focused.*

Let's get personal goals

YOU ARE A SALESPERSON, *and it is important to remember that the word "salesperson" is made up of two words, "sales" and "person". This means that you should actually establish sales goals and personal goals. Identifying, clarifying, and committing to your sales goals is actually half of the equation. The other half is for you to develop and commit to some personal developmental goals.*

Who's minding the career?

Early in the game, you need to think about your career direction, if not your career objectives. Many people starting out in sales say that they would like to move into sales management. However, that automatic response deserves a lot more thought. You are responsible for establishing your career objectives, building the plan to reach them, and making sure that the plan is being followed.

Do not think that your company is going to take care of you and your career.

Sales or sales management?

A sales position is different from a management position, and each calls for different needs, motivations, and sources of satisfaction. For example, in sales you will typically have the following:

- Considerable independence
- Control over your time
- Autonomy
- Rewards often based on your performance

In a management position, on the other hand, considerable time is spent doing the following:

- Being involved in meetings
- Planning and organizing work
- Working out budgets
- Leading the troops
- Handling administrative tasks
- Hiring and firing
- Training the troops
- Fighting fires

Sales management may be the perfect career for you. But equally it may not.

You do not have to decide today whether you want to pursue a managerial career, but take the time to do some exploring to see which is the best direction for you. You can certainly develop some short-term goals to help you explore your options. For example, you can develop and prioritize goals that focus on attending classes and seminars, meeting with your manager, and getting some professional career guidance.

Room for improvement

Your other short-term goals should be directed towards improving your sales skills. This means looking at the key sales areas in which you need to improve, identifying specific and measurable improvement objectives for each, and then identifying and committing to the best sources or resources to make the necessary upgrades, all within a specified time period.

■ **Attending relevant classes** *and seminars is one way of helping you decide whether pursuing a career in sales management would be right for you.*

For some real insight into yourself and the kind of work that you genuinely enjoy, take a look at your hobbies and volunteer activities. Ask yourself whether you gravitate towards leadership positions, isolated activities, group functions, or hands-on work.

An excellent sales rep for an electronics distribution company spent a great deal of his spare time as a volunteer teacher. Upon moving into management, he has found that his abilities to coach, guide, plan, and organize are making his new managerial position enjoyable. In fact, it's practically as enjoyable as his hobby. That is the feeling that you should be seeking at work.

A lot of class

One of the most important areas where you can set developmental objectives is in education. The selection of classes that you attend should be based on work-related priorities, and you will need to commit to taking them within a specified time period. Consider some educational upgrading, such as courses or seminars in prospecting, handling objections, or closing.

An applicant for a sales position who has worked in sales for the same company for 5 years but has never attended any professional growth and development training courses may be viewed as having only 1 year's experience five times over.

Maintaining personal interests

From the standpoint of personal development, you will find that your life is more fulfilling if you pursue some personal activities, interests, or courses that are far removed from selling. It is easy to let selling turn into a 24-hour activity, where you live it constantly. The problem is that those around you may tire of living that way, and you may tire of it as well.

■ **To say that** *you want to do some hiking or pursue another activity such as learning a language or studying the piano is easy, but these are wishes. To make them happen, you need to turn wishes into goals.*

Sales goals for sales gold

TO BE SUCCESSFUL IN SALES, you will need specific and measurable goals in a number of key performance areas. If your goals in these areas are merely optimistic statements of what you want, your success will be wanting.

The hunt for customers

To begin, it is important to have some prospecting goals. The best way to do this is to identify a broad range of target prospects through your business, social, and community contacts. Prioritize your prospects and develop a timetable for contacting them. Expanding your prospecting base is a never-ending function, and you should commit to developing your network continuously and following up on possible leads.

One of the surefire ways to close more sales is to have more customers. The larger your base of potential customers, the larger the number of sales.

Some companies promise excellent leads for their salespeople. The idea is for you to spend your time doing what you do best, namely selling. While various companies actually deliver on this promise, many do not.

Try to check with present employees to determine whether the company produces leads or leads you on.

Prospects today, customers tomorrow

It is wonderful to have a broad base of prospects, but they are not going to be worth much if you do not convert them to customers. To that end, you will want to have some goals regarding the percentage of sales that you seek to close, referred to as your *close ratio*.

Assuming that your close ratio is 20 per cent, it is perfectly acceptable to have a goal of improving that ratio to 30 per cent. You then need to get specific in terms of how and when you do this.

For example, beefing up the ratio may be a function of beefing up your sales skills, and you can establish goals in this area. Or perhaps it is more a function of being more selective in determining and visiting prospects. On a broader basis, you

> **DEFINITION**
>
> The close ratio is *a formula that measures the number of sales that you close in relation to the number of prospects that you contact. For example, if you contact 100 prospects and close 20 sales, your close ratio is 20/100 or 20 per cent.*

will need to establish several specific goals regarding the steps that you will take to increase your close ratio.

At the end of a predetermined period, you will have a clear measurement of your success. If you hit the mark, your next step will probably be to raise your close ratio goals even higher.

£ per sale

Another key area that calls for some goal setting is focused on the amount of revenue per sale. You may have a terrific close ratio, but the revenue generated from each sale may be a little thin. It might even be possible that the reason for your improved sales ratio is that your pricing is on the low side.

■ **Having raised** *your close ratio, set some goals to increase the amount of revenue per sale. Decide on the specific improvements you wish to make, and give yourself a time target for achieving them.*

There are two major ways to raise revenue per sale:

(*a*) If the customer buys more of what you are selling

(*b*) If you maintain higher prices

You can definitely set some goals and plans in both of these areas. For example, you may be able to increase sales through deeper probing of your customers' needs, greater emphasis on the value added by your product, and increased emphasis on your company's incentives associated with larger purchases.

INTERNET

www.easy4gifts.co.uk
www.image2000plus
.com

Many salespeople are totally confused when it comes to handling customer gifts, and it's important to follow your company's policies. These web sites specifically focus on helping salespeople in this area.

If you drop a price whenever customers object to it, you will soon be selling on the basis of price only. And, shortly after that, you will not be selling at all. The customer will demand and receive the lowest price, and you will be a human vending machine.

The big picture and the big money

Ultimately, your broad sales objective is to increase total sales revenues, and you should establish some specific numbers in this category, which is not all that difficult to do. Your total sales revenues will be a natural outgrowth of your success in meeting the sales goals noted above. If you generate more prospects, increase your close ratio, and increase your revenues per sale, your total sales revenue is automatically increased.

When you look at a sales position from a broad perspective, you see that it is actually composed of numerous areas where short-term and long-term goals play critical roles. This means that there should be specific goals covering virtually all aspects of your role as a salesperson, including customer service, reviving dead accounts, number of calls per day, repeat business, customer referrals to new business, and customer satisfaction.

■ **When negotiating prices,** *make sure that you don't always cave in too easily to customer objections. Set yourself a goal to further develop your skills in handling customer objections to price.*

What you expect is what you get

THE FINAL ELEMENT *that will help you meet your objectives is to set positive expectations for yourself. Researchers continue to find that people who truly expect to reach their goals are far more likely to do so than those who have constructed similar goals but do not have strong underlying positive expectations.*

Great expectations for great results

Your positive expectations have a definite impact on your behaviour, causing you to behave and react in ways that are more likely to produce the desired results. And this type of behaviour also influences the behaviour of the people with whom you may be dealing. If you are positive, confident, and optimistic about the way your product will meet your prospect's needs, your prospect is more likely to react in a similar way. At the same time, if you enter the same situation with the same goals, but with less than positive expectations, your behaviour is going to show it, and your customer is going to see it. Most importantly, your low close ratio is going to see it as well.

Programme yourself to win

It is one thing to say to yourself that you are going to have positive expectations, and quite another matter to make it happen. Fortunately, there are some simple steps you can take to increase your positive outlook:

1. Visualize yourself dealing comfortably and persuasively with your prospect, and see yourself closing the sale. One of the best times to do this visualizing is when you are at that edge of awareness, just before you are about to fall asleep. At this point the subconscious mind is highly suggestible.

2. Leave some upbeat notes for yourself that reaffirm your strengths, effectiveness, competence, and aspirations. These notes are similar to the advertising messages you constantly see and which gradually work their way into your subconscious. In addition, there is a motivational value associated with the act of writing out your strengths in the first place.

Trivia...

There are electronic signs on many motorways advising drivers of "traffic ahead" and warning them to slow down. The fact is that even if the road were wide open, this message would have an effect on the driver's expectations and cause him or her to slow down. What would happen if these signs established a positive expectation? For example, "Acceleration zone ahead. Prepare to increase speed." Expectations, positive or negative, affect people's behaviour.

3. It can also be helpful to put up a note or graphic that shows how much progress you have made towards reaching your goal and how much is needed before you reach it. Some companies put up huge visual displays that depict how close they are getting to their sales goals, and you can do likewise, whether it's on your desk or your refrigerator. Sprinters tend to run extra hard as the finishing line approaches, and the same thing happens to salespeople. It is highly motivational to see just how close you are getting to your objectives.

Researchers who study human motivation continue to find that goals can have a strong motivating impact.

When people have a clear idea of where they are going, they are more likely to demonstrate behaviour that will get them there. The motivational impact of goals is even more compelling for those individuals who have either participated in the goal-setting process or have established the goals for themselves.

Other studies consistently find that for goals to be motivational, they should be neither too hard nor too easy. If they are outrageously difficult to reach, the individual typically becomes highly frustrated or ignores them altogether. And, at the other end of the scale, if the goals are altogether simple to achieve, they are perceived as meaningless and will again have no motivational impact.

■ **Keep an idyllic picture** *of a holiday or other pleasurable activity on display in your office as a constant reminder of what you plan to do once you have achieved your sales goals.*

You can continue to develop your positive expectations with the help of pictures that are somehow related to the attainment of your goals, such as photos of you during successful events in your life, or they can be pictures of any of the positive outcomes that will accrue as a result of your successful sales. You can even put up a picture of you as you meet your sales goals.

If you keep sending positive messages to yourself, you are likely to see positive outcomes.

A simple summary

✔ It is nice to have positive thoughts about closing more sales, building your customer base, and improving customer service, but these good wishes have to be transformed into goals. This means that they need to be specific, prioritized, measurable, and supported by dates, deadlines, commitment, and an action plan.

✔ Obstacles can arise at any point on the path to making sales; you will need to be flexible, creative, and tranquil to handle them.

✔ Not every obstacle is a roadblock. Some present real opportunities.

✔ Since you are responsible for your career, you should establish career direction and goals, and set your own plan to meet them.

✔ The easiest way to meet your overall sales goals is to establish basic goals for all of your sales responsibilities, right down to the number of calls per day.

✔ No matter how practical, realistic, and reachable your sales goals may be, you will fall short if you do not have positive expectations about them.

Chapter 4

It's About Time

N O MATTER WHAT YOU ARE SELLING, you have one desirable commodity that just about everyone wants, and that commodity is your time. Your manager needs a few minutes, and reminds you of the Friday meeting. When you get a break, some colleagues want to run a few things by you, and that new associate wants some advice. Be sure to read the e-mail messages and faxes you received this morning. Three phone calls are on hold, too, and don't forget to pick up your daughter. So, how are your sales going? Once time has gone, opportunities disappear with it, so you need an effective time management strategy throughout the selling process. Take some simple steps to put this in place.

In this chapter...

✔ *Current events*

✔ *A simple plan*

✔ *Time-management strategies*

✔ *The power of "yes" and "no"*

Current events

ONE OF THE BEST STARTING POINTS *for developing a workable time-management strategy is to review carefully what you are doing with your time right now. After all, how can you plan your time if you are unsure of what you are doing with it in the first place?*

The week in review

Write down all of your activities each day, from the time that you get up until the time you go to bed, during a 1-week period. Be prepared to be shocked at the amount of time that is taken up by interruptions, waiting, administrative work, meetings, looking for lost items, and chit-chat. This shock is the first tip-off that it's time to manage your time.

In reviewing your week, batch and categorize all of your activities by function. You will probably have categories with headings such as Business, Social, Recreational, Personal, and Other.

The next step is to look at the activities within each of these categories and attach a priority to each. For example, time spent prospecting can be noted as an "A" priority, while time spent reading and responding to e-mail messages and faxes can be labelled as "B" or "C" priorities. One important rule that underlies every step of effective time management is that "A" activities are done before "B" activities and "B" activities are done before "C" activities.

■ **Although prioritizing** *a week's activities takes time, in the long run it will save you even more time.*

One of the simplest yet most important points in all of time management is to ask yourself regularly: "Am I making the best use of my time right now?" If the answer is "yes", continue with what you are doing; if the answer is "no", switch to an activity that will generate a "yes" to this question.

"C" you later

Take a look at those "C" activities on your summary and see if you can eliminate any of them right now. You may get lucky and see a few glaring time traps that can be immediately reduced if not eliminated altogether. Some of the other time traps can be handled through *multitasking*.

Rather than thinking about how many hours you put into your sales work, try flipping this notion around and think of how much work you can put into the hours. Look for more ways to multitask, particularly with the "C" activities.

DEFINITION

A key element of time management for salespeople is multitasking, the ability to effectively handle more than one work-related responsibility at the same time.

■ **While wading** *through your e-mail, snail mail, or faxes, you could simultaneously handle some routine phone calls.*

Taking positive action

Whether you delete your e-mails or reply to your letters and faxes is your business, but you should take action on the spot when possible. When you set these items aside and revisit them later, you are falling back into the time trap.

You can also help manage time by going to the source. For example, if you continuously receive marginally useful correspondence, contact the sender and see if you can get off his or her hit list. In companies where this is not a politically correct move, you should make liberal use of the delete button or recycle bin.

Look at your summary of activities for the past week to see how much time you spent on planning. By going through this exercise of noting your activities for a week, you also establish a benchmark for measuring your time-management effectiveness in the future.

■ **Growing numbers** *of salespeople today are using online applications to plan the weeks ahead.*

Plan on handling all paperwork and electronic correspondence only once a day.

As you build your time-management skills, it is both interesting and informative to repeat this exercise every 6 months. You will be able to keep track of how well you have done, as well as gain insight into any additional time traps that may have emerged.

People who are effective at time management dedicate time every week to planning out the days and the weeks ahead.

PLANNING TRIPS ABROAD

As a member of a consulting team working with a US company that was in financial trouble, I met with many of its salespeople to discuss sales planning, strategies, and objectives. Many of their customers were in Europe, and I inquired about how sales meetings are set up and organized with them. The uniform response was that salespeople travel to Europe and then start setting up appointments. Sometimes there can be a delay of several days before key people can be contacted, and there is always the chance that they might be out of town. So there can be a lot of costly sitting around.

As a group, these salespeople knew how to sell, but they could not do much selling if they were in Antwerp and their prospects were on a cruise in the Mediterranean. In a word, sales skills are essential, but they are meaningless unless accompanied by adequate planning and time-management skills. One could write a book about this company, but the only chapter that matters today is the final one: bankruptcy.

■ **By the time** *you reach the airport at the start of a sales trip, you should have all your appointments planned, leaving you time to review materials for your meetings.*

A simple plan

THE BEST WAY TO MANAGE *your time is through planning. This does not mean sticking compulsively to a rigid track that locks you into specific behaviour every minute of the day. In fact, flexibility is an important part of any plan, as you will need room for changes and adjustments, along with some back-up projects or activities if an appointment is moved, abridged, or cancelled. One way to build in the right amount of flexibility is to start planning roughly 50 per cent of your time and work up from there.*

■ **Whether you go** *high-tech with a palm organizer or low-tech, keep an up-to-date diary with you at all times so you can make appointments while away from the office.*

Always remember that the idea behind time management for you as a salesperson is to organize yourself so that you can spend the maximum amount of time selling.

Planning time

Set a specific day and time each week to do most of your scheduling for the week and weeks ahead. You certainly can make appointments and arrange meetings at any time, and there will be instances where this will need to be done on the hoof, but it is easier to co-ordinate the planning process when the core of the scheduling work is handled at one regular time.

Since Friday afternoons are typically less busy for salespeople, this can be an excellent time for planning. If this is not the case for you, then you will need to find one of the quieter times, perhaps during the less traditional business hours, to make your plans.

The easiest place to start is to look at your existing schedule and see if there are any times that are locked out already, such as pre-existing appointments, commitments, or in-house functions.

Trivia...

Ironically, one of the most common complaints from salespeople who do not do much planning is that they lack the time to plan. Of course they do! The reason is that they spend far too much time reacting and getting bounced from one place to another in their pinball world of sales. The bottom line is that if you are going to set aside some time for planning, you need to plan for that too.

THE FARMER'S TALE

A farmer called his three sons out to the barn and told them he was going to give them a lesson in time management. He then took an empty bucket from underneath one of the cows and started placing several large rocks in it until they reached the top.

"Is the bucket full?" he asked. His sons dutifully nodded. "No, it's not!" barked the farmer as he reached behind the boys and pulled out a bag of gravel and poured it into the bucket. As the gravel filled in the spaces between the big rocks, the farmer again asked the boys, "Is the bucket full?" They looked at each other and reluctantly nodded.

The farmer cried, "No, it's not!" as he picked up a bag of sand and poured its contents into the bucket, watching it fill the spaces between the rocks and gravel. "What about now?" asked the farmer.

The boys looked at each other and nodded guardedly. "Nope," said the farmer as he picked up a hose and ran water into the bucket. When the water started to overflow, the farmer turned off the hose and said, "Now it's full. What does this tell you about managing your own time?"

The first son, a pragmatist, thought carefully and replied, "You can always do more." The father responded, "Not bad, but can you think more creatively?"

The second son, the comedian of the group, replied, "If you keep doing more and more work, you are less likely to kick the bucket." The farmer replied, "Not bad, but save it for a different audience."

The third son, a bit of a philosopher, responded, "Life is a bucket. Fill it." The farmer gave him a look and said, "The real message here is that you need to take care of the big rocks first."

The moral of this tale is that when it comes to actually doing your sales work, find the big rocks and handle them before anything else. Complete your "A" priorities first and then move on to the "B's" and "C's".

The next step is to review and clarify where you are with all of your prospects and customers, starting with those who are the most important as well as those with the highest potential. You will then need to determine which ones should be contacted, and when the best time will be to meet them. Now get in touch with them and make appointments.

After the highest "A" activities have been scheduled, you can then add the other "A's", followed by the "B's" and "C's". By the end of your planning session, the coming week is organized, each day is organized, and so are you.

Ultimately, when you look at your calendar for tomorrow, you should have a clear idea of your activities, along with the who, what, where, when, and how for each.

On the "to do" list

Another important part of the plan is to start each day with a "to do" list. This should not be a vague idea in your head, but rather a written or electronic listing that gives you a clear, prioritized itemization of what you wish to accomplish in a given day.

■ **You could review** *your "to do" list and calendar regularly with your manager. He or she may have some additional activities for you to complete and may even coach and guide you in these areas.*

As you complete each activity on the list, cross it off and move to the next. Many people who use these lists not only rave about their usefulness in helping them get things done, but they also rave about the satisfaction associated with crossing off the completed items. Be sure to check your list at the end of each day, and add new items for the next day.

It is easy to get sidetracked and work on the most interesting, enjoyable, or fun parts of your job, rather than focusing on the main event.

Salespeople are known for procrastinating, especially when it comes to making cold calls. In the business, this is referred to as "call reluctance". One of the best ways to keep from procrastinating is to have a plan, priorities, and targets. If you make a commitment to make cold calls on a regular basis and at a regular time, this highly important activity is more likely to become a habit.

You can also master the procrastination monster by breaking down seemingly less desirable projects into more manageable chunks and handling them on a bite-size basis. Taking half a day to catch up on sales reports is a monstrous project that is all too easy to defer, but even this task becomes much more do-able when it is converted into a few mini-projects. The idea of "divide and conquer" is an appropriate strategy for procrastinators.

Some high-tech options

Advances in software, laptops, desktops, palm organizers, and Internet applications have led to major changes in the way that salespeople are able to organize their work and build relationships with their prospects and customers. These activities all fall under a new term called *Customer Relationship Management*, which is referred to as *CRM*.

> **DEFINITION**
>
> Customer Relationship Management, *or CRM, is a set of high-tech tools that are used to plan and organize all aspects of marketing, sales, and support. It deals with the automation of each of these functions.*

> **INTERNET**
>
> www.crmmagazine.com
>
> *This is the web site for CRM Magazine, and it provides online access to a wide range of information on CRM. One of the most helpful features is easy access to a large number of the magazine's articles and columns.*

■ **Finding out** *about prospects has never been easier or quicker. Accessing company web sites on the Internet will give you helpful background information and also save you valuable time.*

DEFINITION

Sales Force Automation, or SFA, *is the automation of the full range of your sales activities, from prospecting all the way through to the close of a sale. This includes generating leads, managing contacts, preparing reports and quotations, document management, project status, calendars, client information, account history, addresses, daily agendas, follow-up communication, and forecasting.*

If you look at the key components of CRM, you'll notice that one of them has the heading of "Sales". Its full description is *Sales Force Automation*, also called *SFA*, and it is the key part of CRM that applies to you.

You can find SFA support to fit your needs on the Internet, through a combination of software and Internet applications and through various software programs.

INTERNET

www.opportunit.co.uk
www.business-critique.co.uk
www.eurosmartz.co.uk
www.salestalk.co.uk
www.pts.com

For Sales Force Automation, these are some of the major online business applications. They can provide you with all of the SFA functions for a monthly fee.

With SFA, you can quickly and easily manage your time and know exactly what is going on with every item of business in your *sales pipeline*.

A key source of SFA support is available on the Web through what are called "online business applications". They provide the full range of SFA functions, and there is no software involved.

You can also find SFA support on the Web through what are called "CRM client server applications". These sites rely on software that you install on your laptop. You would then access the SFA program on the selected web site. As the software changes, you would need to upgrade.

Another CRM option falls under the heading of "contact managers". These are software-based SFA programs and are somewhat more generic than online business applications and client server applications. They are not accessible over the Web, and they are often used by individuals and smaller organizations.

DEFINITION

Your sales pipeline consists of all of your business that is currently in the works, ranging from the earliest stages of a sale to sales that are right at the point of completion. Think of your pipeline in concrete terms and envision all of your business flowing through it. You need to monitor it regularly and take action every day to keep it filled. In many respects, your pipeline is your lifeline, and you certainly do not want it to run dry.

INTERNET

www.onyx.com
www.crmassist.com
www.telemagic.com

These are some of the web sites that offer a broad range of CRM and SFA software.

INTERNET

www.oracle.com
www.siebel.com
www.saleslogix.com
www.pivotal.com

These client server applications provide the full range of CRM support. Oracle and Siebel are usually used by the more prestigious companies, while Saleslogix and Pivotal are better suited for mid-sized companies.

■ **You can** *install software on your laptop to give you access to the range of high-tech tools available for the complete automation of your sales activities.*

Some basic options

Many salespeople still use traditional paper-based scheduling systems such as weekly calendars and organizers in which they schedule their work. This approach can also include handwritten spreadsheets and a series of individual worksheets for daily and weekly goals, time analyses, and account reviews. Other salespeople use a combination of paper-based and electronic systems.

You should look for a planning system that best meets your needs as well as the needs of your company and customers.

However, if there is a trend today, it is a clear movement towards online business applications to help salespeople sell, manage their time, and manage their customers.

E-mail, phones, and faxes can be valuable tools for dealing with your customers and saving time.

The downside of such useful tools as e-mail, phones, and faxes is that they can be costly, but not necessarily in terms of the money you spend on them. Many customers expect personal service, and overuse of these devices sometimes sends an aloof, flat, uninvolved message that can open the door for your competition.

■ **Today's high-tech options** *to schedule your work are user-friendly and can help you spend less time on paperwork and more time with your prospects and customers.*

Time-management strategies

IN ADDITION TO PLANNING, *many of the most effective salespeople incorporate a few simple strategies that take their time-management skills to a higher level. These are strategies you can implement right now, and their impact can be seen almost immediately.*

All in a day's work

Although it is clear that no one is inventing more hours in the day, some highly effective salespeople have come up with the next best thing. In fact, their approach often gives them at least a couple of extra days each month. All they do is wake up earlier each day. Not only does this give them extra time, it gives them uninterrupted time, a commodity that is even more valuable.

Turning downtime into uptime

Whenever there is a lull, or "downtime", such as an unexpected wait at a prospect's office, salespeople who are conscious of the importance of time management do not sit around and read dog-eared magazines. Rather, they use their non-selling time, no matter where it is, to focus on meeting their objectives. So when there is a delay in the game, make phone calls, listen to educational tapes, catch up on some "C"-level work, or read about a client, your industry, or related topics that will help bring you closer to your goals.

As a preventive measure, many salespeople take specific steps to keep downtime to a minimum. This is accomplished by setting specific times for appointments, setting appropriate leaving times for appointments, keeping a buffer zone between appointments, mapping out the best way to get from one client to another, confirming appointments, and calling ahead if unforeseen circumstances cause you to be late.

■ **If you are running late** *and do not have a mobile phone, use a pay phone and let your prospect know when you will arrive.*

Do not drop in on your customers without advance notice.

Most business people are very busy, and a surprise visit will be viewed as an annoying interruption. In addition, an unannounced visit shows that you do not respect your customer's time, or your own for that matter.

INTERNET

www.mapquest.com

On this site, you list where you are and where you want to go, and it gives you the best way to get from one point to another. You can set up a string of directions to help you navigate quickly from one prospect to the next.

If you are in the neighbourhood and want to drop in on a customer, the best way to do so is to call and mention that you are in the area and would like to stop by, if it is convenient.

Ready for prime time

There are certain times of the day when each of us feels more energized, alert, and focused than at others. To manage your time best, you need to know which hours are best for you, and try to use these premium periods for the most demanding, challenging, and motivating part of your job – in other words, meeting with prospects and customers.

LOOKING FOR LOST THINGS

If you spend an average of 15 minutes per day looking for this or that lost item, can you guess what that will cost you in days over a 30-year career?

1. For a 5-day week, 15 minutes per day adds up to 75 minutes, equalling about 300 minutes per month.

2. Switching to hours, that's 5 hours per month and 60 hours per year.

3. In your illustrious 30-year career, that's 1,800 hours, give or take.

4. If you divide your 1,800 hours by 24, you find that your 15 minutes per day looking for those lost goodies cost you 75 days!

WATCH THE CLOCK

Do not work on "C"-level activities during prime time. Prime time is for the main events.

If you find that your customer is more of an afternoon person or if he or she is rarely available during your peak periods, you may not be able to schedule meetings at the best time for your biological clock. Be sure to focus even more intensely during those meetings. Keep in mind, though, that if you are meeting during your customer's best hours, the session has a greater likelihood of going well simply because he or she is feeling upbeat, energized, and ready for action.

Get out of the mess

The salespeople who manage their time most effectively typically do not have work areas that look like the receiving end of a wind tunnel. When it is difficult to find needed information, documentation, computer disks, and even the computer, a tremendous amount of time is wasted in the hunt.

In addition, when materials are lost, a great deal of frustration is associated with the task of finding them. When the lost items finally appear, the frustration does not drop to zero. The stress lingers, and it can have a negative impact on the way in which the salesperson interacts with others.

Paperwork is filed neatly

Concentration is easier when there are no distractions

Desk is clear of extraneous items

In-tray is cleared regularly

■ **Keeping your desk clear** *of everything but essential items that you use regularly throughout the day, such as your phone and in-tray, will help you focus on the job in hand.*

The power of "yes" and "no"

ONE OF THE BEST WAYS *for salespeople to maximize their effectiveness in managing time is to seek out the word "yes" and to know when to use the word "no". These are two of the most powerful and emotionally charged words in the English language, and using them in the right situations can save time.*

Looking for "yes"

When dealing with prospects, it is important to deal with people who are empowered with the ability to say "yes". Countless hours can be wasted with prospects who are not real prospects at all. For example, at a recent dot com sales session, the prospect had neither the interest nor the ability to say "yes", but he actually turned the tables and tried to sell his wares to the salespeople who were calling on him!

This does not mean that every person you contact must be the final decision-maker. In fact, in selling today, it is quite common to have several sales meetings before getting to the final decision-makers. But, at the very least, the people you meet must have the power to take the necessary steps to move you closer to a meeting with those empowered to make decisions.

You will also save time by being well prepared and providing your prospects with the information they need to say "yes". In fact, the word "yes" plays an important role throughout the sales process, but there's more about this in Chapter 10.

Know about "no"

Another important step in managing your time is the ability to say "no". There are countless ways for people to interrupt you, make borderline requests, throw marginal work your way, and generally pull you away from your "A" activities.

■ **Using negative** *body language, such as turning your head but not your whole body towards the visitor, will help discourage unwanted interruptions.*

People who manage their time well are not afraid to act assertively. If you are busy with "A" activities, you do not have to drop everything when interrupted or targeted for a trivial task. This does not mean that you should be aggressive, hostile, or nasty. Rather, you can directly and politely say that you are in the middle of a very important project and this is not a good time to handle whatever issue or question is being presented.

If it's feasible, you can add that you may be able to help out later in the day. Remember to use your non-prime time for these types of activities.

Many people who feel that they have to respond to every request from others often have a strong underlying need to be liked and accepted. The fact is that if you are friendly and fair in your dealings with others, helping them out when you can and saying "no" when you cannot, you will still be liked, accepted, and respected.

A simple summary

✔ Look at how you are spending your time right now. This is the best way to get a quick snapshot of your current time-management skills.

✔ Prioritize your activities as "A's", "B's", and "C's", and plan your days and weeks with these priorities clearly in mind. The biggest "A" for salespeople is selling, and your plans should be organized around it. Selling is the big rock; handle it first.

✔ Keep asking yourself, "Am I making the best use of my time right now?" If the answer is "yes", press on. If the answer is "no", switch to an activity that generates a "yes".

✔ Have a "to do" list that prioritizes and spells out what you seek to accomplish, and review it at the end of each day.

✔ The most important trend in time management and overall organization for salespeople at each step of the sales process is Sales Force Automation.

✔ Spend your time with customers and prospects who have the power to say "yes", and be willing to say "no" to people who seek to devour your time.

PART TWO

SUCCESSFUL SALES RELATIONSHIPS

NOW THAT YOU'VE GOT your sales job and some realistic plans and goals, you're ready to *find customers* and start *building relationships* with them. In the old days, you would have packed your bag of wares, hit the road, and started ringing doorbells. Well, the process has changed dramatically since then, and now there are numerous techniques to help you target a broad range of potential customers.

When you do find a potential customer, you have to work out if this prospect can and will buy your product. With this in mind, there are some *great questions* you'll be asking. You are then going to have to build *trust and rapport* quickly, and I'll show you exactly how to do that.

Chapter 5

Becoming the Prospecting Pro

I N THE MID-1800s, a miner would get up early in the morning, grab a pick with one hand and a pan with the other, and head for the field. He or she was a prospector looking for gold. In the 21st century, a salesperson gets up early in the morning, grabs a palm organizer with one hand and a cell phone with the other, and also heads for the field. He or she too is a prospector looking for gold – sales gold. If you are a salesperson, you are also a prospector. Here are some simple ways to find gold.

In this chapter...

✓ Your customers come first

✓ Referrals for results

✓ Creative steps to build your network

✓ Being cool with cold calls

BEING A PRO MEANS USING A BROAD RANGE OF STRATEGIES TO SEEK OUT PROSPECTS

Your customers come first

PROSPECTING IS OFTEN SAID *to be the single most important activity for any salesperson. Successful salespeople are* prospecting *every day, since prospecting is the ultimate source of present and future business.*

Many people think that prospecting is just sitting at the phone and making *cold calls* to total strangers. Although cold calls are part of the prospecting process, these calls are but one option in the prospecting arena.

Prospecting is often described in units of temperature, all the way from cold calls to hot prospects. The hot prospects are those who are highly predisposed to buy what you are selling, and the cold calls are for those who have no idea who you are or what you are selling. In between are the warm leads, and they are typically prospects who have been referred to you through your network or your company.

■ **Selling to a hot prospect** *is obviously easier than cold calling, but take care not to be complacent. Express enthusiasm for your product and keep your body language positive throughout the meeting.*

Although salespeople pursue leads across this thermal range, it makes sense to pursue the hot leads first, and then move into the cooler zones. There will still be cold calls, even on a daily basis, but there is no reason for them to give you the chills. They are simply part of your overall set of prospecting tools.

Although it is often tempting to go running about in search of new prospects, the first place to look for new sales is with your present customers. After all, they know you, trust you, feel positive about your products and service, and are typically much easier to access than other prospects.

Casting aside grammatical prohibitions about ending sentences with prepositions, one of the most important points to remember about present customers is that people like to do business with people they do business with.

What else do they need?

You can meet up with your present customers to see if the present levels of products or services that they are purchasing from you are meeting their needs. After all, their businesses are dynamic entities, and, as a result, perhaps there may be an increased need for what you are offering.

New products on the block

As you learn more about your customer's changing needs, there is a real chance that the changes in your products will form the basis for additional sales. It is always a good idea to have at least two contact people at client companies. This can be a helpful source for additional *referrals*, and can make a real difference if one of these people leaves.

Another good reason for contacting your present customers is to let them know about the new products and services that your company is now offering.

> **DEFINITION**
>
> A referral is an introduction to a prospect that is provided by an individual who is known and presumably respected by the prospect. This can range from an indirect introduction, where your contact says that you can use his or her name in contacting the prospect, all the way to having your contact lead you down the hall and personally introduce you to the prospect. Can you guess which is more effective?

Additional referrals

In meeting with your contact person or persons, you can also discuss other areas or departments within the company that may need your products. In this case, ask your contact to provide you with an introduction.

This type of introduction comes with instant credibility, trust, and a proven company-specific endorsement. In addition, your customers can refer you to prospects at other companies, and this too is worth exploring.

■ **Referrals from** *existing satisfied customers are as powerful and influential as any referrals that you may ever receive.*

Referrals for results

REFERRALS ARE ONE OF THE MOST EFFECTIVE *ways to build your base of prospects. Instead of being a random person who contacts the prospect from out of the blue, you now come with a stamp of approval from a trusted source. This immediately puts you ahead of any other salespeople who have contacted the same prospect without such an endorsement.*

As noted above, a referral can be made by an existing customer to other key people in his or her company. At the same time, referrals can come from a wide range of additional sources.

Netting referrals from your network

Your network is not merely composed of friends and family, a couple of co-workers, some former colleagues and associates, a few people you met at a seminar 3 years ago, and your friends from the football club. Rather, your network is all of the people you currently know, all of the people you have known in the past, and all of the people

■ **By keeping your network** *as broad as possible, to include roommates from university, even friends from school, you will have an invaluable source of referrals to prospects.*

you are going to know in the future. Out of all these people, surely there are dozens who can provide you with excellent referrals to potential customers.

After you have contacted a prospect referred to you by someone in your network, be sure to get back to the source of the referral with a brief update and thanks. This can be done by letter, e-mail, or phone call, and it is always appreciated. And it can lead to further referrals.

As you compile your network, think expansively and include people you have met through all of your jobs, your schooling and seminars, trade shows, civic and community work, social gatherings, family gatherings, neighbourhood meetings, holidays, air travel, your children's activities, all the way to the queue in the supermarket.

Your primary objective in prospecting is to find sales leads and set a specific date and time for a sales call.

As a salesperson, you should genuinely enjoy meeting people in any context, and these meetings can be a source of potential referrals.

You do not have to be a back-slapping extrovert to meet people and start talking shop. More typically, when you meet someone, your conversation will naturally gravitate towards what each of you does for a living.

If you like what you hear, you can exchange business cards or get a phone number, and then say that you will give him or her a call during the week. You have now added one more person to your network. This person can be approached as a prospect, a source of additional prospects, a customer, and even a friend.

■ **A chance meeting** *can lead to business cards being exchanged and another person being added to your network of contacts.*

Netting referrals from your company

Many companies have fine-tuned marketing and advertising programmes to help build a base of quality prospects. The programmes often have high visibility, and they occasionally offer various incentives and promotions to entice the prospects and make it easy for them to contact the company. These kinds of marketing efforts can generate a good number of *warm leads* for the salespeople.

> **DEFINITION**
>
> *Prospects that are generated by a company's marketing programmes are typically referred to as* warm leads.

At the same time, if you find that your company's leads are insufficient or of marginal quality, you should discuss the situation with your sales manager. Ideally, you should have an opportunity to discuss these referrals with some of the marketing staff as well.

■ **Discussing the leads** *provided by your company with your sales manager and the marketing staff is encouraged by many organizations. They recognize that the salespeople are the ones out in the trenches and they can have outstanding information, insights, and suggestions as to how to improve the marketing effort and the products.*

Netting referrals from the Internet

With increasing numbers of salespeople using the Internet for a broad range of sales functions, the forums on various sales web sites provide an opportunity to network with other salespeople and build their potential referral base. The participants share ideas regarding any number of sales topics, and some valuable ideas as well as contacts can be shared as well.

In addition to web sites that provide opportunities for salespeople to chat about referrals, there are several web sites specifically designed to provide salespeople with leads. In fact, many of these web sites boast that they have millions of leads, and they can stratify them based upon such factors as product, prospect analysis, company profiles, industry, financial condition, and markets.

INTERNET

www.businessadvice
online.org
www.salestalk.co.uk
www.enterprisezone
.org.uk
www.infospace.com
www.justsell.com
www.imarketinc.com

These sites can provide you with numerous leads, while also helping you narrow them down to those that may be most suitable for you.

INTERNET

www.salesdoctors.com

This web site has an interactive forum for salespeople to network and discuss sales problems, strategies, and solutions, as well as to share leads. It also offers a wide range of sales products and support for users.

Creative steps to build your network

AS A PROFESSIONAL SALESPERSON, *it is important for you to be on the alert for ways to build your network every day. Here are some simple additional steps that can help take your network to the next level.*

The power of public relations

Try to see yourself as a public relations specialist with one client: you. The idea is to try to find ways to get free publicity. This can include writing some articles for an industry journal, newsletter, or magazine, doing some public speaking, and making yourself available for radio and television interviews. All of this gets your name around the community and industry, puts you into contact with people who are either contacts or sources of contacts, and further characterizes you as an expert.

■ **Being interviewed** *by your local newspaper is an effective way of getting free publicity.*

GETTING YOUR NAME KNOWN

Be willing to adopt new strategies as part of your public relations strategy. For example, in some areas you can sponsor a roundabout by donating a specific amount of money to keep it clean. A prominent sign is placed on the roundabout, indicating that you have adopted it.

In southern California an estate agent sponsored a section of freeway in the area where he sells and leases commercial property. Typically, at least 10,000 cars per day travel this stretch of road, and the salesperson's sign is so prominent that he feels it has practically made him a celebrity. When he meets new prospects, they inevitably say that his name is familiar to them. Of course it is, they see it every day!

Let's get involved

You can build your network by joining civic, community, business, trade, and religious organizations. There are great opportunities to learn, grow, contribute, and network in countless organizations such as your local Rotary Club, churches and other religious centres, and youth sports. Your network will expand even faster if you assume a leadership role in any of these organizations.

Triumph at trade shows

Another important arena for building your network is industry trade shows. Try to attend panel discussions that sound as though they could be of interest to prospects.

Trade shows are useful for building your network of contacts, but you have to do more than simply show up and hang out in your company's booth.

As you build your expertise, plan on being a panellist in some of these sessions. Set aside some time every day to "work the show". This means getting to as many booths as possible, chatting with the troops, having meals with new people, and gathering a handful of cards from select people whom you will call during the following week.

Being cool with cold calls

IN ADDITION TO PROVIDING YOU *with warm leads, your company may provide you with lists of prospects with whom no prior relationship or contact has been made, but who might possibly meet the company's criteria as viable leads. At the same time, perhaps you have gathered names from the Internet, industry directories, magazines, journals, newspapers, press releases, advertisements, and newsletters. Either way, you may not have much additional information about them. Rather than picking up the phone and simply pushing buttons (or procrastinating), you can take steps that can make cold calling easier and more effective.*

Before the cold call

The first step is to look over the list of prospects and try to prioritize them as "A's", "B's", or "C's" based on such factors as their size, revenue, location, and potential. You should plan on contacting the "A's" first, and move to the "B's" and "C's" from there. This does not mean, however, that you are going to pick up the phone and call them yet.

One way to make a cold call somewhat warmer is to send the prospect a brief covering letter first, along with a short brochure if you wish. Then, when you make your cold call, you are actually following up on some materials you have already sent, and this can make it easier to approach the prospect and break the ice.

If you want your covering letter to be read, it should never be longer than one page.

A "P.S." message at the bottom of your covering letter is an especially good place to include a key benefit that would be particularly effective in meeting a prospect's needs.

One highly successful direct marketing organization found that no matter what people do with a cover letter, they typically read a "P.S." message at the bottom.

When to cold call

From the planning standpoint, you should try to set aside time each day to make cold calls. It makes sense to batch a good number of cold calls together each day because you can get into a rhythm, and if you have one successful call, there is an increased likelihood that your next call will be successful too.

Although it may sound efficient to take an hour each morning for cold calls, the reality is that the morning may not be the best time for the kinds of prospects you need to reach. As a result, you will have to do some test marketing to find the hot times for your cold calls.

Scripted or not?

You should have a clear idea of what you want to say to your prospect before you call. For some salespeople, this can be a memorized script. A script can work well, but only if it is supported by outstanding content and a good deal of guided practice. The material has to be memorized and rehearsed to the point that you can deliver it in a totally natural style, and that does not happen overnight.

■ **When you smile**, *it helps to maintain a positive tone of voice, which is invaluable when you're making sales calls. Try propping up a mirror in front of you to encourage you to smile.*

Whether you go with a script or not will depend on your company and your personal style. Either way, it is important to know the key points you want to bring out, along with the basic track you want to follow. At the same time, don't be so focused on what you are trying to say that you miss what your prospect is telling you about his or her needs. In a word, keep your remarks brief, simple, clear, and honest, and try to spend more time listening than talking.

Making the cold call

When you cold call, you should be in a comfortable setting, free of interruptions, with any materials you need within easy reach. If you are a person who likes to stand or even pace, you should use a telephone headset.

To make it as easy as possible for your prospects to respond positively to your call, make it easy for you to make the call.

■ **Whether you are a pacer** *or not, a telephone headset frees your hands to write, use your computer, or thumb through materials that may be helpful during the call.*

Tracking down your prospect

If you make a cold call and reach the individual's administrative assistant, a simple format to follow is, "Good morning. I'm John Smith with XYZ Company. I sent some material to Ms. Jones, and I mentioned I'd be giving her a call this week to discuss it. Is she available please?" With this approach, you have built-in credibility by mentioning your company name, along with honesty by doing exactly what you told Ms. Jones you would be doing. If the administrative assistant indicates that Ms. Jones is not available, ask for the best time to call back, and then do so at the suggested time.

If the administrative assistant indicates that Ms. Jones is not the right person to contact, simply ask who the right person is. The next step is to call him or her.

■ **After you have given** *your introduction, you can then ask the classic "How are you?". No matter how the prospect responds, try to react enthusiastically and ask a question that generates a "yes" answer, such as how busy the prospect must be.*

Making contact

If you get Ms. Jones on the line – and, frankly, this may happen in fewer than half of your calls – you should introduce yourself again, state your company name, and indicate that you are following up the brochure or letter you sent recently.

You then ask her if she has had a chance to review the materials you sent. If she says "yes", ask her a question that focuses directly on her needs. For example, "Did you notice the savings with our new X?" At the same time, if she never saw your correspondence, tell her that you will put a copy in the post, and then ask if she would like to hear more about your company's new X that offers considerable savings to companies just like hers.

You then stop talking and listen carefully to anything that the prospect may say or ask. Even if the prospect shows .01 per cent interest, try to set an appointment. "I'd like to show you how this will really work for you. How would Thursday afternoon or Friday morning suit you for a meeting?"

If you feel that you are just inches away from getting that meeting, one of the most powerful ways to land it is to say something like this to your prospect, "I understand how busy you are. If you can give me 15 minutes to show you exactly what our cutting-edge Product X can do for you, I absolutely feel you'll be pleased. After 15 minutes, if it isn't everything I promised and more, we'll call it a day."

From the standpoint of prospecting, the objective of a cold call is to set up a face-to-face appointment.

Keeping time

With all of the above in mind, calculate that you have between one and two minutes to make the entire call and get the appointment. This means that you need to practise with a stopwatch in hand.

Never phone a prospect and tell the administrative assistant that this is a personal call.

It is not a good idea to lie about who you are to your prospect's administrative assistant. Although you may bypass him or her, you are indicating that you are devious and untrustworthy, which is not exactly the best way to start a working relationship. It is, however, one of the best ways to generate hostility and a fairly sore ear.

It is common today to make a cold call and find that you are expected to leave a message on voicemail. One option is to leave a message that is, again, open, honest, and clear, and again focused on following up the materials that were previously sent. At the same time, you can try to make it more enticing, such as by mentioning any special programmes or guarantees that are now available.

Be wary of appointments in the late afternoon on Friday, particularly on Fridays before long weekends, as they have an increased likelihood of being cancelled.

If you keep calling and find that you get the same voicemail or the same administrative assistant, another strategy is to try calling at more unconventional hours and times.

The hidden advantage of such calls is that they also send a message to the prospect that you are a hard-working and diligent individual who puts in long hours, just like the prospect. This shared feeling can be helpful in building a sense of trust in the sales relationship.

After the cold call

If you have had a successful call and have an appointment in hand, the next step is to make another call immediately. The enthusiasm and positive feelings from your successful call can easily transfer to the next call, and this increases the likelihood of having yet another successful call.

■ **To reach** *an elusive prospect, try calling him or her from your home. There are many prospects who are at the office and grab their own phones in the early morning, early evening, and during the weekends.*

As part of your system of managing calls, be sure that you send a confirmation note to any of the prospects with whom you have made appointments.

If a call did not lead to an appointment, whether you talked directly to the prospect or not, the next step is to take a deep breath and recognize that this is part of the sales process and that your product is still as excellent as it ever was. Put the prospect on the list for some follow-up literature and enter a date for another call.

■ **Just as** *good golfers are not always successful with their first putt, so the best salespeople will never make a sale from every cold call they make.*

Handling rejection

It is also important to remember to leave any of your feelings of rejection or dejection behind you as you make the next call. Many salespeople can bring their feelings of distress from one call to the next, causing one unsuccessful call to yield yet another. Fortunately, you can control this.

After a string of unsuccessful cold calls, it is easy for salespeople to become increasingly reluctant to pick up the phone. They procrastinate by engaging in just about any activity rather than make the next call. It is important to remember that these rejections are a normal part of the profession, as well as an entirely predictable aspect of selling.

Look to the future

Just because a prospect does not sense the need to buy today does not necessarily mean that he or she will be as reluctant to make a purchase in the future, particularly with the increased information about your products that you will continue to provide. Instead of looking at the unsuccessful calls as rejections, you can more accurately view them as deferrals. And, most important, never think that they are personal rejections of you.

If you maintain contact with prospects over time, you will certainly have success with some of them.

If you write off these contacts, you will never be successful with any of them. The reality of selling is that it usually takes several calls before a sale is made.

Plan on keeping in touch with these contacts over the long term, and use all sorts of media to do so. For example, in addition to phone calls, you can stay in touch via e-mail, by forwarding articles of interest and congratulations on achievements or promotions, and by sending brochures describing your company's new products and developments.

The bottom line of the entire prospecting process is that the more prospects you contact, the more sales you will close.

How much is a cold call worth?

It is possible to work out how much you earn from each cold call by looking at the total number of calls you make and doing some simple calculations.

For example, if you make 50 calls, get through to 25 prospects, get 10 appointments, and make 4 sales that net you a commission of £400, what do you earn per call?

Here is the equation: 50 calls = £400.

ADDING IT UP

To find the value of one call, divide each side of the equation by 50:

$$\frac{50}{50} \text{ calls} = \frac{£400}{50}$$

When you complete the division, the answer is: one call = £8.

This means that you earn £8 per call. As a result, for each additional call that you make, you are probably going to earn an additional £8. So, if you want to increase the amount of commission you earn, all you need to do is make more calls.

Keeping track

The best way to make prospecting work for you is to have a system that tracks the entire process. This system should:

a Let you know where you are with your prospects

b Keep you up to date on developments with your contacts

c Give you an idea of the best prospects to pursue

d Highlight the dates for communication with prospects and the kind of communication to be sent

(e) Keep schedules on track

(f) Keep you up to date on the progress and potential for each prospect

(g) Analyze leads and sales

(h) Generally keep you on top of the entire process of managing the prospecting function

Although this can be done by hand, it is more easily accomplished through the SFA software and sales portals discussed in Chapter 4.

A simple summary

✓ The first place to look for new sales is with your present customers. Remember that people like to do business with people they do business with.

✓ One of the best sources of new sales is referrals, and these come from your network. Think of your network as everyone that you knew, know, or will know, and remember to take steps to build and monitor it continually.

✓ Keep your marketing department advised of the quality of the leads they may be providing, in addition to any prevalent themes that you are finding in the marketplace.

✓ To build your customer base further, think of yourself as a public relations specialist with one client: you.

✓ With some planning, prioritizing, and practice, cold calls can be a powerful source of new business for you.

✓ The objective of all prospecting is to get an appointment with the prospect.

✓ One of the sources of prospecting success is to have an SFA system that keeps track of the entire process.

Chapter 6

Qualifying Your Prospects

ONCE YOU HAVE SOME PROSPECTS, you have to mind your "P's" and "Q's." In the sales arena, the "P" stands for the prospect, while the "Q" stands for Qualify. Qualifying is the process of determining if the prospect has the needs, wants, authority, and ability to buy the product from you. In short, as soon as you have a prospect, your first thought should be whether or not he or she qualifies. There is no joy in spending many hours with a seemingly excellent prospect, only to learn that his or her company is in no position to buy from you for the foreseeable future. By qualifying your prospects as early as possible, you can spend more time with the better prospects and less time with the questionable ones.

In this chapter...

✓ You already qualify

✓ Check out the company

✓ Check out the person

✓ Other essential qualifiers

You already qualify

YOUR DAILY LIFE IS FILLED *with numerous situations where you use highly developed qualifying skills to "check out" key people, products, and services. Try to think of the qualifying questions you ask when selecting a school, buying a computer, taking a job, ordering dinner, picking a dentist, deciding on a film, selecting an airline, choosing a jumper, or hiring a car.*

Depending upon the specific situation, you probably had questions about such matters as price, quality, availability, reputation, colour, size, endorsements, and warranties. And, if you received a negative response to any of these qualifying questions, you probably moved on. The main reason you did this was to eliminate the unfeasible choices as early as possible in order to spend more time with the feasible choices.

Your qualifying skills are an essential part of your effectiveness as a decision-maker, and without them you would be forced to handle much of your life on a random or guesswork basis. This applies to the selling process too, for if you fail to qualify a prospect, you do not know until it is too late whether you are dealing with a hot lead or a cold fish.

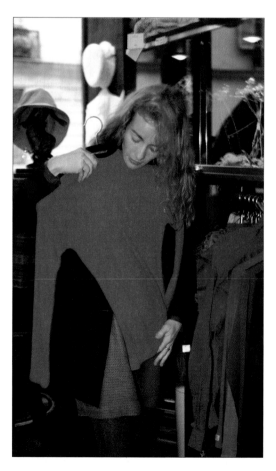

■ **When choosing a jumper,** *you use many of the same qualifying skills as you do when screening a potential customer.*

Check out the company

BEFORE YOU MEET THE PROSPECT, *and in many cases before you even contact the prospect, there are several qualifying steps that await you. The first is to learn as much as you can about the company, and there are a number of simple ways to do so.*

In good company

One way to start assessing a company is to look it up through any number of business directories, such as Dun and Bradstreet, along with checking it out on the Internet.

You may also learn about these companies by contacting the Better Business Bureau, any of your industry associations, and colleagues and associates from your own company as well as from others in your field.

This type of information can also be quite valuable during the sales meeting.

■ **As you read** *newspapers, industry magazines, and various newsletters, it's always helpful to be on the lookout for features about your prospects.*

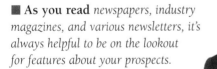

INTERNET

www.dnb.com
www.cpa.co.uk

These web sites can provide you with information about the credit rating of various companies and any investment data.

ARE THEY MAKING MONEY?

Some companies on your "A" list might look like incredibly exciting prospects, and the stories you read and hear about them may glow red-hot. For example, there have been numerous dot com companies that seemed to have everything – a compelling concept, big name support, terrific advertising, solid capitalization, incredible offices, and even more incredible parties.

The only item that is flawed or even missing for a number of these companies is something called a revenue model. In simple terms, this model spells out the way the company is supposed to make money. In spite of their whopping capitalization, several "hot coms" are having a problem with two simple words, burn rate. This rate is the speed at which they are going through their capital. With minimal (if any) revenues flowing in, some of these companies will either burn out or be merely a flicker away from doing so. Many venture capitalists are no longer looking at these ventures as major opportunities, so many of the major chequebooks have closed.

For you as a salesperson, there is a real warning here. You need to be extremely careful when selling to some of the glitzy new companies, no matter how much hype surrounds them. Although these companies appear to be hot prospects, you still need to qualify them very carefully. You can do this in several ways:

a Go to some of the financially based web sites, such as www.fool.co.uk or www.ft.com, and see if there are profits warnings or problematic articles about your hot prospects.

b If you are comfortable reading an annual report, that can be helpful too.

c Speak to some financially savvy people to help give you a better picture of what may be truly going on.

Depending upon what you learn, your own company may want to adjust the payment schedule associated with any sales. If you see some warning flags, you should discuss them with your sales manager.

The dot com marketplace is crowded, and several vendors have already been left holding some very big bags. The consolidation process is going to continue, leaving some players without a home. Many of these companies are in a game of corporate musical chairs, and you will want to be prepared when the music stops.

Your understanding of the company, its operations, and its mission will increase your comfort and confidence levels, and will also increase your credibility.

Your insight into the company will give you a clearer idea of the company's needs, and your ability to demonstrate the ways that your products can help meet those needs can be the primary focus of your sales meeting.

Present company excluded

If you start to find that the information about a given company is not painting a pretty picture, you can rate the company accordingly.

Through your research, you may learn some undesirable facts about a company, including the following:

- Questionable financial condition
- Poor payment practices
- Unethical actions
- Dubious business practices
- Excessive litigation

If warranted, you can drop the company down to "C" level and defer any active contact with it. In a word, as you go through the qualifying process, some companies are going to be disqualified.

At the same time, you should continue to monitor all of the companies on your contact list, as a company may be languishing in the deep blue "C" level, but new ownership, leadership, or recapitalization can easily put it back on your "A" list.

INTERNET

www.google.com
www.yahoo.co.uk
www.hotbot.co.uk

With these sites, you can look up a company by name and then link to the company's web site, if it has one. By entering the company's name in any of these search engines, you can also access news stories, columns, personal web sites, and press releases relevant to these companies.

Internal and external developments can change a company's financial and operational situation quite rapidly.

Check out the person

YOU MAY HAVE QUALIFIED THE COMPANY and found that it is absolutely ideal in terms of finances, location, product mix, and potential. So, does that mean that your qualifying is done? Not exactly. Although the company may meet all of your criteria, this means nothing if your sales meeting is with a part-time summer assistant.

In addition to qualifying the company, it is important to qualify the person you will be meeting. There are three simple qualifying questions that can help you do so. As you talk to your prospects, keep the following in mind: "Can the prospect buy the product?", "Will the prospect buy the product?", and "Will the prospect buy the product from me?"

Can the prospect buy the product?

This first question is structured for you to find out if the prospect has the authority, responsibility, budget, and decision-making capacity to buy the product or service that you are selling. There are people at ideal prospect companies who may be willing to listen to you and be quite open in describing their departmental needs, but have absolutely no influence on the buying process.

When dealing with people who cannot buy your product, there are two options for you to consider. The first is to determine if this person is a "gatekeeper". This means that he or she is the first contact point at the company, and although this person cannot say "yes" to whatever you may be selling, this person can say "no" and stop the process in its tracks. In this case, your objective is to demonstrate how effectively your product will meet the company's needs, and then try for an appointment with those who make the decisions.

■ **If the "gatekeeper"** *doesn't have the authority to buy your products, it is vital that you ask him or her to make an appointment for you to meet the decision-maker.*

As for those who can neither buy the product nor play a critical role in the buying process, your objective is to discover this as early as possible, preferably before any appointments, and then to find the right person.

Some salespeople are so eager to have meetings at the "A"-level companies that they set appointments with "C"-level people who can neither buy nor be of any help. You cannot go on meeting like this!

A question that can help is, "Is there anyone else involved in making decisions with you?" This question automatically compliments your prospect by implying that he or she is part of the decision-making process. In addition, it comfortably opens the door for the prospect to give you not only the name or names of others in the process but also information on how the process itself works.

In selling today, it is common to sell to many levels of people before a sale is consummated. This means that there can be five sales calls or more in many cases. No matter how a company makes its purchasing decision, the salesperson can always benefit from trying to gain an understanding of how it works, not only in terms of timing, but in terms of the roles played by the various participants.

The salespeople who understand and respect a company's buying system will fare far better than the salespeople who overlook the system and try to barge through with their own sales strategies.

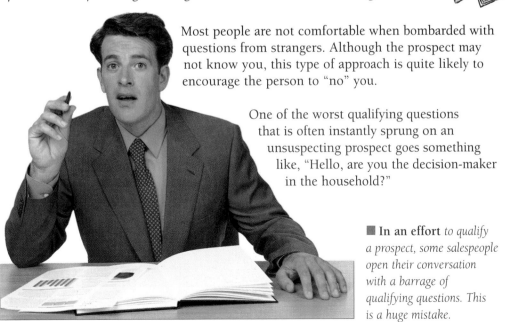

Most people are not comfortable when bombarded with questions from strangers. Although the prospect may not know you, this type of approach is quite likely to encourage the person to "no" you.

One of the worst qualifying questions that is often instantly sprung on an unsuspecting prospect goes something like, "Hello, are you the decision-maker in the household?"

■ **In an effort** *to qualify a prospect, some salespeople open their conversation with a barrage of qualifying questions. This is a huge mistake.*

My response to this question is always the same, "Um, I can't really decide."
I then turn to my wife and ask, "Roberta, am I the decision-maker in
this household?" Salespeople who use this type of approach are
often following a script, and it does not have a happy ending.

*Many of the mistakes that salespeople make could be avoided if
they simply take the Golden Rule and apply it to selling: sell to
others as you would have others sell to you.*

Will the prospect buy the product?

Let's assume that you have found a prospect who can buy your product. You have
asked the right questions and learned that he or she indeed has the title, responsibility,
budget, and full power to purchase what you are selling. All of this bodes well for you,
but now you need to find out if the prospect will buy the product.

Any number of factors can get in the way here. For example, your product may be
something that the prospect neither wants nor needs. A salesperson can ask, "If you felt
that our technology could provide more data than the others in the marketplace, is that
something that would interest you?" The customer may believe that the company has
no need whatsoever for any additional data, other than the masses already being
accumulated, and, as a result, he or she may sense no need to buy. In a word, the
customer neither wants nor needs your product.

By talking *with your manager and some of your colleagues, you may be able to find the decision-makers more easily and avoid the decision-fakers who are unable to commit to buying from you.*

Other qualifying questions in this "will buy" area include, "Does your company already have an X?" and "How satisfied are you with it?"

In addition, there are some prospects who have a hard time buying much of anything. They will meet you, listen to you, express their needs to you, carefully review what you have to offer, ask you to come back, but ultimately cannot commit to buy.

You may be excited about getting to meet a person with the power to buy from you, but unless you hear that he or she is willing to buy, the only buy should be a good-bye.

Will the prospect buy the product from me?

At this point, you have established the fact that this person not only has the power to make purchases, but has actually been making them in the past. The remaining question is whether he or she will buy from you.

Just because you have a prospect who can and will buy, there is no reason to assume automatically that he or she will buy from you.

The sooner you find out where you stand in this prospect's mind, the better. The fact is that there can be any number of business reasons behind a prospect's unwillingness to buy from you.

In order to probe this area, one key question to ask the prospect is, "How have you been making this kind of purchase in the past?" If there are contracts, relationships, or other constraints that may make it impossible for the prospect to buy from you, this is an easy way to learn about them.

For example, you may hear that the account is under contract to another company. You can ask the duration of the contract, and if it extends for a year or more, this prospect should be moved down on your list but should still be sent occasional messages, with a phone call scheduled in 6 months.

When you ask how the prospect has been making the purchase in the past, there are two additional benefits:

1. You are demonstrating that you have been paying attention during the conversation with the prospect.

2. In the event that the prospect is not tied to any particular vendors, you can learn a great deal about selling to this person by understanding how he or she has been making purchasing decisions in the past.

Other essential qualifiers

TO MAKE SURE THAT YOU ARE, IN FACT, DEALING with a *qualified prospect, there are a few other pointers to keep in mind. Although it is always preferable to qualify your prospect as early in the sales process as possible, it is important to remember that you should continue to qualify the prospect throughout the sales process.*

It's about time

There can be any number of issues related to timing that are important to bring out as part of the qualification process. For example, if the prospect meets all of the above qualifiers but is not interested in your product in the foreseeable future, that is worth knowing today.

You can easily ask the question, "What is your timing on making a decision about this?" If the timing falls within your parameters, you continue the process. If, however, the timing pushes the decision beyond a few months, you should try to set a meeting date closer to the decision-making point. Besides, this approach will suit the prospect's needs better.

It is also worth knowing if the prospect absolutely needs the product immediately and there is no way that your company can provide it for months. Naturally, if you have a hot prospect that is ready to go when your company isn't, there may be some internal steps that you can take to expedite things. If, however, you complete the sale and make a commitment that you cannot keep, that sale will cost far more than whatever you made on it.

■ **If your prospects** *are interested in your product but are unwilling to buy at present, arrange to meet them closer to the time when they could agree to making a purchase.*

Since you are not a mind reader

Although there may be any number of company-specific factors that you would like to know when qualifying your prospect, there may be no way of targeting the right questions to ask. For example, there may be unique operational issues, family business or personal matters, or internal procedures that have become inviolate over the years.

Fortunately, rather than going into a random questioning mode, there are some catch-all qualifying questions that can be helpful. For example, one question may be, "Do you see anything else that might get in the way of our doing business together?" This type of question sends a subtle message that already assumes you will be doing business with the prospect, while lightly opening up the way for the prospect to mention other key points that you, as a qualifier, need to know.

Another open-ended question that can be helpful in this area deals more with the product. You can ask, "What improvements to the product would you like to see?" This is a respectful question that implies that the prospect has valuable input regarding your company's product, while at the same time bringing out information that can help you determine if you can truly meet the prospect's needs.

Qualifying by observation

In addition to gathering qualifying data by asking questions, you can also gather this data by being highly observant, paying careful attention to what your prospect is saying and not saying, and looking carefully at his or her body language.

One prospect, a small business owner, mentioned his father-in-law several times during a sales presentation. Every once in a while, he slipped in a comment about his father-in-law's business expertise, and the prospect seemed to fidget momentarily and look away from the salesperson whenever making such a comment. The conversation then continued at its customary pace. Towards the end, the salesperson

■ **Paying close attention** *to the tone and cadence of what is being said will help you make an accurate assessment of your prospect.*

THE SIX PROBES

As you qualify your prospects, there are six easy questions that underlie the information that you are trying to gather.

1 Who? This means to be sure that you are talking to the right person.

2 What? These questions are focused on your product and the prospect's needs. The real issues are what the prospect expects from your product, and how your product can meet the prospect's needs.

3 Where? The issue is the location of your prospect and where your product is to be used.

4 When? This is the probe that deals with the timing. When will the prospect be able to make a decision, and when will the prospect need to take possession of the goods or services that you are offering?

5 Why? Qualifying questions in this area focus on the prospect's needs and wants for your product. If your qualifying questions find lukewarm motivation and desire for what you are selling, you can probe for points that help the prospect recognize more of his or her own needs and the ways that your product can meet them. At the same time, if the prospect truly has neither need nor desire for your product, that prospect should be deferred at this point and contacted later.

6 How? In a word, questions in this area focus on financial and budgetary matters and are designed to help you learn if the prospect can actually afford your product. In other words, how is the prospect going to pay for it?

■ **Use the six probes** *as a checklist to make sure you have answers to all the key questions.*

asked if it would be helpful to meet with the father-in-law. The prospect haltingly indicated that this would probably be a good idea since it was his father-in-law who actually handled all the financial matters for the company.

Perhaps the prospect, as the owner of the business, was embarrassed by this fact and did not want to mention it during the earlier qualifying questions that the salesperson had asked, or perhaps this was the prospect's strategy to defer a decision if the sale appeared to be nearing a close. Either way, if the salesperson had not been observant and truly focused on the prospect, he would not have picked up the subtle cues that told him that there was still more qualifying ahead.

The bottom line on qualifying your prospects is one simple point: the better you qualify, the better your chances of making a sale.

A simple summary

✔ The objective of qualifying is to determine if your prospects have the need, desire, and authority, as well as ability, to buy the product from you.

✔ Effective qualifying lets you spend more time with the better prospects and less time with the questionable ones.

✔ You already use your qualifying skills in many of your daily activities. As a result, it is rather simple to transfer them to selling.

✔ In qualifying a prospect, the key questions are: can the prospect buy the product, will the prospect buy the product, and will the prospect buy the product from me?

✔ Remember the importance of "Who", "What", "Where", "When", "Why", and "How" in qualifying.

Chapter 7

The Pre-Sales Checklist

A S A SALESPERSON, YOU ARE A PITCHER TOO. A pitcher of products. But you need to prepare that pitch carefully. If you randomly walk into a prospect's office and start throwing ideas, questions, or an unrehearsed script at someone, you will never get on. Before every meeting you need to warm up, practise, review the previous meetings, look at the current conditions, and check out the people you will be facing. By following a simple pre-sale checklist, you greatly increase your chances of becoming an ace salesperson.

In this chapter...

✓ What do you know?

✓ Stick to the questions

✓ Product knowledge

✓ Your warm-up routine

BEING WELL PREPARED IS THE HALLMARK OF SUCCESSFUL SALESPEOPLE

What do you know?

THE FIRST STEP, *before you meet with a prospect, is to go back and look at the information you gathered about this individual and his or her company. The idea is to try to get as clear a picture of the prospect's needs as possible.*

Your first contact

Go back to your first conversation with the prospect, whether it was by phone, at a trade show, or at a social gathering. You should have documentation and notes from this conversation in whatever system you selected to track your prospecting. Look over what you entered and try to see if there are any key themes, trends, or comments that point to your prospect's needs.

These kinds of needs can be expressed in any number of ways, including references to revenues, costs, reliability, service, newer technology, safety, security, reliability, or warranties. When you find these kinds of comments, be sure to make a note to mention them in your meeting with the prospect. This will demonstrate that you listened to the prospect and are concerned about what he or she truly needs.

Trivia...

It used to be a compliment to describe a salesperson as someone who could sell snow at the North Pole. But as the North Pole does not need more snow, such a salesperson is being manipulative, self-serving, and unethical. Selling that uses trickery, deception, or high pressure is based on meeting the salesperson's needs, while professional selling is based on meeting the prospect's needs.

Associating with your associates

It is possible that your associates have information about your prospect, and they may have even had direct selling experience with him or her. Perhaps you will learn that the prospect is highly detail minded or visual in his or her thinking, and this type of information can help you prepare what you are going to say, as well as how you are going to say or show it.

■ **Sometimes** *your associates may be able to provide you with extremely useful hints about the best ways to sell to a particular individual.*

Your associates may also know people who have dealt with your prospect, and they may be able to gather some data from them. In addition, your associates may have some updated news about your prospect that can be helpful to know.

Dressing the part

In this era of casual clothing at work, you should wear a neat, clean, and conservative version of the typical attire worn by your prospects and their associates.

Even the business development people, aka salespeople, from some of the most stodgy law firms and accounting firms know to leave off the ties when calling on dot com prospects.

■ **When your attire** *is similar to the prospect's, you are sending a subtle message that you and the prospect are similar to each other, which can go a long way towards building trust.*

Researching your research

Take another look at any of the information you have gathered about the company, whether through the Internet, newspapers, magazines, journals, or your network. By being up-to-date with key developments in the industry and in the prospect's organization, you not only show your expertise, credibility, and dedication, but you also build your own self-image and sense of self-confidence.

In addition, if the company has a *mission statement*, that can be one of the most valuable documents to read prior to any sales meeting.

You can usually find a company's mission statement in its brochures and annual report. These statements reflect the company's most critical needs, and you should try to look for ways in which your product helps the company meet them.

> ### DEFINITION
>
> *A mission statement is a company's expression of its vision, values, and objectives. These statements can be as brief as a sentence or two, or they can run into paragraphs. Either way, they can give you tremendous insight into where the company is going, why it is going there, and how it is going to get there.*

When you meet your prospect, keep the language and expressions from the mission statement in mind.

Having a prospect's mission statement at the front of your mind when you meet will help you phrase better questions, while also helping you respond to your prospect's questions with words that are familiar and positively charged.

■ **Setting aside time** *to read up on your prospect's company and the industry in general will pay dividends. It will not only impress the prospect but also give you extra self-confidence at meetings.*

Stick to the questions

TO BE FULLY PREPARED FOR A MEETING *with a prospect, there are several types of questions to ask yourself first. This step will further help you develop the right kinds of answers to the prospect's questions, as well as the right kinds of questions to ask the prospect.*

The "what-if" game

In this exercise, the objective is to ask yourself the most difficult questions that the prospect could possibly ask. What are the questions that you do not want to hear? Those are the ones to ask and answer now.

Sometimes it is helpful to conduct this exercise with some of your associates and with your manager, as the *brainstorming* approach can bring out many important questions and answers.

> **DEFINITION**
>
> **Brainstorming** *is the process of bringing a group of people together to openly discuss a problem or dilemma, and then develop as many strategies as possible to deal with it.*

■ **A relaxed atmosphere** *among the sales manager and associates will get a brainstorming session off to a good start. The creative juices will flow and no one will feel inhibited putting forward suggestions.*

One of the values of discussing the "what-if" questions with your associates is that many of them have probably dealt with at least some of these questions in the past. Perhaps they have developed some responses that are particularly effective. You do not need to be memorizing any answers, but you should talk them out until you feel comfortable enough to provide a prospect with a useful and productive response to any of them.

One "what-if" question that you should not be asking is, "What if the prospect isn't there?"

This problem can easily be prevented simply by confirming your appointment a day ahead. This is a critical step, unless you are doing a research project on reception-area decor.

Useful to know

This is the time to step back and think about additional kinds of information that the prospect might not have on hand but that could be useful in the sales process. Perhaps there are new figures and findings that relate specifically to the prospect's needs and the strengths of your products. Some of this information can be on the "nuts and bolts" side, but it can just as easily be some rather colourful or counter-intuitive data that truly surprise the prospect.

When prospects are given information that comes as a surprise or even a shock, they typically remember it and the source for a long time. This can be a valuable technique to keep yourself on the prospect's mind.

If you are interested in tracking down the answer to a unique question that could be interesting or even shocking for your prospect, but you are not sure how to access it, you can try the Internet.

All you have to do is ask

Since a great part of successful selling is based upon understanding your prospect, you will need to develop some basic questions to learn more about his or her needs. Although much of this will depend upon your product and your prospect, questions about who, what, where, when, and how can be an effective starting point.

Many of your follow-up questions will be based upon your prospect's responses. You can build your skills in this area by throwing some practice questions to your associates, and then trying to develop some follow-up questions based upon their replies.

INTERNET

www.askjeeves.co.uk

This popular site gives you answers to unique questions. You will be provided with links to all sorts of answers that have something to do with some or all of the words in your question. Quite often, you can find a direct hit. And this can lead to a direct hit with your prospect.

What else?

In preparing for a sales presentation, it is extremely important to consider the supplies, materials, equipment, or other resources that you will need to bring. This can be any item that can help you further demonstrate that your product will indeed meet the prospect's needs.

Although the specific materials necessary for a sales meeting depend upon the product or service that you are selling, some of the items to include are:

- Brochures
- Calculator
- Mobile phone
- Easel
- Pager

- Batteries
- Note pad
- Palm organizer
- Markers
- Sample products

- Warranties and endorsements
- Business cards
- Calendar
- Order forms
- Pens

Your mobile phone or pager should never ring during a sales meeting.

Turn off your mobile phone or pager as soon as you enter the prospect's premises. Taking a call or answering a pager during a sales presentation is the height of rudeness, insensitivity, and foolishness.

■ **If you take a call** *on your mobile phone while with prospects, you might as well be saying, "Whoever is calling me, no matter who it might be, is more important than you."*

If you merely turn off the ringer, but the phone can still vibrate, ignore it. Looking to see who is trying to contact you is equally insulting. Check your messages after the meeting, unless you like meetings that end quickly. Prior to any sales meeting, let your office know where you are. If there is an emergency, you can be reached at the prospect's place of business.

Every one of your prospects should feel that he or she is of primary importance to you.

THROWING LIGHT ON THE SUBJECT

One successful salesperson did the bulk of his selling on the road, and sometimes he would have sales meetings in his hotel room. Inevitably, when he would pack for these trips, he would carefully wrap some 100-watt light bulbs. When asked about this, his response was always the same, "Do you know how many hotels have never heard of light bulbs above 40 watts?".

It is this type of anticipating that can actually make the difference between a successful and unsuccessful sales presentation. Perhaps the presentation could

■ **Before setting out** *on a sales trip, make a note of everything you might need to take with you. If you are well prepared, you will also feel more confident.*

have been made in a shadowy room, but there is no doubt that the salesperson would have been distracted by this, even if the prospect was not. That distraction could be enough to cause the salesperson to miss some of the subtle cues that the prospect may have been sending.

Fast-forward your thinking to the sales meeting and picture it from beginning to end. Try to envision every possible item that you may need, along with replacements if some do not perform. If things look a little shady, perhaps you should think about light bulbs too.

Product knowledge

BEFORE MEETING WITH YOUR PROSPECTS, *it is obviously important to understand your product, but it is even more important to understand how your product will meet the prospect's needs. Although much of this information will be generated during your sales meeting, there are a number of simple preparatory steps that can help accelerate the process.*

From features to benefits

To be comfortable, confident, and effective in communicating with a prospect, you will want to know the ins and outs of your product. This may call for some real studying on your part, and if you find areas where your understanding is a little fuzzy, you should either review them or get some help.

Your product is composed of a number of features. Depending on the product itself, these features can include:

- Size
- Output
- Warranty
- Price
- Technology
- Adaptability
- Speed
- Colour
- Quality
- Uniqueness
- Expandability

As you do your homework, you want to have a clear idea of your product's key features.

DEFINITION

A product's features include virtually every aspect of the product itself, while the benefits are those aspects that meet your prospect's needs. For example, one of the features of your product may be its size, but if the prospect could not care less about the size, it is not a benefit to him or her.

In preparation for a sales meeting, the *features* are only half of the equation. The other half are the *benefits*. This immediately raises the question: aren't features the same thing as benefits? The answer is no.

The purpose of having a high degree of product expertise is not to put you in a position where you can dump a mass of data on a prospect. Rather, your product knowledge is important because it gives you a vast data base of features from which you can select the most appropriate benefits to meet the needs of your individual prospects.

■ **The value-added approach** *to selling lets your prospects clearly see the increased value associated with purchasing your product. Convincing them, for example, that your product will save their company a substantial amount of money will also add value to your effectiveness as a salesperson.*

Adding value

One of the most important concepts to keep in mind when preparing to meet a prospect is the notion of adding value. This means that you should try to think of the ways beyond the price in which your product will bring additional worth to the prospect. For example, if your product can clearly reduce operating costs well in excess of the purchase price, that is an added value that you can demonstrate to the prospect.

If you look over the features of your product, there may be several that fall into this value-added category. Your prospect should understand that buying your product is literally a worthwhile decision.

WHAT IS VALUE ADDED?

One of the simplest ways to understand the notion of value added is to think of it in terms of a formula. Value added is the sum of the benefits that your product brings, minus the cost:

Value added (VA) = benefits (B) – cost (C)

This means that the value added is a function of two factors, the benefits and the cost. If you want to increase VA, there are only two ways to do it. You have to either increase B or decrease C.

From the preparation standpoint, the one cost factor where you have any real control is the price. If there are other prohibitive costs that prevent the prospect from buying from you, this should have already come out during the qualifying process.

It makes no sense to put a great deal of time into working out ways to decrease price at this point in the process. If there is some room for manoeuvre in terms of price or payment options, you should be aware of it right now. If, however, you base your selling strategy on price, that is where your prospect will focus, and soon enough that is where the entire process will focus. That is one of the least desirable outcomes in selling.

When it comes to increasing B, the idea is to make sure that you have a clear idea of all of the benefits that your product brings to your prospect. You can certainly focus on the increased revenues or decreased costs, but don't forget to look at such factors as training, service, support, customization, and warranties.

By taking this approach, you can also put together information to help your prospect see how and when the product will pay for itself. In this way, your prospect is more likely to think of your product not only as a way to meet his or her needs, but also as an investment.

This is also a good time to be thinking about the relationship between the price of your product and increased revenues or decreased costs. For example, if your £10,000 product can save a company £100,000 in its first year, there is a saving of £1,000 for every £100 spent. This is a value-to-investment ratio of 10:1. For some prospects, this type of approach fits directly into their needs as well as into the way they think.

■ **Keep working** *at a clear and concise description of your product to show its superiority over its rivals. It should be no more than a one-liner, without a single superfluous word.*

The one-liner

Before you meet with any prospect, try to develop a concise sentence that describes the superiority of your product and why your prospect should buy it. If it takes you two or three sentences to spell this out, go back and keep sharpening and simplifying until you have a crisp one-liner.

Your one-liner should differentiate your product from the competition, not only in terms of the quality of the product itself, but also in terms of the support that your company provides for it. That support can include service, training, and warranties.

When you meet with a prospect and try to understand his or her needs, be ready to talk about more than just the product itself.

Salespeople who focus exclusively on product often find that the conversation evolves into a discussion of price. This is not likely to occur when you include product support in the discussion.

Once you clearly understand the strengths of your product and the reasons for your prospect to buy it, you will be better equipped to keep your sales presentations focused, and your prospect focused as well.

Your warm-up routine

IN THE FEW MOMENTS *before you actually meet your prospect, there are some simple steps that will help you to be completely ready for action.*

Why am I here?

You need to have an absolutely clear idea of the reason you are meeting your prospect. The reason quite clearly is: you are meeting your prospect to make a sale. It's as simple as that.

Since meetings with some prospects are preliminary in nature, and many sales situations call for five meetings before a sale is actually consummated, that does not change your objective for the first four meetings.

At the same time, if the only way to make a sale is through a subsequent meeting, then you move to your backup objective, which is to get a commitment from your prospect to take specific action to keep the sale moving.

There can be any number of commitments that your prospect can make, depending upon the specific sales situation. For example, your backup objective may be to have the prospect set up the next appointment, meet the key person or persons from the next level to set the stage for that appointment, or supply you with needed information before the appointment.

A little ritual

Salespeople and tennis players have something in common, and this similarity is also apparent in the minutes before a new challenge. Tennis players often have a little routine that they go through before they play. Some need to bounce the ball a set number of times, others tweak the racquet and observe the strings closely, while others take a few deep breaths. This routine helps them focus, clear their head, and positively channel any nervousness.

■ **Adopting a routine** *before a meeting, such as straightening your tie, will help calm the nerves.*

No matter what you include in your brief pre-sale ritual, it is absolutely essential to repeat one word over and over to yourself: listen.

ROUTINE RELAXATION

Before you meet your prospect, you should establish your own little ritual. It can be helpful to briefly close your eyes, take a few deep breaths, relax your neck and shoulders (see the exercises, right), and visualize a successful sales meeting. You can repeat your company's one-liner, quickly review the high points you want to mention, and even repeat your own mantra. The idea is to start each sales session feeling refreshed, energized, enthusiastic, and positive.

a **Massaging the shoulders**

Support your left elbow on your right hand, and drum the fingers of your left hand on your right shoulder blade. Repeat on the opposite side.

It all counts

Remember that once you enter a prospect's premises, everything that you do counts. The person you cut off in the car park could be the company president. Another person who comes running towards the lift and asks you to hold it may be your prospect. When you are in the prospect's domain, be on your best behaviour.

Just prior to meeting your prospect, you may meet another very important person, namely your prospect's administrative assistant or secretary. This is the person who screens your prospect's calls, handles your prospect's calendar, and even mentions a few words to the prospect about your behaviour while waiting for the meeting. It is essential to have this person on your side, and the best way to do so is to be friendly, polite, and professional.

■ **Treat everyone** *at your prospect's offices, from the receptionist to the company president, with the same amount of respect, whether you are in a face-to-face meeting or speaking to them on the phone.*

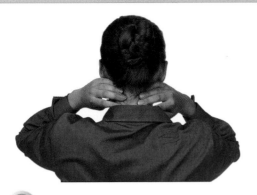

b **Massaging the neck and shoulders**

Place the fingers of both hands at the base of your skull. Apply slow, circular pressure, working down the neck, then across the shoulders.

c **Stretching the neck**

Place your hands on the top of your head. Pull your head gently down, and hold the position. Feel the slight stretch in the back of the neck.

A simple summary

✔ Look at everything you have learned about your prospect and his or her company and identify the ways that your product can meet his or her needs.

✔ Playing the "what-if" game helps you anticipate the toughest questions from your prospect and develop the best answers to them.

✔ Be sure to understand the features of your product and the ways that they translate into benefits for your prospects.

✔ Think about the ways that your product brings added value beyond the purchase price.

✔ Develop a one-liner for your product and keep it in mind before and during sales meetings.

✔ Before you walk into any sales meeting, remember that you are there to make a sale. If that cannot be done, then your objective is to obtain a specific commitment from your prospect that will advance the sales process.

Chapter 8

Building Rapport and Trust

W HEN PROSPECTS FEEL COMFORTABLE with a salesperson and believe that he or she is forthright, honest, and dependable, buying becomes far easier. Buying is an emotional decision – justified later by reason and logic – and a critical piece of the emotional filter is trust. A prospect's uneasy feeling about a salesperson can easily block a sale. After all, if the salesperson cannot be trusted, one has to wonder about the product. Before you start explaining your product and how it will meet your prospect's needs, focus on building rapport and trust. Many of the best salespeople can do this rather quickly, and by following these simple steps, you can too.

In this chapter...

✓ Ready for rapport

✓ Foundations of trust building

✓ Pacing for trust

Trust in your product

BUILDING TRUST WITH YOUR CLIENTS IS A CRUCIAL PART OF THE SALES PROCESS

Ready for rapport

SOME SALESPEOPLE MAKE THE MISTAKE of jumping into a sales pitch the second they meet a prospect. This approach is destined to fail because the salesperson has no idea of the prospect's needs, and the prospect has no reason in the world to trust a verbal vending machine.

Initial impressions are formed quickly, typically in a matter of minutes, and they do not change easily. When a salesperson enters with mouth open and ears closed, it has a lasting impact, even if the salesperson later tries to do that thing called listening.

Use your common senses

As soon as you meet your prospect, all of your senses should be in a high state of readiness. Listen carefully not only to everything that your prospect says, but also to how it is expressed. All of this is data that can help you understand the prospect's needs.

■ **On meeting a prospect** *for the first time, look at your surroundings and make a note of any personal touches in the office. The choice of books, for example, could reveal a lot about your prospect's personality and give you clues to his or her way of thinking and working.*

Be observant of everything going on in your prospect's work area. Take a look at whatever may be on the walls, floors, tables, bookcases, and desks. A person's office can give you a great deal of insight into his or her personality, and this can give you more keys into understanding his or her thinking and decision-making style. Even your sense of smell, touch, and taste can give you all sorts of information as to what may be going on in a company and in your prospect's mind.

Easy icebreakers

It is always a good idea to open your discussion with a prospect by exchanging some friendly words about a shared interest. Maybe you noticed a picture of a youth football team on the wall or perhaps a degree from a particular university. You can easily break the ice by asking a question. For example, if you have any kind of connection to youth football, you can ask, "How'd the football team do?" Your prospect will smile and now you are well on the way to an easy and friendly conversation.

Right from the outset, it is important to try to find areas of similarity between you and your prospect.

■ **A friendly conversation** *with your prospect before you launch into your presentation will help break the ice. People trust others like themselves, and the more you can demonstrate areas of similarity between you and your prospect, the more trust you will build.*

Sometimes it is recommended that salespeople sit right next to a prospect rather than across a desk or table. This is not something you should automatically do, however. It makes far more sense to consider making this move during the course of the conversation, particularly if you have any visuals you would like to share.

If you just plop down next to a prospect, you can actually make the prospect feel uncomfortable.

■ **Sitting next to a prospect** *is supposed to let him or her know that you are a partner, not a vendor, but be sure that your prospect will welcome this move before you make it.*

Widespread agreement

If you have tuned all of your senses up to the maximum and still cannot find one thing in common with your prospect, you can mention a broader subject, one that both of you may have experienced.

For example, if the weather has been unseasonably hot, mentioning this is an easy conversation opener. You could also open with some upbeat or positive developments or events in the community.

When meeting a prospect, do not complain, tell endless stories, argue, use slang or swearwords, interrupt, smoke, criticize, or show any impatience.

CLEARING THE AIR

Once, when I was selling employee-attitude surveys, I met the president of a company who said he was interested in identifying and correcting all sources of employee dissatisfaction. I had met him on two previous occasions, and at each meeting I started sneezing and coughing. This is not the best way to build a healthy relationship with a prospect.

I was not nervous about meeting him, and I did not have a sneezing and coughing problem anywhere else. And I've never been allergic to a prospect. Nonetheless, my senses were being drawn into the sales process. At last I asked the president if he thought the survey might find some complaints about coughing and sneezing at work. He said there did seem to be more than a few people in the company who had allergies.

After the meeting, I did some quick research into possible reasons people might be coughing and sneezing in one environment and not in another. It looked like the culprit might be the air conditioning system.

I contacted the president and mentioned this to him. He was so grateful that our firm was willing to check out the problem in our own time, and with no signed contract with his firm, that he agreed to the survey on the spot. As for the allergies, it did turn out that the air conditioning filters were the problem and ultimately the solution. By using all of my senses in selling, I was able to deliver an employee-attitude survey that cleared the air in many important ways.

■ **Eye contact** *with prospects shows that you are interested in what they are saying, but make sure you don't end up staring, which will make them feel uncomfortable.*

Many experts advise salespeople to maintain eye contact with their prospects, but that too has its limits. Some eye contact is entirely appropriate, but if eye contact evolves into a staring contest, it can be downright distracting. In addition, maintaining prolonged eye contact in some cultures is considered to be rude.

There are still stereotypes about dishonest people being unable to look others in the eye. Unfortunately, there are some notorious con artists who can look you in the eye better than an optometrist, while some of the most honest and ethical sales professionals may look everywhere but in your eye.

The real message is to avoid applying any stereotypes to your prospects. When salespeople buy into stereotypes, their prospects do not buy into much of anything.

Exit strategy

Sometimes you will walk into a prospect's office and your radar will tell you that this is not a good time to meet. If you enter just as your prospect slams the phone down in disgust, stares out the window in anger, or sits there frowning, you should heed the warning. All of this translates into a huge red flag.

Some salespeople will ignore these cues and try to break the ice, but this is a major mistake. If you sense that your prospect needs to be doing something other than meeting you, then you should deal with it. You can say, "If this is not a great time to meet, we can reschedule. It's not a problem."

By taking this approach, you are demonstrating confidence, concern for the prospect, and consideration for his or her needs. Whatever the prospect decides, he or she will have increased respect for you. If the meeting is held, you will have taken some of the negative edge off the prospect's mood. And, if the meeting is rescheduled, you will have already created some credibility.

Remember that selling is based on meeting the customer's needs, not the salesperson's needs.

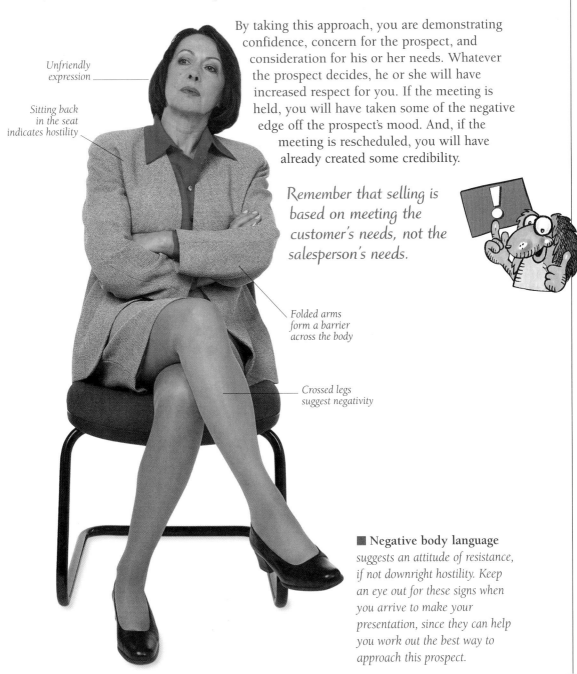

Unfriendly expression

Sitting back in the seat indicates hostility

Folded arms form a barrier across the body

Crossed legs suggest negativity

■ **Negative body language** *suggests an attitude of resistance, if not downright hostility. Keep an eye out for these signs when you arrive to make your presentation, since they can help you work out the best way to approach this prospect.*

145

Foundations of trust building

THERE ARE SEVERAL *simple basic steps that you can take to help you build trust quickly with your prospects.*

By being early for a meeting, you demonstrate that you are not only well organized and diligent, but that you are a person who keeps commitments and has a high degree of respect and concern for your prospect.

One of the best ways to start the trust-building process is to arrive at your appointments a few minutes early.

Other people

You can generate a high degree of trust by mentioning the names of the people who referred you to this prospect, as well as the individuals who have endorsed your product. These names can have a great amount of emotional significance for your prospect, as the thinking is something like, "If Joe thinks so highly of this product, it must really be good." By mentioning these testimonials, you can actually transfer the trust from a credible source directly to your prospect.

In good company

If your company is well regarded in the community or industry, this can definitely build your personal credibility.

Your company can be a major source of increased trust for you.

At the same time, if your company has had some problems recently, you should be the one to bring them up, and do so early in the process. By taking this approach, you are demonstrating that you think similarly to the prospect, since this matter was probably on his or her mind as well. In addition, you are demonstrating honesty, confidence, and candour, all of which can accelerate the trust-building process.

Feeling secure

You can also build trust in the sales relationship by helping your prospect feel that there is a good deal of safety and security associated with what you are selling. If your product is backed by any warranties, guarantees, or assurances, it is important to mention them early in the process. When your company demonstrates a high degree of trust in its product, that in turn can help increase the level of trust that the prospect has in you.

■ **Earn bonus points** *in your prospect's eyes by getting to meetings ahead of time. Being early will also help you be more relaxed, comfortable, and confident.*

OTHER PEOPLE'S OPINIONS COUNT

A salesperson called one of my associates and advised him of the countless advantages of a home water-purification system. In most cases, my associate would have ended the call before the second syllable in the word "water" had been uttered. The salesperson built trust immediately by saying that one of my associate's close friends had just bought the system. My associate then heard the entire presentation and ultimately made the purchase.

As he said, "I know how critical Bob is about any type of product, and if he's buying it, that really means something."

Speaking as an expert

Another important source of trust is your product knowledge. People generally respect experts. The one caveat is that as positive as people may feel about experts, they feel equally negative about know-alls, so do not overplay your expert card.

Do not bluff if you don't know the answer to a question asked by your prospect.

If you are unsure of the answer to a prospect's question, say that you will find it out quickly. With this approach, you are showing honesty, self-assurance, and humility. All of these traits are definite trust-builders.

In addition, when you have to look up a piece of information for a prospect, that gives you another good reason to contact him or her again. That has a real value in itself. And when you do get in

■ **If you have the opportunity** *to briefly demonstrate your depth of knowledge to your prospect, that is well worth doing.*

touch, you will be further demonstrating that you are thorough, diligent, and a person of your word. In terms of timing, always try to have an answer to a prospect's question by the next working day at the latest. If that is impossible, call or e-mail your prospect and let him or her know the status of your search.

No matter how much you may know about your competition, do not waste your time or your prospect's time by running them down.

It is important not to run down the loyal opposition. Your time could be far better spent listening and learning about your prospect and his or her needs. Prospects are not typically interested in your negative thoughts about others' products, and your credibility in this arena is not great. After all, you have a vested interest in making other products sound inferior. When you make comments that have questionable credibility, you undermine all of your efforts to build trust.

To succeed in sales, you need to understand your prospect's needs. Prospects do not just lay their needs on the table when a salesperson appears. Rather, they are willing to share their needs only after they feel they can trust the salesperson.

Pacing for trust

ONE OF THE MOST POWERFUL SOURCES *of trust in the sales process occurs when the prospect senses that he or she has a great deal in common with the salesperson. The reason is that people tend to trust others who are like themselves.*

This means that one of the best ways to build trust with a prospect is to send various messages showing that the two of you are similar. One way to do this is through a process called *pacing*. It is used by many of the great salespeople, and it is quite simple to learn.

Verbal pacing

When you first meet your prospect, listen carefully. As your prospect talks, notice the speed, vocabulary, length of sentences, tone, and volume. Then, as you talk, try to adjust your speech pattern so that it is similar to that of your prospect.

This does not mean that you are trying to imitate your prospect. Rather, if your prospect speaks quickly, you should make sure that you are not talking in a slow or deliberate style. When you speak slowly to a fast talker, that person may think that you are just plain lethargic. That person will also think that the two of you do not have much in common, and that undercuts your trust-building efforts.

At the same time, if your prospect is a slow talker and you are a fast talker, you will need to pull in your reins. When you approach a slow-talking prospect at full speed, you can be perceived as a high-pressure hustler, and that too undercuts trust. When your speech pattern is similar to that of your prospect, you are sending a subtle, even unconscious, message that the two of you have a good deal in common, which in turn sends the message that you can be trusted.

Non-verbal pacing

When you see successful salespeople at work, you will notice that many use the same physical behaviour as their prospects. When the prospect sits forward, the salesperson sits forward; when the prospect leans back, the salesperson leans back. And, once again, the prospect unconsciously says, "This salesperson is like me. I trust people like myself."

■ **Mirroring a prospect's body language** *will help promote successful communication. For best results, this physical mirroring should be continued throughout the sales process.*

Pacing just about everything

Salespeople also pace the overall scene in a way that matches what the prospect doing and feeling. For example, as part of a larger sentence, the salesperson mig interject, "… as we're sitting so comfortably in this great office with that incredi view of Tower Bridge …".

All of those phrases are undeniable truths, and they further demonstrate the salesperson's level of insight into the prospect. In addition, that type of message causes the prospect to nod in agreement, something that successful salespeople do throughout the sales process.

Is it hypnosis?

Hypnosis and selling are both based upon building trust with a client, and this may be one of the reasons why people describe some sales presentations as being absolutely mesmerizing.

Some researchers have found that successful salespeople unwittingly use a form of conversational hypnosis.

Using a type of conversational hypnosis does not mean that these salespeople are putting their prospects into a trance and then dumping inordinate numbers of unwanted products upon them.

However, people who are hypnotized are not asleep, nor does hypnosis cause them to abandon all rationality and judgment. Rather, hypnosis is a state of heightened suggestibility.

Viewed in this way, it is interesting to point out some of the similarities between the techniques of hypnotists and salespeople. For example, hypnotists traditionally use pacing and mirroring as a central component of their procedure.

And many salespeople and hypnotists follow a similar progression that includes grabbing the full attention of the person, expressing several ideas that are absolutely true to generate a good deal of nodding, putting the person into a state where he or she senses a need to take action, and then providing the person with the kinds of actions to take.

Salespeople and hypnotists often use a good deal of repetition, relaxation techniques, emotionally charged words, and a series of suggestions.

Trust in your product

ONE OF THE BEST WAYS TO BUILD TRUST *with your prospects is for you to truly trust your product. After all, if you do not trust your product, why should anyone else? If this trust is lacking, many of your prospects are going to know it.*

■ **If you are selling a product** *that you don't really trust, your customers are going to see it. And so are your sales figures.*

Even if you are able to sell a product successfully in which you do not have full faith, confidence, and trust, sooner or later there will be problems. For example, the trouble may come from customers who find out for themselves why your product should not be trusted. This can lead not only to a loss of business for you, but a loss of goodwill as well. In essence, this will undercut much of your network and source of referrals.

Trouble can also come from within as you start to live with the fact that you are not proud of what you are doing. It is always nice to be able to sleep at night, and if your lack of trust in your product is keeping you awake, perhaps your unconscious is literally telling you to wake up.

If you have trust in your product, your company, and yourself, you will be in a much better position to enjoy the full range of benefits that selling can offer.

A simple summary

✔ One way to separate yourself from average salespeople is to build trust with your prospects.

✔ Buying is an emotional process that is then justified by logic and reason.

✔ When you first meet your prospect, try to find areas of similarity and use them as the basis for friendly icebreaking.

✔ Effective selling involves all of your senses.

✔ When you use verbal and non-verbal pacing, the message to your prospect is that you both have a good deal in common, and that is a major source of trust.

✔ If you do not trust your product, neither will your customers.

PART THREE

LISTENING IS AS VITAL AS POSING THE RIGHT QUESTIONS

THE KEY COMPONENTS

AT THIS POINT, you are moving into the heart of your sales presentation. Now the most important step is to learn about your prospect's *needs*. This means that you will be using specific *questioning strategies*, backed up by strong *listening skills*.

You are going to see how to use compelling *persuasive techniques* such as sales stories and power words to help your prospect see the many ways that your product will meet his or her needs. Certainly there will be *objections*, but you are going to find out about the best ways to handle them. You will easily recognize the signs that tell you when it's time to *ask for the order*, and as soon as that moment arrives, you are going to know just how to seize it.

Chapter 9

Questioning Techniques that Work

MANY SALESPEOPLE TAKE GREAT PRIDE in learning every possible detail about their product, and then feel compelled to discuss each minute point with every prospect they meet. They believe that their boundless scope of knowledge will surely convince a prospect to buy. The salesperson who employs this tactic might as well be talking to the wall, since there is no reason to assume that the prospect is interested in anything he or she is saying. To sell to someone, the salesperson has to know what that person needs. And that can be determined only by asking questions and listening. Asking questions is not difficult or magical, but it can have a miraculous impact on your ability to sell.

In this chapter...

✓ **Why ask questions?**

✓ **Key questions**

✓ **TNT questions**

✓ **Multilevel listening**

ASKING THE RIGHT QUESTIONS IS JUST AS IMPORTANT AS KNOWING THE RIGHT ANSWERS

Why ask questions?

THERE IS A VERY OBVIOUS REASON for basing much of your sales presentation on questions: questions will solicit answers that will let you know about problems the prospect is encountering, what the prospect wants and needs, and acceptable solutions. Armed with these insights, you can then focus your comments, suggestions, and expertise on precisely what the prospect is seeking.

Using questions as the core of your sales presentation has additional advantages, all of which help make your presentation and suggestions far more compelling.

Never assume that you understand a prospect's needs simply because of his or her company, title, position, or predecessor.

Background information is important, but it does not come close to fully delineating your prospect's needs. If you operate on limited prospect data, your chances of success will be limited too.

A positive reflection on you

The questions that you ask your prospect immediately demonstrate that your objective is not to push your product on the prospect, but instead that you respect the prospect and are interested in his or her needs, ideas, and expertise. This approach can help the prospect sense that he or she is actually buying something, as opposed to being sold something.

■ **By asking questions** *you are acting as more than a salesperson. Your behaviour is also that of a partner who is working with a colleague to solve problems jointly.*

■ **Listening closely** *to your prospect's answers to your questions helps you focus your presentation on exactly what your prospect needs and wants.*

Studies of the workplace continually show that employees at all levels react positively when treated with respect and trust. This applies to the way prospects prefer to be treated, as well.

Your questions also allow you to demonstrate your expertise. To ask good questions, you need to know a great deal about the prospect's company and industry, your own products, and the links between them. Good questions can easily highlight your broad range of knowledge and understanding.

Increased acceptance

The lecture method of selling tends to generate resistance, rejection, and objections. Alternatively, when prospects are actively involved in a sales presentation, they are far more likely to demonstrate increased levels of ownership, commitment, and acceptance of whatever is being presented.

> ### Trivia...
> *Management theorists have known for a long time that employees are more willing to accept company decisions if they have been allowed to present their ideas, input, and suggestions in the process. This is far more effective than the unilateral or dictatorial managerial approach, which typically generates resistance, rejection, and objections. By being consulted as part of the decision-making process, employees are left with an increased sense of ownership, commitment, and acceptance of the decision.*

Increased understanding

Asking your prospect a broad range of questions also helps the prospect understand his or her own needs.

Even if you clearly understand the prospect's needs, it is not going to do much good in the sales process if your prospect is unaware of them.

■ **Your prospects' active participation** *in the sales presentation will ensure that their ultimate buying decision will truly reflect their own feelings, interests, and needs.*

Key questions

ALTHOUGH IT IS IMPORTANT *to use questions as the basis of your presentation, this does not mean that any old questions will do. In the sales context, three simple types of questions make up the core of a presentation, and each helps support the other as you gather your information.*

Open-ended questions

Some of the most powerful questions in the sales process are those that are specifically designed to get the prospect talking. They are known as *open-ended questions*.

For example, if you want to learn about your prospect's level of satisfaction with a current product, you would not learn much by asking, "Do you like product X?" The "yes" or "no" answer will tell you nothing about the strengths, weaknesses, problems, difficulties, or other concerns that are truly important to the prospect.

DEFINITION

Open-ended questions are questions that cannot be answered with a "yes" or a "no". They typically start with "Who", "What", "Where", "When", and "How".

■ **Be ready** *with specific open-ended questions to ask your prospect, and take note of the answers. By doing so you will soon find out what your prospect really thinks about the product and service.*

More effective questions would be:

(a) "How satisfied are you with product X?"

(b) "What do you see as the product's strengths?"

(c) "When has it worked best for you?"

Questions such as these give the prospect the opportunity to think about the product and the ways in which it has or has not been up to scratch.

These types of questions are also helpful when following up on your prospect's answers. If you are uncertain about what a prospect is saying, you can ask probing questions such as:

(a) "What else?"

(b) "When did this start?"

(c) "How did you deal with that?"

(d) "Where did that take you?"

Of all the open-ended questions, those that begin with "Why" should be used sparingly.

"Why" often has a judgmental or even accusatory tone, and it can be misinterpreted as a challenge. It is safer to ask the prospect something like, "How is that?" This means the same thing as "Why" but is a softer way of asking.

The sales approach of asking open-ended questions implies that the prospect, not the salesperson, controls much of the sales session. The salesperson does not know exactly what to say or ask until the prospect has responded to his or her questions. Each successive step of the presentation is based upon what the salesperson has learned by probing the prospect's needs.

Your sales presentation should be tailor-made for each prospect, and this will allow it to fit each prospect perfectly. You cannot grab some presentation off the rack back at the office and think that it will wear well with any prospect. When it comes to professional selling, one size does not fit all.

Many salespeople still try to control the sales situation. Their hope is to direct the prospect to wherever the salesperson wants to go, and then move in for the close. This

■ **Trying to control** *a sales presentation regardless of the prospect's wants or needs is not wise. Your prospect will resent being pushed down a path he or she is not willing to take, and will probably not buy.*

calls for a structured sales presentation that goes down a pre-planned path in a predictable way. The problem is that this may not be the path that the prospect wants or needs.

When you use primarily open-ended questions, it is your prospect who will select the path. And this path is paved with the prospect's needs and wants. Rather than being pushed to a destination that ultimately may not be acceptable, the prospect is likely to lead the salesperson to a far more acceptable place.

The path to follow in sales is customer based rather than salesperson based.

Leading questions

The open-ended questions that you ask the prospect are similar to a lasso. They grab the overall issue, but it is still jumping around so much that it can look like a blur. To really see what you are dealing with, you need to ask *leading questions* that can actually tie the matter down.

For example, a salesperson may ask an open-ended question such as, "What was the main problem that you were having with that application?" The prospect will then describe the problem, and may do so in some detail. Once he or she has finished, a leading question can be, "Was that the only problem?"

DEFINITION

Leading questions *typically have answers built into them, and they are designed to generate "yes" or "no" responses to narrow down specific points. These questions also link one open-ended question to another.*

163

If the prospect responds with a "yes", the salesperson can then move to an open-ended question that focuses on this problem. Such a question might be, "What steps did you take to deal with it?"

On the other hand, if the prospect replies "no" when asked if that was the only problem, the salesperson can then ask an open-ended question, such as, "What other problems were you having?" This can then lead to another leading question, "Were there any other problems?" If necessary, this too can be followed with an open-ended question.

Sooner or later, by being asked a sequence of open-ended and leading questions, the prospect is going to come to the end of the problems. That point will be indicated by a response of "no" to the leading question that asks, "Were there any other problems?" Through this approach, the blur of problems is now clarified and tied down.

Confirming questions

Many salespeople also use *confirming questions* to generate agreement and understanding, while simultaneously building trust with the prospect.

Examples of confirming questions are, "It's important to save money, isn't it?" and "You'd like to see productivity increase, wouldn't you?" By asking these types of confirming questions, you are subtly telling the prospect that you think similarly to the way that he or she does. This type of shared feeling can clearly play a trust-building role.

> **DEFINITION**
>
> Confirming questions *are placed at the end of a statement and change it into a question that automatically generates a "yes" from the prospect.*

By eliciting "yes" responses throughout a sales presentation, you are increasing the likelihood of ending the presentation with a "yes" as well.

However, when salespeople attach these types of questions to practically every statement, they can be perceived as manipulative, insincere, and slick. As a result, they should be used with discretion. If you sense any resistance or negative reaction to your confirming questions, you should drop them at once, shouldn't you?

If confirming questions are overused, they can come back to haunt you.

TNT questions

SOME DYNAMITE QUESTIONS you can ask fall into a simple TNT classification: Then, Now, and Tomorrow. By focusing your questions in these three areas, you will have a complete picture of your prospect's wants and needs.

Questions about Then

To get a foundation of your prospect's needs, ask historical questions. It is important to know how the prospect made earlier purchasing decisions, the rationale behind those decisions, and his or her current level of satisfaction with the outcome.

Examples of typical historical open-ended questions include:

a "What made you interested in product X?"

b "How did you decide to buy this product?"

c "What did you hope it would do?"

d "How satisfied have you been with it?"

e "How did you measure its effectiveness?"

f "What kind of difficulties did you experience with product X?"

g "What else was dissatisfying to you?"

■ **Asking historical questions** *establishes in your mind the rationale behind a prospect's earlier buying decisions and helps you set the stage for future sales.*

You can also generate a good deal of information with questions that start with, "Tell me about", "Describe", and "Give me an overview of". Your open-ended questions can be followed with any number of leading questions, such as:

(a) "Did you find what you were looking for?"

(b) "Were there any other problems?"

(c) "Was that the only time this occurred?"

Questions about Now

The next step in TNT questioning is to learn about your prospect's current needs and wants, which can be accomplished by asking Now questions. Be on the lookout for problems that were first mentioned when you asked the Then questions and are still in the forefront of the prospect's mind.

Some examples of open-ended Now questions include:

(a) "What are you looking for?"

(b) "What are you using now?"

(c) "How satisfied are you with product X today?"

(d) "What do you like most about product X?"

(e) "What do you like least?"

(f) "What kinds of problems are you experiencing?"

(g) "What are the improvements that you would like to see?"

(h) "What effect does that have on your revenue?"

(i) "How would you describe the solution?"

These questions will help your prospect open up and more freely discuss the current situation and his or her thoughts about the ways to correct it. It is important to notice that the questions move from the prospect's view of the problem to the prospect's view of the solution, all in the prospect's own words. With this approach, you will be able to get a clear snapshot of the prospect's needs and the path that he or she would like to follow to have them fulfilled.

The idea of fulfilling your prospect's needs is based on classic psychological research that has found that unfulfilled needs are motivational, while fulfilled needs are no longer motivational.

If a person is hungry, the need to eat will motivate him or her to find and consume food. Once fed, that person is not motivated until hunger sets in again. Research has also found that people fulfil their more basic needs, such as for food, safety, and shelter, before they fulfil their higher-level psychological needs, such as for recognition or achievement.

Some prospects may actually be operating at a very basic need level, such as those who seek a product that absolutely must reduce costs. If you focus on the service aspects of your product, while the prospect's needs for your product are at the cost-reduction level, your prospect may not see how your product can meet his or her needs. Then your prospect will not buy.

You cannot actually motivate your prospect to buy anything, but you can create an environment in which the prospect can take action to meet his or her needs.

■ **Knowing that** *unfulfilled needs are motivational, your quest is to identify the needs that your prospect is trying to fulfil, and then demonstrate the ways that your product can meet them.*

The motivation to act comes from within, but if you have helped your prospect understand his or her unfulfilled needs, and if you are offering a product that will fulfil those needs, your prospect will probably be motivated to act.

There can be any number of leading Now questions that can help you gain additional understanding of your prospect's current needs. Examples include:

(a) "Do you see how this works?"

(b) "Do you understand what you will save?"

(c) "Do you see what you will gain?"

Questions about Tomorrow

The final component of the TNT, the Tomorrow questions, is to learn more about what your prospect seeks in the future. The idea behind these questions is to understand not only your prospect's needs but also his or her objectives and vision. Some helpful open-ended Tomorrow questions include:

(a) "How would you describe a perfect relationship with a supplier?"

(b) "If you were to make a change, what would you want from a new company that you are not receiving right now?"

(c) "What kinds of future problems do you anticipate?"

(d) "What would an improvement in X mean to your company?"

(e) "How would you describe the ideal product?"

(f) "How will you measure it?"

(g) "What do you see as the long-term solution?"

Other powerful, open-ended Tomorrow questions include those that start with "Just suppose", "What if", and "In a perfect world". In addition, some of the leading Tomorrow questions include:

(a) "Is that all you need?"

(b) "Is that your real goal?"

(c) "Can you see that happening?"

Multilevel listening

AS IMPORTANT AS IT IS to ask the right questions, all of them are useless if you do not listen. Multilevel listening has all sorts of advantages, including the opportunity to build trust and credibility, understand your prospect's needs and vision, and focus your expertise on issues that are truly important to your prospect.

The three "R's" of listening

A simple way to make sure that you are listening with all cylinders is to think of the three "R's". In the listening arena, the first "R" is to Repeat the information back to your prospect.

From the standpoint of asking a question, you can take your prospect's statement and repeat it with a question mark at the end. For example, when your prospect says, "We were not happy with the outcome", you can respond, "You were not happy with the outcome?" The prospect will then continue the discussion, and you have indicated that you are listening.

■ **Make sure** *that your prospect can see that you are listening closely to what he or she is saying by nodding when appropriate and pacing his or her behaviour.*

The second "R" of listening is for you to Rephrase what your prospect has said. Using the same example, when the prospect says, "We were not happy with the outcome", you can respond with, "There were some problems with the outcome?" This again shows that you have been listening, and you are opening the door for the prospect to elaborate.

The final "R" in listening is for you to Remember. This simply means for you to pay careful attention to what your prospect is saying. Do not let yourself be distracted by any kind of *noise*. If necessary, you can take notes and ask more questions to clarify what the prospect has said.

> **DEFINITION**
>
> *In the communication process, anything that interferes with communication is referred to as* noise. *It can be people talking in the next cubicle, a leaf-blower outside the office, or even your own daydreaming.*

Speak with your body language

When your prospect is communicating, it is important not only to listen, but to show you are listening. If you are sitting with your eyes focused on the floor or if you are fiddling with your pen, your prospect is going to sense that you are not paying attention. That means you will not be getting much of a hearing with your prospect.

Crossed arms indicate disbelief

Forward posture suggests attentiveness

Hands on chin shows thoughtfulness

■ **Always be aware** *of the way that your body language can be interpreted by your prospects. By appearing interested in what your prospect says, you, in turn, are more likely to be listened to.*

Avoid some of the main listening blockages in the sales process. These include:

a Interrupting your prospect

b Finishing his or her sentences

c Criticizing

d Non-stop talking

e Jumping to conclusions

f Focusing on what you are going to say instead of what the prospect is saying

g Ignoring the prospect's body language

A simple summary

✓ The core of selling is based on understanding the prospect's needs, and the best way to do that is to approach the prospect with questions, not answers.

✓ Selling today is based on the prospect's needs, and not on the salesperson's needs.

✓ Open-ended questions, typically those that start with "Who", "What", "Where", "When", and "How", are an easy way to encourage a prospect to talk about his or her needs.

✓ Your sales presentation should be tailor-made for each prospect, with much of the content determined by the prospect's responses to your questions.

✓ To understand fully where your prospect has been and wants to go, ask TNT questions that focus on Then, Now, and Tomorrow.

✓ All of the information you gather about a prospect's needs will mean nothing if you do not practise multilevel listening and the three "R's" of listening: Repeat, Rephrase, and Remember.

Chapter 10

The Language of Sales

B Y THIS POINT, you have built a solid base of trust and credibility with your prospect and gained insight into his or her needs. Now you are ready to use your product knowledge to selectively access the precise information that will best meet your prospect's needs. The most powerful way to do this is not only to present and demonstrate the product benefits that are tailored to your prospect's needs, but also to do so as persuasively as possible. Fortunately, the key elements of persuasion are easy to learn and apply.

In this chapter...

✓ Sales stories
✓ Power words
✓ Between the lines
✓ Climate of concurrence

TAILOR YOUR PRESENTATION TO MEET YOUR CUSTOMER'S NEEDS

Sales stories

ONE OF THE MOST POWERFUL TECHNIQUES *used by highly persuasive salespeople is sales storytelling. If you think back to any sales situation that truly impressed you, the odds are you can also remember a story or two that the salesperson told.*

> ### DEFINITION
>
> Sales storytelling *is the art of introducing stories into your presentation. Sometimes these stories are anecdotal and other times they are based on fact. Either way, they should be brief, ranging anywhere from 10 or 20 seconds up to about a minute.*

A sales story can help your prospect understand the points you are trying to make far more efficiently than a detailed presentation would.

Many salespeople fill their presentations with so many facts, figures, and comparisons that the result is head spinning. A sales story does the opposite. It paints a clear and simple picture of what you truly want your prospect to remember.

If a picture is worth a thousand words, sales storytelling is a way to get the value of thousands of words while using only a few.

■ **Telling a sales story** *is a powerful selling tool. It is one of the most effective ways to make your presentation highly compelling, memorable, and persuasive.*

Story behind the stories

Sales stories have a number of advantages over the more conventional methods of presenting information to a prospect. For example, just about everyone likes to hear stories. The whole process of hearing a vivid story brings back pleasant youthful memories and creates a more comfortable atmosphere. Stories are fun, and that is a positive element to introduce into your sales presentation.

When a prospect is geared up for a classic sales pitch, sales stories can help him or her relax quickly and feel at ease. In addition, the story not only allows the prospect to visualize what you are saying, it also helps him or her visualize how your product will meet his or her needs.

Winning story lines

Stories should be used throughout the sales process, all the way from icebreaking to closing.

If there is a true story you would like to include in your presentation, but it really did not happen to you, do not present it as something you experienced. You never want to be in the position of lying to a prospect or customer. If the story dealt with one of your friends, then that is how you should present it.

You've learned about your prospect's needs through your questions, so now you should tailor your stories to address those needs. If you sensed that your prospect has fairly strong needs for safety and security, some stories about warranties, guarantees, company responsiveness, and service excellence could be compelling. For example, rather than going through the warranty chapter and verse, it is far more comforting, motivational, and memorable if you tell a brief story about a customer who relied on the warranty and was satisfied.

Depending upon what you have learned about your prospect, you can add stories about family, money, cutting costs, increasing revenues, personal recognition, and even a story if the prospect reminds you of someone else. For example, if a prospect reminds you of a particular person or sales situation that you previously encountered, you can certainly tell that story. And further, if the person who is seemingly so similar to your customer is now enormously satisfied with your products, that should be part of the story.

When telling sales stories about your product, be sure to focus more on benefits than features.

Hidden advantages

In addition to the apparent advantages of storytelling, there are some less obvious benefits as well. For example, sales stories are one of the best ways to help build a positive emotional reaction to your product. Stories can do this not only by the very nature of storytelling itself, but also by reminding your prospect of a pleasant experience or situation that he or she may have experienced in the past.

Your stories can take your prospect back to the feelings that come from a great accomplishment, receiving an award, or a restful day in the country.

A salesperson may say, "I remember as a child there was a toy aeroplane that I always wanted. I'll never forget the feeling when I got it. Do you remember how happy and excited you felt when you got a special toy that you always wanted? Well, you are going to feel the same way after you buy this product." By merely bringing up this experience, you are unleashing some of the deep-seated positive feelings that your prospect has about the event.

■ **Your sales story** *can take your prospect back to a special day from childhood, such as opening birthday presents.*

In addition, by lacing your story with words that draw from all of your senses, you are more likely to reach your prospect on an emotional level. Since so much of the decision to buy is based on emotion, your ability to connect with your prospect on this level is particularly important.

Sales stories are also an excellent vehicle for transferring your positive feelings about your product to your prospect. By helping your prospect feel as emotionally charged about the product as you are, you are making it easier for him or her to make the decision to buy from you. An upbeat and lively story that is linked to your prospect's needs and wants can actually help your prospect have a level of enthusiasm that equals yours.

The transference of positive emotions is one of the most critical elements of effective selling, and sales stories are one of the best ways to make this happen.

One of the lesser known advantages of sales stories is that you can make suggestions in them that you could never make in a typical sales presentation. After all, do you think that you could turn to your prospect, look him or her in the eye, and bluntly say, "It's time to stop messing around and buy this!" Of course not. But you can say it through storytelling.

Assuming that the salesperson actually experienced this situation, he or she could turn to a prospect and say, "You know, yesterday I was working with a young couple in pretty much the same situation as both of you. I showed them a property that seemed to be perfect, and the young woman turned to her husband and said, 'It's time to stop messing around and buy this!'" When saying that final phrase, the salesperson looks directly at the prospect.

Sales stories provide a salesperson with the opportunity to send any number of suggestions, hints, and even commands directly to a prospect.

■ **Through a sales story,** *you can paint a vivid picture that helps these prospective home buyers see themselves living happily in this home.*

CAN YOUR PRODUCT SELL ITSELF?

Some products easily lend themselves to a demonstration, while others do not. Nonetheless, no matter what product you are selling, you should always look for ways to demonstrate it.

The old days of a salesperson standing in front of the customer and seamlessly demonstrating the whiz-bang aspects of a product are all but gone. Customers in these scenarios typically feel that the salesperson can get any gizmo to work, but who knows if that is just a big act and the product is impossible to operate.

This means that your product demonstration should always include hands-on participation by your prospect. Let the prospect get behind the wheel, sit down at the keyboard, try on the coat, play the guitar, listen to the speakers…. It is one thing for you to say that your product is user friendly, but it's an altogether different matter when your prospect tries it out and learns that fact on his or her own.

On a more subtle level, when your customer gets involved, your product is proving that everything you said is true. This revelation further increases your credibility and trust, as it verifies that you are a person of your word. In addition, as management theorists have found for many years, participation in decision making reduces resistance, and this same principle applies in selling. When your prospect has become directly involved in the sales process, many of the unknowns are reduced, along with your prospect's resistance.

■ **Allowing your prospect** *to match a shirt and tie is part of the product demonstration. The more a prospect is involved in the process, the more likely he or she is to buy.*

Power words

THE NUANCES OF THE WORDS YOU SELECT *when communicating with a prospect can change the entire message that you are sending. The better you understand your prospect and his or her needs and wants, the better you are able to incorporate words that are particularly meaningful and persuasive.*

Emotionally charged words

Some words set off an instantly positive reaction when people hear them, and others can do the opposite. Your insight into your prospect is going to help you work out some of the key emotionally charged words to use as well as those to avoid.

To get an idea of the emotional power of a word, notice your reaction to the following words:

- Taxes
- Bankruptcy
- Drug addiction
- Funeral
- Kidnapping
- Toxin
- Root canal

Just as they may generate negative feelings for you, these words and many others can generate conscious or unconscious negative reactions in your prospect.

Now notice your reaction to such words as:

- Love
- Baby
- Money
- Power
- Serenity
- Peace of mind

These words often trigger a more positive emotional reaction and help keep a prospect's mind open to other thoughts and suggestions from you. To figure out more of the words that are linked to positive or negative emotions for your prospect, study your prospect and his or her environment.

For example, if you are going to mention something about the picture of the basketball team on the wall, notice the difference in the following: "Your kid plays basketball?" In the first place, the question is phrased as a statement, and that can be perceived as being somewhat aggressive.

Secondly, the word "kid" is not a flattering description of a child and could be interpreted negatively, particularly to a family-orientated individual. And since your prospect has a picture of the basketball team on the wall, that may be a tip-off to his or her strong family orientation.

Wording the question slightly differently can trigger a more positive emotional reaction from your prospect. Notice the difference in the question, "Do you have a child on the basketball team?" In the first place, this is phrased as a question, not as a statement. Secondly, the word "child" tends to be far more positively charged than the word "kid". And, finally, the word "team" often triggers a positive emotional response, particularly among people in management.

■ **If you comment** *on a personal photo, such as a school basketball team, choose your power words carefully.*

Looking specifically at positively charged words for people in management, you should also think about including some of the following:

- Achievement
- Profit
- Pounds
- Performance
- Growth
- Advancement
- Power
- Resources
- Success
- Innovation
- Influence
- Productivity

Or, if you are dealing with a person whose comments and behaviour point to a need for security and stability, some of the positively charged words and terms include:

- Guarantee
- Well established
- Widely endorsed
- Safety
- Predictable
- Warranty
- Historically proven

It is interesting to note that some of the positively charged words for one prospect may be negatively charged for another. If you approach your relatively insecure prospect and use the vocabulary that worked so perfectly with your high-achieving manager, you are going to destroy that emotional bridge that is so critical in selling, and you'll probably burn a few other bridges as well.

Since the buying decision has such a strong emotional component to it, many successful salespeople tend to stay away from words that deal with thinking.

For example, they will not ask, "What do you think?" Instead, they will ask, "How does that feel?" or "How does that sound?" You will not hear them using words such as rational, analytical, deductive, or reasoning. Their word selection is heavily focused on building an emotional attachment to the product. They'll make statements such as, "You're going to like this benefit", or "Everyone loves this."

Metaphorically speaking

Another particularly effective source of word power in selling is through the use of *metaphors*. For example, notice the compelling difference between the following two phrases, all because of the addition of a simple metaphor: "Our equipment is different from what you are using now" versus "There is a world of difference between what you have now and what we are offering."

By using metaphors throughout your presentation, you are using language that is clear, memorable, colourful, and enjoyable.

Action words

Words that imply action are very effective in the sales process. Or, expressed metaphorically, action words can propel your sales presentations to new heights. These words imply a high level of activity, energy, and enthusiasm, and they too are highly visual and memorable. Action words also give a subtle suggestion to your prospect that it is time for him or her to take action.

Look at the actions implied in the following: "All of our customers jump at this feature", "Let me throw you an idea", "How does this grab you?", "Let's run with this for a minute." All of these phrases could have been easily expressed with passive words, and the prospects' reactions would have been equally passive.

> **DEFINITION**
>
> *A metaphor is a figure of speech where a word or phrase that typically means one thing is used to convey another, forming a comparison. For example, rather than saying that sales metaphors will help you become more successful, it is more compelling to say that they are the building blocks for a fortress of success. If your stories are the pictures in the sales process, metaphors are the colours.*

When you use action words in selling, your prospects tend to reply in kind, and this increases the likelihood of their taking action.

A school of thought contends that there are three distinct thinking styles, and to communicate effectively with an individual prospect, you need to determine if his or her dominant style is visual, auditory, or kinaesthetic. Although the research in this area is still somewhat uneven, the message is clear:

To communicate persuasively with others, you need to use language and speech patterns that are meaningful and significant to them.

With that in mind, if you are selling to a person who seems to be more visual, you will want to use expressions such as "I see what you are saying", "Picture this…", "Look at these advantages…." If your prospect appears to be more auditory, you may want to use expressions like, "I hear what you are saying", "This has an interesting ring to it", or "How does this sound to you?"

Prospects who think on a more kinaesthetic basis tend to process information based on the way that it relates to their physical body. For such a person, the kind of language that may be more meaningful includes, "You're walking a tightrope on this", "That must have been hard to stomach", or "This is a way to get a leg up."

WRITING YOUR NAME

One highly successful salesperson never asks his prospects to sign their name on the dotted line. When I asked him why, he said that people have such negative feelings about the word "sign". He mentioned that it is often linked to such phrases as "Signing your life away" and "That's a bad sign."

Instead of asking prospects to sign their name, he asks them to write their name. He feels that the word "write" has such a comfortable and appealing sound, particularly since it has the same sound as the word "right". The subtle connotation is that writing one's name is the right thing to do.

■ **Asking your prospects** to *"write", not "sign", their name on an agreement may make them feel more at ease about finalizing a deal.*

Between the lines

IN ADDITION TO *selecting power stories, words, and phrases that are particularly compelling for your prospects, there are other simple parts of the communication process that can add further persuasive power.*

Hold it

One of the most effective ways to make your words even more convincing is to slowly hold and stretch them. For example, that new system you are selling is not just "very powerful". Rather, it is "verrrrrrrrry powerful". Just that subtle difference in the word "very" can help it sink much deeper into your customer's subconscious.

The technique of slowly holding words and then stretching them has a relaxing and comforting tone, and it clearly adds to the suggestibility of what you are saying.

Subtle suggestions

Let's assume that you have a customer named Dave, and somewhere in the middle of your presentation you say, "Dave, buy this product." After all, this is certainly a suggestion that you would like to give Dave, and if your product is so good, he should buy it. Of course, the problem is that your lack of subtlety is probably going to lead to a lack of sales.

There is, however, a simple way to state these exact words to Dave and for them to be positively received. In fact, they will come across as a subtle suggestion that may actually help energize Dave to make a decision to buy.

Rather than dropping the phrase on Dave from out of the blue, you can put it in a larger sentence such as the following: "When you, Dave, buy this product, you are going to see that it will do all that we discussed and more."

There it is, right after the first two words of the sentence, a subtle suggestion for Dave to buy the product. He will definitely hear it, but probably on a subconscious level. Either way, this suggestion is one of many in your presentation that can help him decide to buy from you.

What are you implying?

You can also send powerful messages to your prospects by describing your product in a way that automatically attaches any number of powerful attributes to it. For example, if you want your prospect to know that your product is durable, you could easily say, "Our product is known for its durability." There's nothing wrong with this, but you can embed this point in a sentence, and then move on to discuss the fit between the product and your prospect's needs.

With this approach, you would say, "Our durable product is…." In this way, instead of having to say that your product is durable, the notion of durability is simply part of your product's definition. And by consistently describing your product in this way, durability is more likely to become part of your customer's definition of it as well.

A few choice words

Some key words that can keep your sales presentation alive and focused on matters that will truly help your prospect meet his or her needs are:

- Here
- Right now
- Now
- Then

At the same time, it is important to avoid using the word "but" in your presentation. If your prospect makes an inaccurate point and you respond by saying, "I know what you mean, but there's more to it", you have put down what he or she has said. This typically results in disagreement and defensiveness.

The word "but" often throws a big spanner in a conversation, and your entire message can be sidetracked.

Fortunately, there is an easy way to avoid this problem. Rather than using the word "but", simply use the word "and" in its place. You can see how much better it is to respond with, "I know what you mean, and there's more to it." Now you are in a state of agreement with your prospect, and the two of you can then work together on whatever the question may be.

Climate of concurrence

WHILE USING SALES STORIES and power words throughout your presentation, remember that you want to generate as many "yes" responses as possible. In addition to the pacing techniques and confirming questions that were discussed earlier, verification is an additional word power technique that can help you hear "yes" more often.

One way to continue to generate a "yes" response at any time in the presentation is by verifying what you already know about your prospect. The kinds of statements that can do this typically begin with, "I see you have X", or "Over the past three years, you bought Y", or "This means that you will have X more." Verifying what you know about a customer will help keep your knowledge about him or her current, while automatically generating a positive response.

A simple summary

✔ Sales stories are an interesting, fun, and memorable way for you to present and support the benefits of your product.

✔ Use sales stories to transfer your positive emotions about the product to your prospect.

✔ You can get a tremendous amount of sales action by using action words.

✔ Customers are most likely to be influenced by language and speech patterns that fit their individual styles of thinking and communicating.

✔ You can send compelling subtle messages by placing them within larger sentences.

✔ Along with your sales stories and power words, make sure that you use pacing, confirming questions, and verification to generate numerous "yes" responses throughout your sales presentation.

Chapter 11

Handling Objections

WHENEVER YOU SELL, you are going to hear objections from your prospects. Objections are normal and common features of any sales session and have probably been around since the first prehistoric salesperson tried to sell a newfangled rock called a wheel. Some salespeople collapse at the first hint of an objection, assuming that the deal is over. But there is no reason to jump to this conclusion. Although objections are indeed obstacles on the way to a sale, there are many ways to turn them into building blocks rather than roadblocks.

In this chapter...

✓ A few ounces of prevention

✓ Classic objections and responses

✓ You go first

✓ Icing on the cake

A few ounces of prevention

BEFORE YOUR PROSPECT EVEN COMES CLOSE *to thinking about objections, you can take a number of steps to anticipate them, prepare for them, and even prevent them.*

Back to "what-if?"

One of the most effective ways to deal with a prospect's objection is to plan for it. When you played the "what-if" game (described in Chapter 7) before your sales call, you tried to come up with every difficult question or issue your prospect could raise. Objections should be at the top of that list.

Although anticipating a potentially endless list of objections may sound like a daunting task, most of the objections you will hear generally fall into five or six key categories.

You will find that, rather than hearing many different objections when you sell, you will probably hear variations of the same objections. This is good news for two different reasons. In the first place, if you are hearing basically the same objection over and over again, you may be able to alter your sales presentation in order to prevent an objection

■ **As well as discussing** *the most common objections raised by prospects with your sales colleagues, find out the best language and strategies they have developed to deal with them.*

from even being formed. And secondly, by dealing with the same objections over time, you can anticipate them and develop a few highly compelling responses.

The most effective way to do this is to meet up with a few fellow sales professionals and your sales manager to discuss the most common objections they hear. This should not be a casual discussion over lunch, but rather a formal meeting that includes an in-depth discussion of the objections, the most effective ways to handle them, and practice sessions where you try out some of the proven strategies. The ultimate outcome of this type of meeting can be a *sales script book*. If used properly, it can be a productive tool for dealing with objections. In fact, some companies use script books for every part of the sales process, from the opening line to the close.

> **DEFINITION**
>
> A sales script book *is a line-by-line summary of the actual language you can use to respond to the most common objections you are likely to face during the sales process.*

If it is professionally prepared and supported by guided practice, a script book can be a powerful sales tool. The one caveat is to make sure it is not either overly focused on what the salesperson is supposed to say, or inadequately focused on listening to the prospect. Either way, when it comes to anticipating and planning for objections, sales script books can be particularly effective.

■ **Before using a sales script** *in an actual presentation, try it out in front of a few of your peers. Your use of language from the script book should be seamless and sound completely natural. Anything short of this is going to turn your sale into a mockery.*

Never use a script in your sales presentation unless you are comfortable, confident, and relaxed with it.

When using a sales script book, you need to spend a good deal of time practising, as there is nothing worse than a mechanical response. Take the language of the script and go over it, learn it, and then tailor it to fit your style of speech, delivery, and pace.

LIVING THE SALES NIGHTMARE

A salesperson had been speaking easily and glibly through an entire presentation. When the prospect raised an objection, the salesperson thought back to the script book and responded accordingly.

Unfortunately, he had thought it would be easy to apply the powerful language of the book, and had not sensed much of a need to rehearse. The result was that he stumbled through the points in the script and used unnatural vocabulary, inappropriate pauses, and forced gestures.

With that, the prospect looked at him and said, "It sounds like you are talking from a script or something." This totally undermined the salesperson's credibility as well as the prospect's interest in the product.

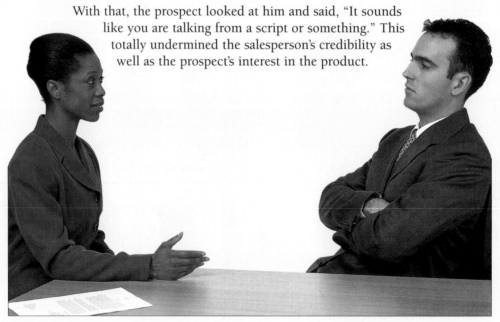

■ **If the beautiful writing** *in Shakespeare's plays can come off poorly because the actors have not rehearsed adequately, you can imagine what inadequate rehearsing can do to a sales script.*

Your questions have the answer

A good number of objections can be avoided by qualifying your prospects, as discussed in Chapter 6, and by using questioning techniques, such as the ones presented in Chapter 9. Your TNT questions (Then, Now, and Tomorrow) have the distinct advantage not only of reducing the number of objections, but making it much easier to handle the ones that are raised.

When you use a questioning approach in the sales process, the sales conversation goes in a direction that is determined by the prospect. One automatic outcome is that the prospect tends to lead the discussion in a direction that typically avoids areas in which objections may be found.

Secondly, when the prospect leads much of the conversation, he or she may in fact raise an objection and may just as quickly provide an acceptable response to it. In this context, you and your prospect are working as partners, and as objections arise along the way, the two of you can also work together to resolve them.

Silence is not golden

Some salespeople assume that it is a good sign if a prospect does not raise objections. The lack of objections, however, can also indicate a lack of interest, involvement, and enthusiasm.

Never assume that a prospect has no objections just because he or she hasn't voiced any.

Hearing no objections, you may have left your meeting feeling happy, but your prospect may have been smiling for an entirely different reason. And your competition may be smiling too.

In a broad sense, your sales session with a prospect contains some of the features of more personal relationships. Therefore, some research findings, specifically those from marriage counselling, apply to it.

■ **The prospect who smiled** *and seemed to go along with what you were saying may have mentally dismissed you long ago and was just waiting for you to leave.*

For example, when a couple has been arguing, many marriage counsellors take the position that there is still interest in the relationship and concern about holding it together. However, when there are no arguments, and then one partner walks out, this calm façade can be an indicator that at least one of the partners has lost so much interest and concern that he or she feels it is not even worth arguing about the marriage. Interest, motivation, drive, and passion are gone. These are the relationships that are the most difficult to salvage.

In the sales relationship, a similar principle applies. If your presentation goes without a hitch, it is entirely possible that your prospect does not feel that raising an objection is worth the effort.

The fact is that some objections and disagreements in any relationship are healthy, and when the individuals can jointly resolve them, the relationship becomes that much stronger.

When your presentation is going along without an objection, be on the lookout for behaviour that may be pointing subtly to hidden objections.

If you have been studying your prospect with all of your senses, you will be able to tell when he or she changes behaviour. For example, you may notice a slightly different speech tone, a hint of a frown, sitting back instead of leaning forward, a squinting of the eyes, glancing away from you, or perhaps a pause.

Whenever you see a behavioural change, no matter what it may be, you should immediately ask a question to find out what may be causing it. For example, you can ask, "Is there something I neglected to go over fully?" If you have hit a real objection, the prospect typically responds with, "Well, I was wondering about…". Once his or her issue is on the table, the two of you can work to resolve it.

Trivia…

One highly successful salesperson uses what he calls "the flinch factor". Throughout the presentation, and particularly during discussions about price, he watches his prospects very carefully. As soon as he sees the prospect flinch, he knows he has hit an objection. He addresses it immediately, works with the prospect to resolve it, and then moves on to the next question or point.

■ **When a smile** *becomes a frown, don't ignore it. Such behavioural changes in a prospect indicate that something is wrong. Find out what the problem is.*

Classic objections and responses

AS A SALESPERSON YOU WANT TO MAINTAIN *a climate of goodwill by keeping the door open and working out ways to deal with any objection as it comes up.*

Listen carefully to whatever your prospect's objection may be. Your response should be positive, such as, "I'm glad you brought that up."

Many salespeople think an objection is actually the prospect's way of expressing criticism, aggression, or rejection. When a salesperson assumes that an objection is a rejection and responds defensively or appears dejected, the sales session can spiral downwards by bringing out a similar reaction from the prospect.

The best way to approach an objection is to treat it as a request for more information.

Although you may find a variety of recurring objections in your sales sessions, the following are among the most common:

- "The price is too high"
- "Let me think about it"
- "We are pleased with our current suppliers"

The price is too high

This is one of the most common objections, and it causes far too many salespeople to throw in the towel.

Most buying decisions are not made on the basis of price.

Just think about your home or office right now and ask yourself if you paid rock bottom price for every single item. If price is your prospect's real point of concern, your first comment is to agree that it is indeed on the high side. Your next step is to draw on your knowledge of everything that adds value to your product. Next, explain how these benefits are far in excess of the cost.

Show your prospect how, by paying more at the outset for the product, he or she will eventually receive cost-saving benefits such as higher quality, fewer breakdowns, higher productivity, less wasted time, and a longer product life. In fact, you may be able to demonstrate that the higher price of your product makes it cheaper in the long run than the less expensive alternative.

Another way to deal with the issue of price is to *extreme it out*. By pushing the price issue to its extreme, you can make it easy for the prospect to understand the true cost and value of your product.

■ **If you can**, *demonstrate how the higher price of your product will actually lead to a lower cost and translate into measurable savings for your prospect.*

When dealing with a price objection, you can extreme it out on the minimum side by saying, "This will cost you only 10p a day." Or, you can do likewise on the maximum side by saying, "Your annual savings will be X, and over the next 3 years they can jump to 5X."

Let me think about it

When your prospect says, "I want to think about it", your first response should be to encourage him or her to do so. You can respond by saying, "I want you to think about this, because when you do, you are going to feel good about the product." This type of response has several advantages: it maintains the climate of goodwill, focuses on the prospect's positive emotional reaction by using the word "feel", and gives a strong suggestion regarding the prospect's attitude toward the product.

Having established this type of foundation to the objection, you can then say, "Let's talk about it." The next step is to ask a question that focuses on the product and the prospect's needs, such as, "Based on what we've discussed, do you feel that product X is what you're looking for?" This should generate a "yes" response. Your next statement can focus on helping the prospect right now.

For example, you can ask, "How can I help you here?" In this way, you are not pushing the prospect, but rather playing a partner/associate role and offering your support and guidance. In addition, use of the word "here" sends a message to the prospect to do something now.

It is important to try to narrow down the issues that are holding your prospect back.

One way of determining the issues that are holding your prospect back is to use the "other than" technique. With this approach, you can say, "Other than X, is there anything else that's on your mind?" If the prospect says "yes", you will need to discuss those matters. If the prospect says "no", then you can go back and fill in the gaps about X.

Another approach is to present specific reasons why the prospect should act now. This does not mean turning on the pressure cooker. On the contrary, there may be various incentives associated with purchasing during a certain time period, or there may be matters of product availability or delivery schedules that can also help the prospect accelerate his or her thinking.

As the prospect responds, an additional approach that many salespeople use is called "feel, felt, found". In this mode, the salesperson says something like, "I know exactly how you *feel*. Many of my satisfied customers *felt* the same way. Let me tell you what they *found*...".

■ **If your prospect** *raises any objections, remember that this could simply be his or her way of asking for more information.*

We are pleased with our current suppliers

This type of response, along with its cousin, "We already handle this internally", often sends timid salespeople packing. This need not be the case. Once again, your initial response in this situation should be positive. For example, you can say, "I'm glad to hear that. I hope you'll be as pleased with us at some point." The next step is to look for ways that your product can complement the goods or services that the company is already receiving. An example of the complementary approach is, "Let me show you the ways our cutting-edge product can help make their application even more powerful."

If you sense that your prospect is highly committed to his or her current suppliers, you can acknowledge this relationship by saying, "I understand your commitment to them, and I hope we can build the same level of commitment with you." You can then use the prospect's thinking about the word "commitment", and take it to the next level by saying something like, "We feel that the real commitment is to your company." Your prospect is going to agree with this. So the next step is to add a statement that is linked to his or her needs, such as, "If I can show you right now how our product will reduce costs by X per cent, would you like to take a look at it?"

I want to compare it

If your prospect says that he or she would like to compare your product with others in the field, you should respond once again that this is a good idea. You can then paraphrase the objection and turn it into a "yes" statement, such as "You want more information before you make a decision." Your prospect will nod, and you can then say that you compare products all the time. Tell him or her that you have brochures that you would be glad to share. You can then offer a suggestion to the prospect, such as, "After we review these, it will be easy for you to decide."

■ **If your prospect** *expresses a commitment to present suppliers, look for ways that your products can complement their products.*

How did you know you needed to have this information with you? The answer is the "what-if" game.

Offering to share competitors' brochures further demonstrates your expertise, professionalism, preparation, and partnering with the prospect.

■ **Be as helpful as you can** *towards your prospect in searching for information on competitors' products. This may include taking him or her to the appropriate sites on the Internet.*

You go first

ONE OF THE MOST EFFECTIVE WAYS *to deal with objections is to bring them up yourself. You might wonder why a salesperson would ever be the one to mention an objection. There are many good reasons for doing so.*

For one thing, an objection is not likely to go away by itself. Sooner or later it is going to come up, and the longer it festers, the more serious it will become. Another good reason for bringing up an objection is that you can control it.

You can express an objection in positive language and phrase it in a way that is appealing to your prospect.

While bringing up an objection yourself, you can also demonstrate that the problem is either currently being resolved or will be resolved soon. Your words are going to sound better than any language a prospect would use when bringing up an objection.

For example, let's assume your company has had a chequered history, and there are lingering concerns in the marketplace about its reputation and ability to honour

■ **When you voice an objection,** *you are demonstrating your confidence in yourself and your product, as well as your honesty, integrity, openness, and desire to work with the prospect as a partner.*

commitments. Even if your prospect does not bring this up, don't assume that it isn't on his or her mind. Your best approach is to mention it: "You know, we're a completely different company today compared with even as recently as two years ago." Although this statement brings out the objection, it is more of a positive response to an objection than the objection itself.

Also notice that this statement contains a strong implied suggestion that the prospect already knows about the improvements in the company. As soon as you make this type of statement, support it with information regarding changes in the company, such as new leadership, new infusion of capital, new structure, or new improvements in operations.

Bringing up an objection shows the prospect that your thinking is similar to his or hers, and this sense of communal purpose further strengthens your credibility and the overall working relationship.

Icing on the cake

THERE ARE A NUMBER OF ADDITIONAL *strategies for handling objections that can give you the extra edge. Many of the best salespeople use them, and they are easy to incorporate into your presentation.*

Say it again

A prospect may use an absolute term, such as "never" or "always", to phrase an objection. For example, your prospect may say, "We never use X." Some salespeople might view this statement as an opening for a debate and respond by asking, "Why?" All this will do is lock the prospect even further into his or her absolute position.

When you hear a prospect use absolute words, the best approach is to repeat the word in the form of a question. When a prospect says, "We never use X", a powerful response is, "Never?" This makes the prospect stop and think. Don't be surprised if then you hear him or her say, "Well, sometimes we…".

Just suppose

One of the most powerful ways to deal with a broad range of objections is to respond with "Just suppose". This can be particularly helpful when a prospect says, "I'm not ready to buy right now." Rather than responding, "Why not?" or "When will you be ready?", you can reply with a simple "Just suppose" comment, such as "Just suppose you were ready to buy. How would the situation be different?"

At this point, the prospect will naturally think ahead and put him- or herself into a buying mind-set.

■ **By responding** *with a "Just suppose" to an objection, you are helping your prospect mentally put him- or herself into a buying state of mind. The information he or she provides next may tell you what you need to do right now to preserve that mind-set.*

Just what the prospect needs

If you have been using all of your senses to understand a prospect, you should be able to see a link between objections and needs. For example, if your prospect has been sending direct or indirect messages pointing to a need for achievement and recognition, make sure your response includes words and terms that will be particularly meaningful to him or her, such as:

- Growth
- Rewarding
- Success
- Profit
- Accomplishment
- High visibility

Rather than being blocked by an objection, this approach further demonstrates to the prospect that your product will indeed meet his or her needs.

Profiting from objections

The best salespeople view objections as an opportunity rather than a problem. Viewed in this light, an objection presents an opportunity for you to work closely with your prospect to resolve a problem or difficult situation. Going through this type of experience together is a way to accelerate the process of bonding, building mutual trust, credibility, and respect.

Rather than using objections as opportunities, many salespeople still resort to strategies that are virtually guaranteed to turn any objection into a rejection.

When a prospect raises an objection, do not deny it, argue the point, respond defensively, rationalize it, become impatient, or try to overpower it.

INTERNET

www.salesdoctors.com

This web site is filled with excellent articles on a broad range of sales topics, including ways to handle objections from prospects.

A simple summary

✔ Let your prospect know that you are glad he or she brought up an objection, and then listen carefully to it. An objection is your prospect's way of asking for more information.

✔ One of the best ways to handle an objection is to plan for it, which isn't too difficult since most of the objections you'll hear are going to fall into a few basic categories.

✔ You and your sales team can build a sales script book that can be highly effective in dealing with objections, but it won't be of much use to you unless you take the time to practise and work it into your own personal style.

✔ Never assume that the prospect who does not voice objections has no objections.

✔ One of the most powerful, persuasive, and compelling ways to deal with an objection is to bring the objection up yourself.

Chapter 12

Closing Time

PICTURE THE PERFECT sales presentation. The prospect, Jennifer, is enthusiastically answering the questions that Matt, the salesperson, is posing. Matt understands Jennifer's needs and has clearly aligned himself as a partner in the sales process. Matt tells Jennifer that he enjoyed chatting with her and will be in touch soon. They shake hands and Matt leaves. The perfect sales presentation? Not even close. The session worked well in terms of building trust, assessing the prospect's needs, joint problem solving, and handling objections. However, the perfect sales session must end with the salesperson asking for the order. There are many ways to close a sale, and the best ones tend to be natural, brief, and simple.

In this chapter...

✓ How to close

✓ When to close

✓ Add-ons add up

✓ Ringing up sales on the phone

KNOWING HOW AND WHEN TO CLOSE ARE ESSENTIAL SALES SKILLS

How to close

ALTHOUGH YOU DO NOT WANT TO PRESSURE or badger your prospect into buying your product, closing the sale should be on your mind throughout your sales presentation. Be on the lookout for opportunities to close, and seize them whenever they arise.

The best way to close a sale is to use two related techniques: *trial closing questions* and *closing questions*.

Using these types of questions to close the sale should fit easily, comfortably, and naturally with the questioning mode you've already established. Some salespeople are actually afraid to ask closing questions. Their reluctance is often based on fears of rejection or appearing to be too pushy.

If you are making a professional sales presentation that includes building trust and learning your prospect's needs, it is quite easy to ask closing questions. In fact, if you do not ask these questions, your prospects are likely to be confused, concerned, and even disappointed.

> **DEFINITION**
>
> Closing questions are the specific questions that ask for the order. They range from subtle questions, such as "What do you want to do from here?" all the way to not-so-subtle closing questions, such as "How about if I take out a contract and sign you up right now?" There is a broad range of closing questions, yet all have one objective in common: to finalize the sale.

> **DEFINITION**
>
> Trial closing questions are asked throughout a sales presentation to measure the prospect's opinion and point of view as well as to deal with objections that he or she might raise. These questions do not call for a decision. Typical trial closing questions are "How does this sound so far?" or "Do you see how this can help you?" or "Does this seem like what you wanted?" These questions typically generate a good number of positive responses and set the stage for the closing questions.

Failure to ask for the order is one of the main reasons salespeople fail. If you never ask for the order, you'll never make the sale.

It would be nice if there were one surefire closing technique that worked in every sales situation. Unfortunately, it simply does not exist. The most effective salespeople vary their closing strategies to fit the various sales situations they encounter.

The best closing technique is the one that fits your prospect's needs, style, and objectives. The more you understand your prospect, the better you'll be at closing the sale.

The direct approach

Some closing questions clearly, succinctly, and directly ask the prospect for the order. One example of this approach is the "Why not?" With this type of close, the salesperson starts by saying, "You like the product…" or "The product does exactly what you want…". The salesperson then says, "…so, why not give it a try?" or "…why not set a date to get this going?" This is directly asking the prospect to make a decision to buy the product, and the prospect may indeed respond with, "Okay, let's do it."

Another direct close option is simply to assume that the sale is already completed. With the Assumption Close, the salesperson says, "We can start on Tuesday", or "If we get it to you by the end of the week, is that okay?" If the prospect agrees, the sale is closed.

The Alternative Close is another direct way to try to finalize the sale. The salesperson gives the prospect a choice, either of which automatically implies that the sale is made. For example, the salesperson may ask, "Do you want the larger or smaller model?" or "Which colour do you prefer, the red or the blue?" This approach assumes that the purchase decision is made, the sale is completed, and all that remains is the finishing touches.

Another direct technique is to Hit the Scales. This is where the salesperson attempts to close the sale by asking the prospect, "On a scale of one to ten, where are you in your thinking?" If the prospect answers any number but ten, the next question is, "What will it take to get you to ten?" Once this question is asked, the salesperson says nothing and awaits the prospect's answer. This answer can be particularly revealing, since it can provide the prospect's own personal road map to direct the salesperson towards a sale.

■ **If your direct question** *doesn't work and your prospect is unwilling to proceed, your next step is to deal with that objection and then try another closing question.*

■ **An aggressive approach** *to closing will not automatically result in a sale. In fact, it is far more likely to alienate your prospect, and the only thing that will close will be your relationship with him or her.*

At the same time, there are some salespeople who are far too eager to close, and their entire sales approach is based on meeting their own needs rather than the needs of the prospect. At any point in the presentation that suits them, these salespeople push too hard to close the sale. And, whether by persuasion or intimidation, they sometimes succeed.

DEFINITION

Buyer's remorse is a prospect's serious regret at having made a particular purchase. It frequently occurs when prospects feel that they have been pushed, tricked, or manipulated into buying something that they really did not need or want.

Overly aggressive closing can be more expensive than might meet the eye since it can cost you dearly in terms of professionalism, credibility, goodwill, reputation, referrals, and future business.

Another little gift that can come to you courtesy of overly aggressive closing is called *buyer's remorse*. In many situations, this feeling of "I wish I hadn't bought that" can lead to a cancelled sale. And, in virtually all situations, it will lead to a cancelled relationship with your prospect.

The indirect approach

There are closing options that are softer, more prospect-based, and not quite as direct in calling for a purchasing decision from the prospect. But make no mistake, the indirect questions are still clearly designed to close the sale.

One of the easy ones to use is the Recap. This is where the salesperson reviews the sales presentation, links it to the prospect's needs, and then waits for the prospect to respond. For example, the salesperson might say, "… and that summarizes what we've discussed.

You said that you wanted a product that can do X, and that is what this will do, and more." Notice that the salesperson is not asking a direct question here, but clearly a question is implied. Then the salesperson waits quietly. The next words from the prospect will either be "yes" or another question. If it's a question, the salesperson responds to it, and then selects another closing option.

A similar indirect technique is the Logical Next Step. With this approach, all the questions have been asked and answered, final points presented, and the prospect seems to be satisfied. The salesperson looks at the prospect and asks, "What do you want to do from here?" An offshoot of this question is a statement, such as, "It looks like we're there."

You can see that this technique is highly focused on the prospect, and it is up to him or her to figure out what to do next. At the same time, much of the presentation has been led by the prospect, and only one logical step remains. The sale will be sealed when the prospect takes that step. With this approach, the prospect definitely feels that he or she is buying something, rather than being sold something.

Another indirect technique is the Embedded Close, which places the closing question in a sales story. For example, the salesperson can relate a story about a similar prospect who reached the same decision-making point as in the current sales situation. The story may include something like the following, "And he was unsure about the decision, but he knew it was time to act. So I said to him, 'My feeling is to go ahead and do it. How do you feel?'" The salesperson then stops, looks at the prospect, and waits.

■ **The indirect approach** *to closing a sale is just as powerful as the direct approach – but it is done in a softer, less heavy-handed way.*

The twist

There are a number of closing questions that twist the presentation and present a closing question in a slightly unusual format.

One of these techniques is the Reverse Close. If the prospect seems to be indicating that the product is more than he or she can handle, the salesperson can respond by saying that perhaps the prospect should not buy it. The salesperson would say, "Maybe this is more powerful than you need." This type of statement automatically implies the tremendous power of whatever the product may be, and in many cases the prospect responds with something like, "Wait a minute! I wouldn't say that…". In this type of case, the prospect often responds that he or she needs that much power. When this occurs, the sale is not far away.

■ **Using the Reverse Close** *with a reluctant prospect, such as suggesting he or she might be happier with a less powerful model of your product, can help him or her focus more carefully on the decision at hand.*

However, if the prospect agrees that the product may indeed be more than what he or she needs, the next question from the salesperson focuses on identifying the model that best fits the prospect's needs. As the discussion on this model continues, the salesperson again uses a closing question to wrap up the sale. On a more subtle basis, this approach further demonstrates the honesty and credibility of the salesperson.

Another twist in closing questions falls under the heading of Trading Places. With this method, the salesperson not only asks the prospect how to close, but actually asks the prospect to close it. A sample of this type of wording is, "If you were selling this product to yourself, what would you say now?" At this point, many prospects ask themselves a direct closing question, and they may well respond with a "yes". After all, it is rather difficult to turn down your own request.

Another set of compelling questions in this area is premised on wording that includes "If" and "Then". In essence, if the prospect agrees to the If, he or she is Then committing to buy. In such a case, the salesperson would say, "If we agree to do all that, will you then agree to buy?" The salesperson then waits. If the prospect says "yes", then the sale is closed.

Using "If" and "Then" in a closing question is particularly effective when your prospect starts asking for special changes, additions, or treatment.

Similarly, if the prospect says "no", the salesperson follows up with a question such as, "What else would you need to make this work?" When the prospect adds another item to the wish list, the salesperson repeats the If-Then question. With this approach, it will not take much longer to find out if the prospect is the real deal or no deal at all.

A further twist in closing is the Perfect Timing approach, which shows the prospect the value of acting now. On the one hand, this can mean closing by mentioning some special incentives or benefits associated with buying today. For example, "For people who buy today, we are including several free add-ons." This approach can focus on incentives for acting now or disincentives for waiting, such as in terms of impending price increases, product changes, or availability. The salesperson may say, "This is a particularly good time to buy because we've been told that a 9 per cent price increase is in the pipeline." If a salesperson has established a credible working relationship with a prospect, this kind of information can be helpful to the prospect, while also helping to close the sale.

One of the most crucial parts of any closing question is what you do not say.

After you ask a closing question, keep silent until the prospect responds. The ball is in the prospect's court. If you start talking, you may lose this opportunity to close the sale. It is also important to keep your replies to the prospect's questions brief, clear, and simple.

When your prospect asks you a question that you could answer with incredible detail, resist that temptation. When you give a brief response, your prospect will automatically fill in the blanks with the specific data that meet his or her needs. For example, you could respond to a product safety question by saying something like, "The system is equipped with the TRC System 80l, the XS restraint package, extra tracks on dual safety monitor, all tested with 31.18 sensory meter…". Or you could say, "This has all the latest safety features, and I know you're going to be happy with it." With this second statement, your prospect will do his or her own mental search and develop a picture of this product's safety that perfectly fits what he or she wants.

■ **By giving longwinded answers** *to any questions, you are likely to bore your prospect and discuss matters that don't interest him or her.*

What if it doesn't close?

If the sale does not close, perhaps it is a matter of timing. That being the case, you should continue to work with the prospect and try other closing techniques along the way. Some sales, however, are just not going to happen, at least not right then. When this occurs, you should work with the prospect to reach an agreement as to the next step to take, such as a follow-up meeting. As part of this process, you will also want to make sure that there is complete agreement over the issues that have been resolved as well as those that remain. It will also be helpful to commit to work on some of those remaining issues before the next meeting.

If the issues appear to be insurmountable and there does not even appear to be a possibility for a next meeting, the prospect still remains a prospect. This means that you thank the prospect for his or her time and interest, and then indicate that you will be staying in touch, and that is exactly what you should do. Although this person might not be an active prospect today, he or she will remain a prospect permanently, and may become an active prospect sooner than you think. In addition, he or she can also be a source of valuable referrals.

If a sale does not close, you should think about ways to build bridges rather than burn them.

When to close

YOU SHOULD ACTUALLY BE CLOSING *throughout your presentation by placing trial closes at several points along the way. At the same time, you should be paying careful attention to your prospect so that you can spot the signals that tell you when he or she is ready to make the decision to buy.*

There is no best time to close a sale: if you pay attention to your prospect, he or she is going to let you know when it is time to close.

Verbal signals

When your prospect is at a point where the sale can be closed, he or she will typically give you some clear verbal signs. You are likely to hear "yes" frequently, along with the increased use of the word "I", particularly in such expressions as "I see", "I get it", and "I understand".

Sometimes your prospects are going to ask direct questions that clearly indicate it is time to close the sale.

These types of questions imply that your prospect has already taken psychological ownership of the product. Typical examples include "How much is it?", or "When can it be delivered?", or "How many are available?", or "Do you have special rates for larger quantities?" When you hear these types of questions, you should move immediately to close the sale.

There are times when a prospect's questions and comments indicate that he or she is ready to buy, but the salesperson still feels compelled to talk more about the product, the company, the service, or any number of additional topics. The problem is that when a salesperson proceeds down this path, the prospect may well raise other issues, questions, or concerns, and this means that the opportunity to close the sale is deferred or even lost.

Avoid missed opportunities by remembering a simple yet critical rule of closing: when you've made the sale, close it.

Physical signals

Your prospect's physical movements can also let you know when it is time to close the sale. To receive these messages, all you have to do is look for the obvious changes in your prospect's body language. These changes usually include more smiling, nodding, leaning forward in enthusiasm, uncrossed arms, or rubbing hands together.

As you get to know your prospects over time, you are going to learn about individual changes in body language that tell you when they are ready to buy.

However, be careful about trying to read too much into body language during a sales presentation. For example, some theorize that a prospect who touches his or her face is ready to buy, but the prospect could just have an itchy face.

Reading body language beyond the basics can move into pop psychology and steer you down the wrong path.

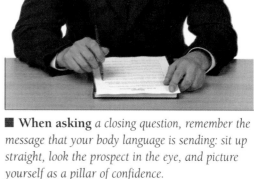

■ **When asking** *a closing question, remember the message that your body language is sending: sit up straight, look the prospect in the eye, and picture yourself as a pillar of confidence.*

211

Add-ons add up

ONCE YOUR PROSPECT HAS AGREED

to buy the product, you have a unique opportunity to sell some accessories and add-ons. Your prospect is in a buying mode and you have established sales momentum. Not only are you helping your prospect fully meet his or her needs, you are also generating more revenue per sale. You are not dumping additional products on the prospect, but rather providing him or her with additional goods and services to gain maximum effectiveness and satisfaction from the product.

DEFINITION

Accessories are specific items that help your product do what it is actually supposed to do. For example, if you sell a computer, the accessories can include software and disks. Add-ons *are additional related products that the prospect may want. In the sale of the computer, add-ons can include a surge protector or an extended warranty.*

Other forms of add-ons include offering a better package for a nominal increase in price, discounts for purchasing more than one item, and savings for purchasing additional years' worth of items.

Be sure to consult with your fellow sales professionals and manager about the kinds of accessories and add-ons that work best for your product.

DIGITAL CAMERA

CDs

■ **Once your prospect** *agrees to buy the computer system, you have an excellent opportunity to sell add-ons and accessories that will help meet his or her needs.*

SCANNER

It's the rational thing to do

Now that your prospect has made the emotional decision to purchase your product, he or she is looking for ways to rationalize this decision. You can help him or her out by emphasizing the wide range of benefits associated with the purchase, and you can show him or her additional products and services that can save money and help the product function at peak efficiency so that the benefits you described can be maximized.

Ringing up sales on the phone

IN ADDITION TO USING THE PHONE for prospecting, the telephone is often used for sales per se. While all of the previously discussed elements of selling apply to telephone sales, there are also some specific sales skills that can help when trying to close sales by phone. One of the most important basic steps in selling by phone is to do everything in your power to contact prospects in senior-level positions.

Part of your sales strategy will depend on whether you are handling an *inbound* call or an *outbound* call.

Taking the inbound call

Inbound calls have some distinct advantages, not the least of which is that the prospect seemingly has a need for your product or he or she would not have contacted you in the first place. In addition, the prospect would not have called your company if there had been some questions about your company's credibility and trust. This is a positive way to begin a sales call.

DEFINITION

An inbound sales call is one that is made from a prospect to you. It is typically the result of company advertising, promotions, and publicity, but it can just as easily come from referrals, satisfied customers, Internet links, or general interest from a potential consumer.

An outbound sales call is one that a salesperson makes to a prospect. These prospects can be generated from any number of sources, including the company's marketing efforts, company listings, and Internet leads. Refer to Chapter 5 to learn more about outbound sales calls and cold calls.

■ **The simplest strategy** *for inbound sales calls is to open with a friendly greeting and thank the prospect for calling.*

YOUR VOICE

One of your most valuable tools in selling by phone is your voice. You can train it, develop it, and build it into an instrument that can make a real difference in the sales process. Listen to the voices of people who are highly trusted, and then listen to a tape recording of your own voice. Are you doing everything in your power to make your voice interesting, trustworthy, and captivating? Are you projecting your words with strength and confidence, particularly when you ask closing questions? The overall tone of your message is at least as important as the content.

It can certainly help to vary your pitch, pace, tone, and points of emphasis. Try saying the following sentence in a monotone, and then say it again with some variations in your delivery: "I think you will be very satisfied when you see what this product can do." Try holding the word "very" a little longer, and put a little more emphasis on the word "this". Can you hear the difference? So can your prospect.

This also counts when you are leaving a voicemail message. In essence, you are going to leave a 10- or 15-second commercial. As enticing and compelling as your message might be, your voice should be even more so.

If you have ever practised a musical instrument, you will know what it takes to get a better sound. Well, as a salesperson, the instrument that you are playing is your voice. So, don't forget to practise tonight.

When you answer an inbound call, make sure that you get the prospect's name and use it when asking, "How can I help you today?" From this point, continue just as you would with in-person selling by asking questions and further identifying the prospect's needs. Be sure to ask about products that the prospect is using and the problems he or she is currently experiencing. All of the elements of pacing, building trust and rapport, handling objections, and closing apply in these calls.

No matter how the call goes, be sure to obtain the prospect's company name and phone number. Even if you did not make a sale today, this is a real prospect, and you should plan on staying in touch with him or her over time.

Find out how the prospect heard about your company and note the specific reason for the call.

Your messages in telephone sales should be simple, brief, and clear. Do not try to focus on an array of products, and make sure that you do not get muddled in details. Your information is basically coming to the client through a tiny earpiece, and if you start presenting highly detailed information, quantitative comparisons, and varied products, your prospect will be lost, and so will the sale. The best approach in selling by phone is to focus on one item that sounds as though it definitely meets the prospect's needs, and focus later in the call on some possible add-ons.

A simple summary

✔ Ask trial closing questions throughout your sales presentation to measure your prospect's opinion and set the stage for your closing questions.

✔ There is a broad range of closing questions, but all have one goal: to finalize the sale. Be sure that the questions you use fit your prospect's needs, style, and objectives.

✔ Depending upon the prospect and the overall sales situation, you may want to close with the direct approach, the indirect approach, or with a twist.

✔ After you ask a closing question, stay completely silent until your prospect responds.

✔ Closing time is an excellent time to sell accessories and add-ons.

✔ In telephone sales, all of your skills in pacing, asking questions, using power words, handling objections, and closing still apply. Remember that the tone of what you are saying is just as important as the content.

PART
FOUR

LOOKING BACK

N O MATTER HOW your sales session went, you can gather invaluable information by *reviewing* what happened. Even if the session went beautifully, you can still learn from it. If the session ends with a commitment to meet again, be ready with your best *negotiating* skills for that return visit.

Sometimes a prospect asks for a *written proposal* or perhaps a *presentation before a group*. Don't panic! You are going to learn some simple techniques to handle these like a pro. And should you face *difficult customers* along the way, you are going to learn how to handle them like a pro, too. When all is said and done, you will know how to easily apply a full range of services to develop *long-term relationships* with all of your customers.

Chapter 13

How'd It Go?

I N THE WORLD of professional sports, one activity that typically follows every game is a review of the tapes. It is important for players to understand what worked and what didn't. They need to take a second look at the unexpected moves pulled by the other team, and their own adjustments. And, most importantly, every player needs to have a clear idea of the steps to take to play even better next time. As a professional in sales, you also need to conduct a thorough review of each session. Did you achieve the goal you were seeking? If you want to improve your average, take a second look at your performance after every outing.

In this chapter...

✓ Instant reaction

✓ Self review

✓ Deal with the data

✓ Now they want a proposal

TAKE A LESSON IN SELF-IMPROVEMENT: ASSESS HOW YOU DID AFTER EVERY SALES SESSION

Instant reaction

YOU HAVE JUST FINISHED YOUR SALES PRESENTATION and *now you are back in your car, or perhaps you have just hung up the phone. Either way, you have a sense of how the presentation went. There are probably a few crystal clear images that stick in your mind, and perhaps some key phrases that you said or should have said.*

Right after a sales call is the best time to write down your feelings and briefly note what happened. If you wait until the next day or even later in the day, your memory will become diluted and blend into other sales calls, and any insights you could have gathered will be lost.

Summing it all up

Writing down a brief summary of your presentation does not mean you should compose a fully annotated historical report. All you need to do is make some brief notes about what happened, and then rate your presentation on a few key factors that we'll discuss shortly.

■ **Directly after a meeting** *with a prospect, listen to the thoughts that are running through your head and quickly jot them down.*

There may have been one key phrase that really piqued your prospect's interest, or perhaps there was something you said that inadvertently upset him or her. Were there questions you should have been able to answer but could not handle?

Analyzing your feelings

Whenever you wrap up a meeting with a prospect, you will be left with a gut feeling as to how things went. Try to identify and note any of the factors that are either giving you a positive visceral reaction or turning your stomach. This will provide you with data to improve your sales skills. In addition, many people do not realize the powerful psychological impact that writing down one's feelings can have.

When people are frustrated, upset, or stressed, taking the time to write out negative feelings not only relieves emotional tension, it actually seems to push out the source of these feelings.

Writing down your negative feelings can also help you set up the next call and possibly prevent some of the problems that occurred in the previous one.

■ **The process** *of taking notes about what happened during your last sales call can help put you in a better state of mind to make the next call.*

GIVING IT ALL

Did you know that when opera singers reach the end of a performance, they are completely drained? They draw from deep within and give every bit of their physical and mental energy to each performance. This is what it means to "give one's all", and this is what happens when great professionals aspire to great goals.

How does this apply to the professional salesperson? Naturally, you do not want to expend every ounce of physical and mental energy on one sales call or there will be nothing left for the next one. But it does mean that when you are on a sales call, all of your physical and mental attention must be fully focused on selling.

When you are done with each call, whether you make a sale or not, you want to be able to look back and say that you truly gave your all in pursuit of your great sales goals.

■ **When presenting to prospects**, *you must give your all, both physically and mentally, in the pursuit of sales. If you don't give your all, don't expect to get it all.*

Self review

YOU CAN BREAK DOWN *every sales presentation into a beginning, middle, and end, and there are self-assessment questions for each segment that can be helpful in focusing, assessing, and fine-tuning your performance. After you make a few notes on a sales session, just look over these questions and rate yourself with a "+" for excellent, "0" for average and "-" for poor. In considering your self-rating, also try to think of the rating your prospect would give you for each question, since your prospect will be the ultimate judge of your performance.*

In the beginning

The beginning of the sales process includes your first contact with the prospect and the way that you set the framework for your sales presentation. You would give yourself a "+", "0", or "-" for each of the following:

- Punctuality
- Initial contact with secretary or administrative assistant
- Icebreaking
- Getting off on the right foot
- Building trust and rapport
- Early questions
- Looking and listening
- Reading body language
- My initial impact

Somewhere in the middle

As you move beyond the introductory comments and casual conversation into the body of your presentation, use a "+", "0", or "-" in assessing your performance in each of the following areas:

- Listening
- Understanding my prospect's needs
- Letting my prospect take the lead
- Acting as a partner
- Maintaining trust and rapport
- Pacing
- Trial closing questions
- Getting "yes" responses
- Quality of my questions
- Quality of my answers
- Demonstrating product knowledge
- Displaying confidence
- Using power words
- Using sales stories
- Avoiding excess detail
- Keeping the presentation simple
- Focusing on benefits, not features
- Handling objections
- Setting the stage for the close

Nearing the end

When you move into the closing stage of your sales presentation, there are a number of actions unique to this phase for you to assess with a "+", "0", or "-", including:

- Closing the sale
- Helping prospect justify the purchase
- Using a closing technique that fits prospect's needs and style
- Selling add-ons and accessories
- Finishing on a positive note
- Agreeing on a next step

- Understanding all points that are resolved
- Understanding all points that remain open
- Taking accurate notes on the meeting
- Obtaining referrals

Deal with the data

AT THIS POINT IN THE PROCESS, you have three sets of information. The first is your set of notes from the sales meeting itself. This is the information that came directly from the sales session. It may be a signed contract, or it may be your own summary that spells out the points of agreement, points in contention, and the next step to take with this prospect. This next step may be setting up a shipping date, setting up a date for a second meeting, or scheduling a follow-up phone call in 6 months.

After every sales session, you should have clear documentation of not only what happened in the meeting but also what is supposed to happen next.

The second set of information is the brief write-up you put together after the sales session, and the third set of information is the checklist on how things went in the beginning, middle, and end of the session.

Check it out

Before you make your next sales call, take a look at your brief summary and see if there are any problems that you can fix on the spot. For example, if your "gut feeling" was that you could not really work out what the prospect wanted, try to do more listening and less talking in your next sales call.

Towards the end of the day, after you have amassed data from several sales calls, take a look at your self-assessment scales. In doing so, you are most likely to find all sorts of pluses, a few zeros, and even fewer minuses.

You can certainly dwell on all of the well-deserved pluses that you gave yourself, but if you want to improve as a salesperson, you have to take a look at the zeros and minuses as well. In particular, look for any of these ratings that are repeated in several of your presentations. By doing so, you can identify the area or areas where you will need to set an action plan for improvement. Some of these

■ **A thorough and honest review** *of your sales performance each day is one of the most effective ways to improve your sales performance tomorrow.*

problem areas are easy to fix, such as not being punctual. On the other hand, if your closing techniques are not closing, your action plan may call for some formal training and guidance.

One of the additional values in assessing your performance in this way is that you are conducting what is called a needs analysis. This is going to be highly valuable to you in selecting the kinds of training and educational programmes that will best upgrade your sales skills.

■ **Formal training** *may be what's called for if your sales techniques fail to generate any business. If your company doesn't arrange courses for its staff, there are many independent organizations that do.*

SHOULD YOU ASK FOR REFERRALS?

Some companies expect their salespeople to gather additional referrals after attempting to close a sale, whether the sale has closed successfully or not. The theory behind this is that if the sale has closed, the customer's satisfaction with the salesperson and the product is clearly in mind, and the customer can also help rationalize his or her purchase by referring others to the product.

At the same time, if the sale falls apart, it is believed that there is nothing to lose by asking the prospects if they know others for whom your product would be more suitable. And, if some of these significant others ultimately buy, this would be yet another reason to go back to the original prospect with an updated presentation.

There are some, however, who feel that asking a customer for a referral at this time is a little tacky, particularly when your focus as a salesperson is supposed to be on the prospect and his or her needs, rather than on you and your need for future sales. After all, if you closed the sale, you can always come back to your prospect after he or she is fully satisfied with the product and then generate more meaningful leads.

So, what should you do?

The answer to this conundrum is a simple one. First, see if your company has any expectations in this area. Second, if the decision is up to you, try asking for referrals at the point of sale. Most likely, the answer is going to jump out at you either in the form of a flinch or a nod. That will be all you need to know.

■ **The look on your prospect's face** *will tell you immediately if he or she is willing to pass on the names of contacts who may be interested in your product.*

Don't be disappointed if you find that you have given yourself more than a few low ratings. Studies have found that when high-achieving people look back at their performance, they tend to focus on the areas where they could have performed better, rather than focusing on the many areas in which their performance was excellent.

Set up for the next meeting

If the next step with a prospect is another meeting, take each point of disagreement from your previous meeting and list as many alternative approaches as you can. With a little homework, you may be able to discover ways to turn these points of disagreement into a point of agreement. However, if your prospect is locked into some of his or her points of disagreement, you will need to be ready for some on-the-spot *negotiation*.

Speaking of negotiating

Depending upon your prospect and his or her needs and style, you may need to do some negotiating to keep the sales process moving. Although your collaborative sales approach is based more on joint problem solving than negotiating, some of the basics of negotiating can be useful tools to have in your sales kit.

■ **Noting previous points** *of disagreement with your prospect and different ways of solving them will give you a full menu of options from which you can, with luck, reach the perfect solutions.*

Keep in mind at the outset that with a collaborative approach to selling, your objective in negotiations is to reach a *win-win* solution where the seller and buyer are both happy. If you go with any other approach, all of the trust, credibility, and goodwill that you have built will be lost, and your relationship with the prospect will probably be lost too.

The collaborative approach to selling tends to generate less game playing than a sales approach that calls for one party to win and the other to lose. As a result, although you may be doing some negotiating, your dealings with your prospect are typically more like joint problem solving.

If there is a major sticking point and your prospect has placed you in a position where the only card you can play is your negotiating card, the following are three simple points to remember:

 1 To negotiate a satisfactory solution, you need to have a clear idea of the relative *power* that you bring to the sales session.

Some aggressive negotiators assume that bluffing about one's power is an altogether acceptable option. The idea is that your actual power is not important, but what is important is a prospect's perception of it. The only problem is that if your prospect calls your bluff, your credibility and the sale are both out the window.

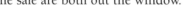
In sales negotiations, as well as in life, truth wins out.

Your power is going to affect what you do if your prospect locks on to one point of disagreement. It is your power that will heavily determine if your negotiating strategy is to stick with your original proposal, offer a counterproposal, accede to the prospect's demand, or end the whole session.

 2 Have a clear idea of the best price that you can reasonably expect for your product, the minimum price and terms that you are willing to accept, and

WINNERS AND LOSERS

There are four possible outcomes to sales negotiations. These are:

Win-Win

The salesperson is satisfied with the selling price and terms, and is further satisfied at having successfully met the prospect's needs. The prospect is pleased that he or she purchased a product at a fair price that fully meets his or her needs.

■ **The best possible outcome** *in any sales negotiation is a win-win situation. Strive for this always, not only for your benefit but also for that of your prospect.*

Win-Lose

The salesperson has extracted a huge amount of money from the prospect, far beyond a fair market price. The prospect feels that he or she has lost out.

Lose-Win

The prospect worked the salesperson so hard that the prospect ended up buying the product for a fraction of its fair price. The salesperson feels like a loser.

Lose-Lose

In this scenario, there can be a number of outcomes, none of which is particularly appealing. For example, perhaps a sale that should have been made was never consummated, in which case neither the prospect's needs nor the salesperson's needs were met. Another lose-lose outcome occurs when the salesperson and prospect are both dissatisfied with the final price. And, perhaps this sale was consummated with an alternative, lesser product. This outcome fails to meet the prospect's needs for a quality product at a fair price, while also failing to meet the salesperson's needs to deliver it. Lose-lose is the classic bad deal.

the actual price objective that you are trying to meet. Not only do you need to know your absolute minimum, you also have to be willing to end the transaction if your minimum is not met.

Sometimes a prospect will wait until the very end of a presentation and then throw in a seemingly harmless point that makes the sale far less acceptable to you. When this occurs so late in the game, it is tempting just to go along with it. Do not make this mistake.

If necessary, reopen the entire sales discussion. A lose-win outcome is not a happy ending for you.

As part of your negotiation strategy, do not be afraid to ask for a break or a moment to call your office. You may need a few minutes to step back and review or reframe whatever may be going on.

■ **Sometimes more can be accomplished** *over a cup of coffee than in a formal negotiation session. Both you and your prospect may benefit from a change of scenery or a breath of fresh air.*

3 One of the most powerful negotiating techniques is to build outcomes that will help your prospect feel successful. This in no way means giving in to all of the prospect's demands, but focuses more on listening, empathizing, and seeking out the specific criteria that the prospect wants in a successful resolution. The sticking point in negotiations is typically composed of several lesser points. Breaking down the sticking points and then negotiating an agreement on a few important ones may spell success for the prospect.

By helping your prospect to be successful, you are helping yourself to be successful as well.

If the sales session falls apart, always keep your tone friendly and positive, and be sure to maintain contact with the prospect over time. You never know when your prospect will need a product just like yours. When this occurs, you want your prospect's memories of you and your product to be totally positive.

INTERNET

www.negotiation.com

If you are interested in further developing your negotiation skills, this site offers a broad range of highly regarded seminars, books, videotapes, audiotapes, and software programs.

Now they want a proposal

SOMETIMES YOUR SALES PRESENTATION *will end with the prospect asking you to submit a proposal. This should not send a pang of fear through you. After all, your company may have some procedures to help you out. In fact, perhaps your manager will step in and take care of this.*

Some salespeople reckon that they can pull an old proposal off the shelf, dust it off, move a few phrases around, and the work is done. While the format and structure of previous proposals can be helpful, you need to tailor your proposal to fit the needs, standards, expectations, and objectives of your prospect.

Do not submit a rewrapped old proposal to your prospect unless you want to send a message that you and your company are not particularly industrious, inventive, or diligent.

231

The proposal that you send to a prospect is actually their first sample of your work. If it reeks of *boilerplate* language, questionable comparisons, and force-fitting data, you are going to short-circuit your chances for a sale by the time the prospect reaches page 2.

If you are called upon to write a draft or even the proposal itself, there are some simple steps that can help you prepare a highly professional proposal.

Introducing the proposal

Your sales proposal should be introduced by a brief and friendly covering letter that states how pleased you are to present the attached proposal.

> **DEFINITION**
>
> *Boilerplate is a printing term that refers to a plate that contains items that are repeated in print, such as a newspaper's masthead. In the context of a proposal, boilerplate language refers to sections from one proposal that are dropped in their entirety into another proposal.*

Although there are no hard and fast rules, your proposal should be somewhere in the range of two to ten pages. Some proposals certainly run longer than this, but if you see yours starting to turn into a tome, think about adding some appendices.

■ **Write a brief but friendly** *covering letter to accompany your proposal. It should conclude with a comment indicating that you look forward to discussing the proposal with the prospect.*

Your proposal should definitely include a title page, table of contents, and an executive summary that gives a brief overview of the overall themes and objectives. It should also include an introduction that gives the prospect a quick overview of each of the sections that follow.

It should be written in a clear, focused, and concise style. Crisp short sentences sell much better than those that ramble. When the language of a proposal starts to wander, it is just a matter of time before the reader's mind starts to wander too.

The heart of the matter

Now that the overall introduction of the proposal has been presented, the next step is to provide the body of the proposal. In this middle section, the first important component is your overview of the prospect company and the specific problem or problems that are currently being encountered. This is a chance to demonstrate not only your listening skills and understanding of the business and the industry, but your insights into the prospect's specific needs as well.

This section should also spell out the benefits and solutions that your product will provide, with specific emphasis on how the product meets the prospect's needs. It is also important to include a complete breakdown of all aspects related to the timing of your product, including start dates, benchmark dates, objectives, and review points.

If the language in this section starts to get too technical, consider putting it in an appendix, while keeping the body of the report clear and simple.

By reading this section, your prospect will have a complete understanding of what your product will do, how it will do it, when it will do it, what specific problems will be solved, and how its success will be measured.

INTERNET

www.salesproposals.com

This site provides articles on proposal writing, design tips, books, and proposal design software to take you step-by-step through the process of writing a sales proposal.

In conclusion

Issues related to the price of your product should be placed in the later sections of the proposal. If pricing matters are placed at the beginning, some prospects may put down the report before they understand the price and the value that your product adds. When you present information on price, be sure to support it with specific detail so that the prospect understands precisely how the various figures and totals were reached.

This final section is also the place to provide the prospect with information about your company. Let the prospect know about the company's history and objectives, and include selected testimonials, awards, and references. Your goal in this section is to let the prospect see your company's strengths, stability, experience, expertise, and any other points that indicate that your product is obviously the best choice.

A personal appearance

Once you have completed your proposal, do not just simply post it.

If posted, the proposal can be routed here, rerouted there, and lost somewhere in the great corporate abyss. And, even in the best case scenario,

■ **Discussing your proposal** *in person allows you to answer questions and clarify any confusing issues. You can also observe your prospect's reaction and place appropriate emphasis on key parts of the proposal.*

if it gets right into your prospect's hands, he or she may have questions, but you are not there to answer them and guide him or her persuasively through the proposal.

When the proposal is done, make an appointment with your prospect to deliver it yourself, and go over it point by point. At the very least, if you cannot meet your prospect at the time the proposal is delivered, be sure to make a follow-up call to review it.

A simple summary

✔ After you complete a sales call, make a few notes about what happened, particularly in terms of what worked and what did not. Be sure to look this over before you make your next call.

✔ Doing a self-assessment after a sales call can be very helpful. You can use this information to identify and ultimately correct parts of your sales presentation that need some fine-tuning or upgrading.

✔ When negotiating with your prospect, your objective is to reach a win-win solution.

✔ It is always helpful to have a clear idea of your own power and that of your prospect.

✔ Look at your sales proposal as a representative work sample from you and your company. It should have crisp and clear phrasing, a minimum of boilerplate language, and maximum tailoring to show how your company and product will meet the prospect's needs.

✔ The most effective way to get your proposal to your prospect is to make an appointment, deliver it yourself, and go over it at that time.

Chapter 14

Dealing with Difficult Prospects

As you go out and sell, you are going to meet some difficult prospects. There are plenty out there, and their behaviour can cover a very broad spectrum. Nonetheless, they are still prospects, and even if they behave a little differently, they still have needs that you as a salesperson can fill, provided that you know how to deal with them in the first place. While some prospects are just plain difficult, others can actually become difficult as a result of the way that they are treated by a salesperson. Fortunately, in any case, there are some strategies to help you deal easily with difficult prospects.

In this chapter...

✓ Is it you?

✓ Selling to the classics

✓ Dealing with rejection

✓ Getting out of a slump

THE BETTER YOU UNDERSTAND A DIFFICULT PROSPECT, THE BETTER YOU ARE ABLE TO DEAL WITH HIM OR HER

Is it you?

IT IS ALWAYS EASY to attribute problems in a sales presentation to your prospect, but, frankly, the first place to look when you encounter seemingly difficult prospects is at yourself. Is there anything that you may be doing to bring about some of this problematic behaviour? If you are the source of the problem, that's good because it is much easier to change your own behaviour than someone else's.

What did you expect?

As we have discussed earlier, your expectations have a profound impact on your performance in all aspects of selling, and nowhere is this more apparent than in dealings with your prospects. If you are expecting difficulties with a particular prospect, the likelihood of encountering difficulties is increased dramatically.

Your expectations are going to alter the full range of your behaviour and comments. When you expect problems from a prospect, your body language can visibly tighten up, and your facial expressions and head gestures can easily show how you feel.

When you are in a negative expectation mode, your choice of words tends to be rather unimaginative and uninspiring, and the tone of your voice becomes noticeably harsher.

And further, your negative expectations are going to alter the way you interpret your prospect's behaviour and comments. For example, if your expectation is that your prospect is going to be nasty, even a friendly "Hello, nice to see you" can be misinterpreted as an act of hostility.

■ **It could be** *your body language that is at the root of any selling problems you may have.*

Once you misinterpret that friendly "Hello", your response and accompanying body language will send a nasty message in return. Perhaps it will be in the form of a condescending or aloof "Oh, hi. How are you doing?" Your prospect is certainly going to pick up these cues, and his or her response will probably be equally nasty. With that, you will probably say to yourself, "Aha! Just as I thought. This is one nasty prospect."

The key to preventing this type of problem rests in your hands. The best step is to approach all prospects and sales situations with positive expectations.

If you expect a prospect to be upbeat, friendly, and positive, your own behaviour will help bring out these qualities. If you expect a prospect to be difficult, that is probably what you are going to get.

■ **Greeting your prospect** *in a friendly way with a smile and a firm, but not rigid, handshake can help set the right tone for the rest of the meeting.*

Snap judgments

Another way that you can turn a neutral prospect into a difficult one is by making snap judgments, which are usually based on stereotypes, biases, or preconceived ideas about the prospect. If you act on these beliefs, your behaviour is not going to fit the prospect's needs, style, and expectations. As a result, the prospect may react negatively, and this can cause you to incorrectly assume that the prospect is difficult.

For example, some young salespeople can look at an older prospect and decide that grey hair has something to do with grey matter. This can lead to a sales approach that is condescending, arrogant, or even impatient. When the prospect responds with a high degree of technical expertise, the salesperson then inaccurately assumes that this is a difficult prospect, known in the trade as a know-all. The real know-all in this session was the salesperson who, like most know-alls, did not know much at all.

Avoiding pseudo-science

There are some pseudo-scientific writings claiming that you can make accurate judgments about other people in a matter of seconds by looking at their features, gestures, and body types.

The "research" behind this claim typically has slick packaging and enough psychobabble to sound credible. The only problem is that there is not a shred of scientific evidence to support this claim. These types of personality instruments are party games at best. And, as such, they belong at the party, certainly not in a sales presentation.

When salespeople draw instant conclusions about prospects based on pop psychology, they misread the prospect and generate a negative reaction.

The best way to avoid the traps that are set by making instant judgments about your prospect is to do more listening. By taking your time and approaching your prospect with questions as opposed to answers, you are far more likely to gain accurate insights into him or her as an individual. And you are far less likely to meet a difficult prospect.

What did you do?

Another way that salespeople can turn friendly prospects into problem prospects is by making basic selling errors. These include showing up late, criticizing the prospect, interrupting, complaining, talking too loud, and using inappropriate slang.

There are many types of inappropriate behaviour by a salesperson, and any of them can cause a salesperson to incorrectly assume that the problem is with the prospect.

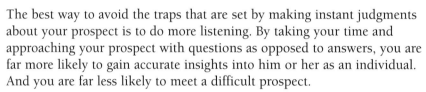

If you seem to be encountering a particularly high number of difficult prospects, consider the possibility that you may be drawing this behaviour out of them. If this is the case, go back to the basics of building trust and rapport, asking questions, using the most powerful language, and listening.

Selling to the classics

YOU ARE GOING TO FIND *that most of your difficult prospects fall into two classic categories:* evaders *and* warriors. *With a few simple and straightforward steps, you can make some real headway in dealing with all of them.*

DEFINITION

Evaders *are prospects who are difficult to pin down, while* warriors *seem to be intent on pinning you down.*

Recognizing evaders

There are several types of evaders out there – the duck, torpedo, short cutter, delay of gamer, slow speaker, and wall – and there are just as many effective strategies for dealing with them.

The duck

The duck is one of the major forms of evaders. This is the prospect who ducks your calls and does not respond to your messages or voicemail. You believe that he or she has a real need for your product, and if you could have a meeting, you may well be able to make a sale. If there is no contact, though, there is no meeting.

The best way to deal with the duck is to go duck hunting. You will need to aim your calls during off-peak hours, including early in the morning, later in the evening, and at the weekends. Target your prospect with varied media. Try sending your prospect some informative or newsworthy e-mail, the newest brochures, and voicemail that concisely presents the clear benefits of your product.

■ **If your prospect** *proves to be elusive, don't give up the hunt. Try to befriend his or her secretary or administrative assistant, if there is one, but make sure you don't overdo the charm.*

The torpedo

It is also important to have some strategies to deal with another classic evader, the torpedo. This is the prospect who cancels meetings with you, often at the last moment.

While there certainly can be legitimate reasons for a prospect to torpedo your meeting, there are less acceptable reasons as well. One of the common reasons that a prospect does this is his or her belief that a meeting with you is not that important. In other words, the prospect does not see the need for your product or the value that your product adds. As a result, when you are dealing with the torpedo, make sure that he or she has a clear idea of the real benefits provided by your product.

When setting a date for a sales presentation with a torpedo, try to set appointments on Tuesday, Wednesday, or Thursday, preferably in the morning.

There are also some administrative steps that can reduce the likelihood of having your sales presentation cancelled. Early morning appointments tend not to fall prey to the delays and cancellations that occur as the day wears on. The problem with setting up Monday appointments is that prospects are often consumed with issues that have backed up over the weekend, and Fridays can end early in fact and in spirit.

The short cutter

Another evasive tactic is that deployed by the short cutter. This is the prospect who will actually meet you but, unfortunately, has to cut the meeting short. Prospects who do this are demonstrating their power as well as a lack of understanding of the need for your product.

When meeting with the short cutter, be sure that you clearly present the key benefits of your product as early in the session as possible, without undercutting the time you need to fully understand his or her needs.

When your prospect cuts a meeting short, be sure to obtain a commitment for future action from him or her as well as a commitment for the next meeting.

■ **Constantly checking the time** *and then cutting short your meeting is behaviour typical of evasive prospects who want to demonstrate their power.*

STOP PLAYING GAMES

A salesperson called on a high-tech company and was asked to wait for a few minutes. He took out his laptop and was pecking away when the prospect appeared. At first glance, the salesperson appeared to be handling this delay quite professionally, but things did not look so professional when the prospect noticed that the salesperson was deeply involved in a game of solitaire. The salesperson went on to make the presentation, but after he left, one of the first comments from the prospect mentioned the solitaire. Unless you want to be playing a lot more solitaire, this type of activity during your wait is not a great idea.

Do not be discouraged by the short cutter, as it typically takes a number of meetings to make a sale. If a meeting is cut short, that should not present a problem for you. In fact, if the prospect had to cut your presentation short because of a bona fide emergency situation, he or she will appreciate your flexibility and understanding, and may well feel a need to take an extra step to hear you out at the next meeting.

The delay of gamer

Another evasive tactic is used by the delay of gamers, whose typical approach is to keep you waiting well past the time for your appointment. When this occurs, it is easy for salespeople to become upset and stressed, but there is no need for this reaction. Since you are well organized, you have built enough flexibility into your schedule to handle this type of delay. In fact, you can profit from it by making some phone calls, handling some administrative details, or further preparing for the present call.

Do not waste time reading a bunch of old dog-eared magazines while sitting in the waiting area. If your prospect comes out to greet you, he or she may be surprised that you have nothing else to do.

The slow speaker

You should also be prepared to deal with the slow speakers. These are not necessarily difficult prospects, but they can be if you deal with them incorrectly. Their speech style is very, very slow, deliberate, and ponderous. You may hear "I... have... several... questions... about... this... product." If you respond rapid fire with "Right, now let me run through the key issues for you...", this prospect is going to be bewildered.

When you try to rush slow speakers, they may rush you to the door.

The best way to deal with slow speakers is to speak slowly yourself. They are used to a deliberate style of speech, and it is actually a source of comfort and assurance for them. If you start speaking quickly, you will be perceived as a slick, high-pressure huckster. Speak slowly and you will find that this potential problem prospect is not a problem at all.

The wall

A final evasive technique that is used by some prospects is the wall. Selling to this type of prospect is like talking to a wall. This prospect may indeed simply be quiet by nature, or perhaps he or she is playing a negotiating game with you in which you weaken your position every time you speak.

The best way to deal with the wall is to use your questioning technique and wait for him or her to answer. Sometimes the wait can be rather long, but part of that is a matter of perception. When you are sitting in silence with a prospect, each second seems like several minutes.

■ **When you come up against** *"wall" prospects, use open-ended questions and extreme patience. They will reply eventually.*

Recognizing warriors

Warriors are the prospects who deal with you more forcefully, directly, and aggressively. If you roll over, they will flatten you, but if you dig in your heels, they will confront you. So, is it impossible to sell to them? Not at all. With a few adjustments in style, you should be able to keep the peace and make the sale. The most common warriors include the debater, ego puff, picky player, chronic complainer, and the fast forward.

The debater

One of the more typical warrior prospects is the debater. He or she is the prospect who is ready to debate or argue every point of the sale. This desire may emerge from his or her desire to control the process and you, or perhaps your prospect is just in an argumentative mood.

Either way, when you are face to face with a debater, you are not in the gallery. You are in the debate. This does not mean that you should lock horns and argue every point. It does mean, however, that you should not be afraid to respond in a professional, confident, and factual way to his or her assertions. Comments such as, "I agree with your point, and there are some interesting ways to look at this…" can set the stage for you to present your points, without setting the stage for a battle. In this way, you can work with, rather than against, your prospect.

You don't want to cave in on every point, either. Your prospect will respect you less, and you will end up making less of a sale, if you make a sale at all. Not only do you lose in this scenario, but your argumentative prospect loses as well because he or she will probably not buy the best-fitting product.

The ego puff

Another interesting warrior prospect is the ego puff, a person with a vastly inflated vision of his or her importance, knowledge, and power. This prospect is likely to talk non-stop, interrupt you, and try to impress you with his or her vast realms of knowledge and technological verbiage. One of the tip-offs that clearly indicates this type of prospect is frequent use of the word "I".

In dealing with the ego puff, there are two key strategies. The first is to let this person talk. After all, some of this prospect's thoughts are actually going to provide insights and be productive, and they will give you additional understanding of his or her needs. If you try to make a point or interject a comment during one of this prospect's verbal deluges, all you are doing is giving him or her a chance to take a deep breath and recharge. Once you are done, your comment will be left on the floor, and this prospect will be off and running again.

You will fare better if you listen carefully, mirror the prospect's speech pattern and body language, and then rephrase his comments to line them up with the benefits of your product. Linking the prospect's points to your points will further demonstrate increased shared feeling between the two of you.

When you agree with an ego puff, he or she invariably thinks you are brilliant.

■ **Ego puffs** *like to work with salespeople who respect them. They enjoy hearing comments that show respect, recognition, and even amazement at their vast storehouse of information.*

The picky player

You should also be ready to deal with the picky players who are too keen to focus on the detailed minutiae of your product. When you ask a question, they typically return to one small point or another and latch onto it. You might hear, "I thought this had the 4.2 over the 3.337, but instead it appears to max out at 3.1. How was this decided? When was this change made? I thought the tests in 1998 that called for 3.1 were overruled in 1999? And why is it that…?"

When you are selling to a picky player, remember that you, too, must be very concerned with detail. Through your questioning, find out exactly what may be concerning him or her, and then go straight to the detailed information in your response and work through it, point by point. This is the only way to get information to this type of prospect, and by using this approach, you are building trust and credibility as well.

Some picky players try to break your product into smaller parts and get you to commit to selling smaller parcels along the way. This is generally a bad idea, as you can make commitments and concessions early in the process that will come back to hurt you when you try to close the sale.

The chronic complainer

Another warrior prospect that you are likely to find is the chronic complainer. This is the prospect who never seems to be happy.

The first step is to let chronic complainers know that you understand their concerns and agree with them in many important respects. If you agree with your prospects, then there is no point in them complaining to you. "I know exactly what you are saying, and that's just what I want to talk to you about…." This is followed with several open-ended questions to find out what the real problem may be. By using questions in the body of your sales presentation, along with a partnering sales approach, you are forming the foundation to work with your prospect to respond jointly to each of his or her complaints. And when there are no more complaints, you guess what the next step is.

■ **The chronic complainer** *will always find aspects of your product to complain about, and if there is absolutely nothing to complain about, don't be surprised if you hear complaints about that.*

The fast forward

Another prospect out there who may be difficult, but does not have to be, is in fast forward. This person cruises along at an extremely high rate of words per minute, with minimal pauses for commas, full stops, or even air intake. In fact, everything about this prospect seems rushed.

Some salespeople find it rather nerve-wracking trying to sell to this verbal whirlwind, but you really should have no difficulties. The main problem is that salespeople are often advised to speak slowly to these kinds of prospects, with the theory that this will slow the prospect down. In fact, putting the brakes on your speech rate will only make matters worse.

Fast forward prospects probably grew up in fast-talking households, and they are typically most comfortable when dealing with people who speak fast. When you speak slowly to a fast forward prospect, he or she is likely to become impatient with you and actually wonder why your brain is not operating as fast as his or hers. Thus, the best approach with these prospects is to step on the verbal accelerator and make the pace of your speech closer to theirs. Once you have built a level of trust and comfort with this person, you can then try to slow things down, but for what purpose? If the prospect is comfortable dealing with you at full speed, it is foolish to take a detour.

Dealing with rejection

ONE OF THE MAJOR CONCERNS
about selling to difficult prospects is that your presentation is more likely to finish with a rejection. However, there are ways to work with so-called difficult prospects and you can even take steps to prevent some from becoming difficult in the first place.

> **DEFINITION**
>
> In sales, a rejection is when your prospect refuses to buy what you are selling. It can come early in the sales process or after any number of sales presentations and meetings. No matter when it comes, it is never welcome.

Rejections can come from any prospect. There are certainly situations where difficult prospects become easy, while easy prospects can become difficult. In fact, some of the best salespeople in the world are facing rejection right this minute.

One of the absolute truths of selling is that you are going to face rejection, regardless of your experience, expertise, and drive.

Just the sound of the word "rejection" is hard on any salesperson's ears. It easily conjures up images of being a failure, loser, or idiot. That is not how the great salespeople see it. When faced with rejection, they keep a few simple points in mind.

What's being rejected?

Although it is easy to think that the prospect is rejecting you personally, he or she is actually rejecting your product. If you used a partnering approach but your prospect still firmly believes that your product does not meet his or her needs, then that is the basis of the rejection.

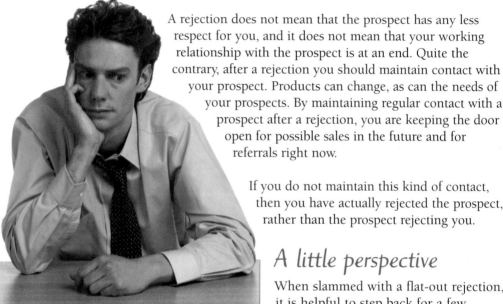

A rejection does not mean that the prospect has any less respect for you, and it does not mean that your working relationship with the prospect is at an end. Quite the contrary, after a rejection you should maintain contact with your prospect. Products can change, as can the needs of your prospects. By maintaining regular contact with a prospect after a rejection, you are keeping the door open for possible sales in the future and for referrals right now.

If you do not maintain this kind of contact, then you have actually rejected the prospect, rather than the prospect rejecting you.

■ **Do not take it personally** *when your sales presentation ends with a rejection. It is your product that is being rejected, not you.*

A little perspective

When slammed with a flat-out rejection, it is helpful to step back for a few minutes and catch your breath. Try to get to your car or a private area where you can close your eyes, take a few deep breaths, stretch your neck, relax your shoulders (see Chapter 7), and give yourself some positive messages. If you let any negative messages in, you will be setting up an expectation of failure for your next call. Your behaviour will show it, and your next prospect will know it. The larger problem is that this can go on, call after call, as a self-fulfilling prophecy.

The truth is that you are still the same successful, high-achieving, knowledgeable, likeable, and service-oriented professional that you always have been. That is the type of message to repeat to yourself.

Each sales call is an independent event, but your mind-set, mood, and expectations from one sales session to another can clearly carry over to the next. When salespeople have a successful presentation, the chances of the next presentation being successful increase. Equally, when salespeople face a rejection, the chances of having a less-than-positive outcome on their next presentation increases.

No matter what happened on your last call, think back to a successful sales call, try to relive it in your mind, and then take those attitudes, feelings, and strengths to your next call.

The silver lining

A rejection need not be a dark cloud that hangs over you. In fact, as you look back at the rejection and summarize what happened, you may find that you can actually profit from it.

One of the best ways to handle a rejection is to view it as a source of valuable data. You can actually learn a great deal from it, not only from the standpoint of improving your sales skills, but also from the standpoint of identifying problems with the company's products, services, and overall marketing.

Getting out of a slump

AS HAPPENS TO MANY PROFESSIONALS,
whether in the sports arena or the sales arena, you may fall into a slump. *You have fewer and fewer winning sales presentations, and you may even start to question your abilities. The real question you should be asking yourself is how to get back on track.*

> **DEFINITION**
>
> *A slump is a prolonged period of time in which your sales performance is in a state of decline.*

One of the problems about being in a slump is believing that you are actually in one. This belief can erode your self-confidence, self-image, and even your level of ease with other people, particularly prospects.

If you believe that you are in a slump, you are likely to act in a way that verifies that belief. You can tweak that belief system slightly and establish a far more positive set of expectations by saying that you are working your way out of a slump.

At the heart of the matter

If you see your sales declining, one of your first steps to get out of it is to look for any possible causes.

A slump in performance may be the result of some distractions in your personal life or work life. It can emerge as a result of any number of personal factors, such as a move to a new residence, financial problems, or inadequate balance between work and family life. At the same time, a slump can result from issues at work, such as changes in management, a redesigned territory, or changes in products or policies. If you can get a handle on the cause of the slump, you will be able to get a better handle on the solution.

■ **Acquiring new skills** *can cause a slump in performance until you have learned how to apply your newly acquired skills. If the training has been effective, performance should improve significantly.*

Many people do not realize that a sales slump can also be caused by sales training. Before anyone goes out to hunt down the trainer, the fact is that such a decline is a normal part of learning.

As a new skill is learned, there can be a slippage in performance during the adjustment period when the individual is first applying what he or she has learned.

Back to basics

One of the ways to help get yourself out of a sales slump is to go back to basics. Try to remember some of the simple techniques that you were using when your sales were going well. Perhaps you have tried to learn and incorporate so many new strategies and approaches that there are too many ideas rattling around in your head when you are sitting with your prospects. In other words, you may be thinking too much.

Some people in a slump believe that the way to get out of it is to practise, practise, practise. This is a waste of time. If a golfer has a horrible swing and can hit a ball only 9 feet, there is no point in going to the driving range and hitting 1,000 balls with that horrible swing.

When you are in a slump, do not just go off and practise. The problem in doing so is that you are going to be practising the very things that got you into your slump in the first place, so your practice will do no good.

When your manager has given you some insights, or you have been able to recall some of the basics of selling that used to work for you, that is what you should be practising. The expression "Practice makes perfect" is simply untrue. If you want to practise your way out of a slump, remember the expression "Perfect practice makes perfect."

A simple summary

✓ When you encounter a difficult prospect, take a look at yourself to determine whether your own behaviour may actually be bringing out some of your prospect's problematic behaviour. Look particularly at the expectations that you bring to a sales presentation.

✓ With prospects who use evasive behaviour, try a combination of persistence, varied approaches, and clear delineation of the broad range of benefits provided by your product.

✓ In dealing with the more aggressive warrior prospects, do not be afraid to act assertively. This type of response actually builds the bond of sharing and trust with them, while a more deferent response pattern will be interpreted as weakness.

✓ All salespeople face rejection, and the best salespeople do not take these rejections personally. It is the product that is being rejected, not the salesperson.

✓ Do not carry the negative emotional reaction from a rejection to your next sales call.

✓ Be sure to use rejections as a source of valuable information regarding your sales skills, your company, and its products and services.

Chapter 15

Presentations that Grab

THE PHONE RINGS. One of your best prospects has great news. "We want you to come in and make a full presentation to the group. These are the people who'll be making the decision. How about next Tuesday?" At this point, many salespeople break into a cold sweat, complete with churning stomach, but it's important to stay calm and get prepared. There are some simple steps that can help you turn your bundle of nerves into a bundle of sales.

In this chapter...

✓ The big picture

✓ Preparing your presentation

✓ Do sweat over the details

✓ The final countdown

✓ It's show time

PROPS AND OTHER VISUAL AIDS CAN BRING A PRESENTATION TO LIFE

The big picture

NOT ALL SALES PRESENTATIONS IN FRONT OF A GROUP are *alike. Sometimes you will be appearing before a small group of two or three top people, and other times you may be addressing 25 people or even more. This may be your first personal contact with the company, or perhaps you have been there several times. There could also be a discussion of your proposal. Before you make any group presentation, you need to know as much as possible about the who, what, when, where, and why of the group and the meeting itself.*

Who are the players?

Prior to making a presentation, you need to know about the participants. As far as possible, you should be able to answer the following questions about them:

(a) How many will be attending?

(b) What are their titles and positions?

(c) What is their role in the decision-making process?

(d) What is their level of expertise?

(e) What do they know about your product?

(f) What is their attitude towards being at this meeting?

(g) What is their attitude towards your product and company?

(h) What are their goals for this meeting?

Your objective is to put together a presentation that will meet the needs, expectations, expertise, and objectives of the participants. The more you know about them, the more successful you will be.

If your prospect can provide you with some of the attendees' demographic data, such as age, gender, and education, that too can be useful.

■ **Knowing who the players are** *in advance will help you understand their needs better and tailor your presentation to meet them.*

Why are we here?

In addition to having a thorough understanding of the participants, you need to know the purpose of the meeting itself. Is this an introductory meeting? Is this some kind of audition? Is this a real sales meeting? If you make a presentation without this knowledge, you could do an incredible job and never hear from the prospect again. The reason is that you may have done a wonderful job giving them something that they did not want. It is as if you loaded a customer's truck perfectly with oranges, but they wanted apples.

It is also important for you to understand clearly your own goals for the presentation. For example, depending upon the expectations and objectives of your prospect, is it feasible for you to try to close the sale during this meeting? In many cases, that is not the most likely outcome when you make a presentation to a group, but this is where it is so important to speak to your prospect before the meeting.

Regardless of the possible outcomes, you should have two minimum objectives for every sales presentation to a group:

(*a*) The participants can only conclude that you, your product, and your company are the best for their needs.

(*b*) The prospects will commit themselves to a specific action to move the sales process forward, even if this is as basic as setting up the next date to meet.

INTERNET

www.presentations online.com

This is the site to visit if you need help putting together a sales presentation. It provides a full range of advice and support, including guidance on making graphics and animated slide presentations.

WHAT ABOUT CD-ROM SALES PRESENTATIONS?

The image of a salesperson heading off to a presentation lugging a bulging briefcase and stack of catalogues, binders, handouts, flip charts, and an overhead projector is becoming a thing of the past. A growing number of companies are turning to CD-ROMs to handle all of this data and other parts of the sales presentation as well.

The software is here

There are software packages that give you a full range of tools to develop all of the charts, slides, and graphics that you might ever need for your sales presentation. It is then a matter of customizing your presentation and downloading it to your laptop. When it's time to make your presentation, just bring your laptop and a lightweight projector. In fact, many prospect companies have projectors of their own, and then all you need to do is plug your laptop into their projector.

CDS FOR PRESENTATIONS

By using such software as Microsoft Power Point, Adobe Persuasion, and Harvard Graphics, you can develop and download a presentation that you have customized to meet your prospect's needs. It can include graphics, images, videos, sound, interactivity, virtual reality models of your products, product demonstrations, live testimonials, a message from your company president, your company history, technical information, product specifications, pricing information, or just about any other customizations that you may wish to add.

CD-ROMs instead of salespeople?

Some companies are going a step further and putting a virtual presentation on a CD-ROM and sending it to prospects and/or making it available on their web sites. This "virtual salesperson" actually makes the first presentation, and if the prospect shows interest, then the real salesperson makes a call. Many companies like the consistency, cost effectiveness, visual appeal, ease of customization, and innovative image that this type of presentation projects.

Something old, something new

There are still prospects who are more comfortable with flip charts, slides, overhead transparencies, and printed materials than with high-tech software. In addition, there can be occasional technical problems that may prevent your high-tech presentation from working.

Even with technological advances, it is still important to bring at least some backup materials to your presentation, particularly if this is what your prospect prefers.

Preparing your presentation

BY TAKING A FEW SIMPLE STEPS IN ADVANCE, you can greatly increase the likelihood of making a far more compelling, memorable, and effective group presentation. With some basic planning, you will feel more confident when you make your presentation, and this will help you inspire a good deal of confidence and ease in your prospects.

Your main message

By understanding the audience and objectives of the meeting, you are ready to frame your main message. One of the easiest ways to do this is to answer this question: what is the one thought that you would like each person at this meeting to have clearly in his or her mind by the time the meeting ends? Your answer should not be some vague, general, or rambling point about your company and product, or some abstract idea about meeting needs.

■ **Keep narrowing down** *your main message to one targeted sentence with as few words as possible.*

You should develop one brief, simple, and clear sentence about the excellence of your product and the ways in which it will definitely meet the needs of your prospect. This is a message that you will want to repeat several times throughout your presentation.

You should be open to questions at any point in your presentation.

A SIMPLE STRUCTURE

Your presentation can follow this simple six-step format that will easily help you get your message across:

1   **The opener:** it is always a good idea to have an opening that quickly grabs and focuses the participants' attention. This can be a story, an anecdote, or even a joke. In all cases, make sure that these openers are in good taste, interesting, and appropriate for the group that you are addressing.

2   **The highlights:** in this section, you provide the participants with a brief snapshot of your overall presentation. This will give them an idea as to where you are going, and it will provide them with a framework to understand and retain your message.

3   **The needs:** this is where you demonstrate your understanding of the industry and the company itself, and then identify the key needs, problems, or issues that the company is facing.

4   **The solution:** now is the time to provide the group with the ways in which your product can not only solve the problems and meet the company's needs, but can do so much more effectively than any other options available. Make sure that you have some factual data to support any assertions that you make. A product demonstration at this point can help substantiate what you are saying, while also helping the prospects become more involved in your presentation.

5   **The next move:** now that you have identified the problems and demonstrated that your product is the solution, this is the point where you provide the group with some specific information on the steps that they can take to acquire the product.

6   **The wrap-up:** now you are ready to give the group a summary of your comments, and then conclude on a positive and upbeat note. The idea is to have a powerful finish, often with a vivid story, that leaves the prospects with a clear, compelling, and positive image of your company, your product, and you.

Although some salespeople prefer to have all questions held until the end, this approach may meet the salesperson's needs, but that is not why you are appearing before the group. It makes far more sense to answer participants' questions when they arise.

In answering such questions, and, in fact, in all aspects of your presentation, be sure that your sentences are brief, clear, and simple, and that your tone is friendly, courteous, and confident. This is a good time to use vocabulary and terminology that are particularly appropriate to the industry and to the prospects' company. At the same time, there is no need to be overly serious, as some light comments and tasteful humour can actually be quite effective.

Smart charts

Charts, graphs, slides, and other visual aids can be important elements in your sales presentation. By using a variety of visual aids, you are far more likely to maintain the prospects' interest and attention. Whether you use a CD-ROM presentation or traditional slides, flip charts, or overhead projections, there is one critical point to remember if you want any of your visual aids to be effective: keep them simple. If you need more detail, you should have some backup tables available.

It has been found that the visual aspects of a sales presentation, including the salesperson, the slides, and the graphics, are remembered more than any other aspect of a sales presentation.

The next element that prospects remember is the style and tone of the presentation. Then, in distant third, the prospects recall the actual content of the presentation.

■ **Be sure to use** *big print for your visual displays and avoid cluttering them with masses of numbers, colours, and symbols.*

Practise, practise, practise

The only way to make a first-rate sales presentation is by doing some first-rate
practising. This means that you will need to put your entire presentation together
and actually do it aloud several times. You can also learn a great deal about
your presentation style by audiotaping and videotaping your practice sessions.

*As important as it is to practise, do not memorize your
entire presentation.*

Memorizing your presentation typically leads to a rigid and mechanical delivery,
and can cause some stumbling and awkward pauses when you are asked questions
and then try to return to your memorized portion.

The idea is for you to sound natural, as if you were talking with
the group, not at them. If you are going to do any memorizing
at all, it should be focused on your opening story and on your
upbeat conclusion. You will be far more effective if you know the
key points and overall direction of your presentation, and then
use a conversational style to stay on track.

■ **It would be ideal** *if you could
rehearse your presentation in front of
your manager or your peers, then
take the feedback that they provide
and incorporate it into your
next practice.*

Do sweat over the details

YOU CAN DO A GREAT JOB PREPARING YOURSELF *for a sales presentation by having the big picture clearly in focus, but all of that preparation can go down the drain if you do not focus on the little picture too. There are all sorts of details that can trip you up just as you are about to make the presentation of your life. In order to prevent this from occurring, here are some of the most common nagging details and the steps to deal with them.*

It's about time

Make sure that you know how much time is allotted for your presentation. There is no way you can effectively prepare for a presentation if you are unclear about its length. And when rehearsing your presentation, you should use only approximately 75 per cent of the allotted time, as there tend to be additional questions and issues that easily consume the extra minutes.

From the timing standpoint, if your prospect is having several salespeople make presentations during the day, you have an advantage if you are the last presenter.

One of the main bonuses of being the last speaker is that you now have a chance to effectively handle any questions that were missed, overlooked, or mishandled in the earlier sessions. If you do really well, there may be no need for the prospects to go back to the others.

In addition, people tend to remember recent events more vividly than earlier events. By going last, you have the opportunity to make that final and lasting positive impression.

Although it is rather obvious, be sure that you know the precise time that your presentation is scheduled to start.

■ **Enter the date** *and time of your presentation into whatever planning system you use, and enter a reminder to confirm the meeting one day in advance.*

Attuned to attire

Find out ahead of time if the attire is casual or formal. Your attire should be just slightly more conservative than the attire of the participants. If people are noticing what you are wearing, they are being distracted from your presentation.

Where are you going?

If you ask any salesperson if he or she has ever had a mix-up on the address for a sales presentation, you are likely to hear a horror story. There's nothing quite like showing up at a dark room to make a sales presentation. This outcome can easily be avoided by confirming the address for the site of the meeting. You will be shocked to find how many times you will hear, "Oh, I'm glad you asked. It's not here. It's at the such-and-such hotel."

Even that may not be enough information. After all, there can easily be hotels that are part of the same chain within a matter of blocks of each other.

If you are planning on addressing a group, make sure that you get the address in advance.

Make sure that you have the mobile phone number of the contact person at the company.

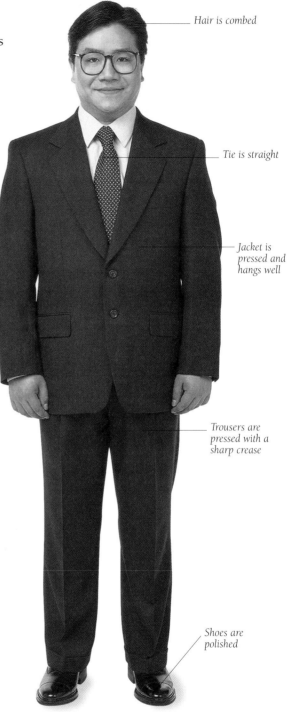

Hair is combed

Tie is straight

Jacket is pressed and hangs well

Trousers are pressed with a sharp crease

Shoes are polished

■ **Although wearing a suit** *for a presentation is not essential, looking neat and well groomed is.*

What are you bringing?

It is always helpful to set up a checklist that spells out the specific materials you need to bring to a sales presentation. This list should include:

- Equipment (e.g. laptop, cables, projector)
- Visual aids (e.g. slides, overheads, flip charts)
- Written materials (e.g. handouts, product literature, brochures)
- Product samples

Before you leave your office, make sure that you have an ample supply of business cards.

As a salesperson, it is important for you to carry some cards wherever you go. And, when you are going to a group presentation, be sure to bring more than enough for everyone in the room. Some of the participants may want an extra card for an associate, a friend, or a referral.

Saying that you are out of cards and then scribbling your name and phone number on a scrap of paper is not the kind of visual image that you want to leave with a prospect.

As is the case with sales presentations, business cards today are undergoing a transformation. Of course, there are still the printed cards, but now there are CD-ROM business cards as well. They are small but fit right into a standard CD-ROM tray on a computer. These New Age cards can have interactive buttons about you, your company, and your products, and they can also provide a link to your company's web site. Some salespeople are already bringing a stack of these cards to their presentations.

> **DEFINITION**
>
> Serendipity *is the ability to find an unexpected positive, fortunate, and pleasurable outcome from a situation that seemed to hold no such outcome in store.*

On a "just in case" basis, try to think of the kinds of things that can go wrong at the presentation, and then see if you can plan out some strategies to handle them. Then, if any of these problems arise during your presentation, follow the advice of one great salesperson and view them as an opportunity for *serendipity*.

By deftly handling a problem situation right before your prospects, you are giving a real-life demonstration of your professionalism, planning skills, and composure. This is a visual that certainly says more about you than words could possibly express.

The final countdown

ON THE DAY OF YOUR PRESENTATION *there are some last-minute pointers that are important to remember. These are the kinds of finishing touches that can actually make all the difference to your presentation.*

Be the early bird

Try to get to your presentation at least 15 minutes ahead of your scheduled time. With these extra minutes, the first step is to do a brush-off and brush-up. Head to the cloakroom to check out your grooming and brush off any dust or lint that has found your clothing along the way. Now take a couple of minutes for a quick brush-up on the key points of your presentation. Do a quick review of the opener, the main message, the key points of the track

■ **Checking your appearance** *and making any last-minute adjustments before a presentation will boost your self-confidence.*

that you are going to follow, and the final closing comments. Tell yourself to speak slowly and keep your message clear, brief, and simple.

Nice to meet you

Your next stop is the meeting room. Your first priority is to meet the participants who are already there or are just arriving. Go up to as many people as possible, introduce yourself, and let them know how pleased you are to have the opportunity to address them today. You can ask them about their work, the company, or the industry, and then listen, listen, listen.

When you meet your audience before a sales presentation, you are instantly more relaxed and comfortable during the actual presentation.

One of the major sources of fear in speaking before a group is the unknown element of what the group will be like. By meeting a good number of the players ahead of time, most of that anxiety is markedly reduced.

Remember that, for most presentations, you are going to find that you will be addressing good people, just like yourself, and there is nothing to be nervous about at all.

Try to remember as many of the names of the participants as you can. If you can absorb all that technical information about your product, you can certainly remember the names of the people you meet. Most of the memory experts who are able to learn the names of hundreds of people simply associate a person's name with something about his or her appearance.

For example, when they meet Mr. Brooks, they instantly picture him wading across a stream. You can form the same kinds of association patterns for remembering names, and you will not only amaze others, but you will amaze yourself as well. In addition, it is impressive when you respond to members of the group by name, and this subtly shows a strong sense of partnership and commitment to the prospects.

Check out the scene

If you pay careful attention to what is going on just prior to your presentation, you can pick up some bits of information that you may be able to tie in to your remarks. Even something as basic as a broken coffee cup that has caught everyone's attention can be incorporated into your presentation, further demonstrating your humour, observation skills, and similarity to the prospects.

For example, if someone asks about the durability of your product, you could say, "I'll tell you this. Our tests have proven that we're stronger than a coffee cup." After a pause, you would then give a brief, simple, and direct response about the strength of your product.

Ready to go

You should also use the minutes before the meeting to make a final check of your supplies, materials, and equipment. Be sure that everything you need is now accessible and in the right order, and that all the necessary plugs are plugged in, cables are connected, and power is on.

Now you are completely ready. If all systems are working and the starting time has arrived, take a deep breath and tell yourself to relax. Await your introduction, smile politely, and then hit them with your opener.

It's show time

WITH ALL OF THE HOMEWORK that you have done in anticipation of your sales presentation before the group, you have already laid the groundwork for success. There are, however, a few simple pointers that can take a good presentation and turn it into an excellent presentation.

The eyes have it

When you are speaking to a group, your eye contact with the various players is important. You do not want to get into a staring contest, but make sure that you connect visually several times with as many of the participants as possible.

Spend a minimum of time looking down at your notes while speaking.

Ideally, you will occasionally look down and see one key word that will trigger several key points for you to bring out. If you need to see more than this in your notes, you are likely to lose your place and lose the group as well. When you have to keep looking at your notes, it appears that you do not fully understand your product. The less apparent message is that if you have neither the time nor interest to understand your product, why should your prospects?

You should be spending far more of your presentation time looking at your prospects. By studying them carefully, you will be able to see if their body language is telling you that they are interested or uninterested, impressed or unimpressed, or awake or asleep.

Where is the power?

Every group has *formal leaders* and *informal leaders*. By meeting a good number of participants prior to your presentation, and by using your observation skills during your presentation, you should be able to spot some of the key decision makers. You can learn about an individual's power and influence by the way that the rest of the group reacts to him or her.

DEFINITION

In a group, the formal leader is the individual who has the established title, role, and responsibility to provide direction, guidance, and influence over the group. An informal leader is the individual who, by virtue of such factors as his or her own charisma, expertise, or personal relationships, has a high degree of influence over the group.

INTERNET

www.toastmasters.org

This is the Toastmasters International web site, and if you are looking for more speaking tips and related educational materials, this is the site to visit. It offers a broad range of information and programmes that can help you continue to develop your communication and presentation skills.

As you identify the leaders in a group, it is important to try to use the same trust-building techniques that you would use in a one-to-one presentation. This means that you should try to pace their speech rate, vocabulary, and body language, while incorporating comments that generate a nod or a "yes" response.

One of the most powerful ways to sell to any group is to persuade the leaders to buy. Once this occurs, they will then try to sell your product to the rest of the group. You could not have better salespeople on your side.

Where's the passion?

If you are passionate about your product and its ability to meet your prospect's needs better than any other option, your entire demeanour should reflect this. One way to do this is to be sure that your speech pattern incorporates a varied tone, action words, and sentences that are simple, short, and clear. At the same time, your body language will also convey a good deal of this enthusiasm.

Look at your posture, particularly your back, shoulders, and head, to see if you are projecting a confident image. If you are shifting from one leg to the other, with your arms resting on a lectern and your body slumping forward, you are not sending much of a positive message. As a result, you should not expect one in return. Instead, stand up straight with your shoulders back as you smile and look across the room. When you want to emphasize a point, try using some gestures with your hands.

■ **One lesser-known outcome** *of an improved posture is that when you look more confident, you automatically speak more confidently.*

If the group senses that you are confident, comfortable, observant, and are even having some fun, they are likely to respond in kind. You are going to set the tenor for the presentation and the reaction of the group to it. If you are interested in a warm and supportive reaction, do not come in with an ice-cold presentation.

The great barriers

There are all sorts of barriers that can block your message, passion, and enthusiasm. One set of barriers is your body language and speech patterns, and the other set is made up of actual physical barriers.

When you are addressing a group, try to put any projectors, computers, or tables to the side so that there is nothing between you and your group.

One of the best things to do with a lectern is to lose it. A lectern creates a major physical and psychological barrier between you and the group, and you will not believe the difference in your energy level as well as the group's response when you eliminate it.

If you are asked to present your sales proposal, a key barrier can be the proposal itself. Fortunately, this only occurs if you give it out at the beginning of your presentation.

In such a case, you will start talking, but the group will be thumbing through the proposal looking for the price and pet issues or concerns. In the meantime, your presentation becomes little more than background noise.

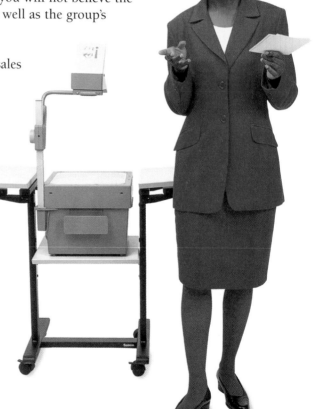

■ **A sales pro** *does not let anything get in the way of his or her presentation.*

Never give out your proposal at the beginning of a presentation.

You will have a far more effective presentation if you first discuss the highlights of your proposal, including an overview of each section, and then give it out. This approach is not only fair to you, it is fair to the group as well, as it will give them an opportunity to understand the full proposal.

A simple summary

✓ Before you make a sales presentation in front of a group, try to learn as much about the group and the purpose of the meeting as possible.

✓ The movement to sales presentations and business cards on CD-ROMs has already arrived, and it is clearly picking up steam.

✓ When making a sales presentation before a group, it is essential to be well prepared, well organized, and well rehearsed.

✓ No matter what visual aids you use, the most important point to remember is to keep them simple.

✓ One of the best ways to make sure that your sales presentation goes well is to arrive early and check out the players, the setting, the equipment, and yourself.

✓ Be sure to focus on the leaders of the group, as they can be highly effective in selling your product to the rest of the group.

Chapter 16

Long-Term Customer Relationships

WHEN YOU CLOSE A SALE, it is often tempting to give a sigh of relief and assume that the end has finally arrived. In fact, all that has happened is that the prospect phase of the selling process has ended, and the customer phase has begun. One objective of this new phase will be to increase your sales with your customer. Another related objective will be to provide a high degree of service and support to build a long-term working relationship based on loyalty, quality, and value. It may sound like a tall order, but it is something that you can do quite easily by keeping the essentials of customer service in the forefront of your mind.

In this chapter...

✓ **At your service**

✓ **Let's get together**

✓ **Staying in touch**

✓ **The finishing touches**

✓ **Dealing with upset customers**

SERVE YOUR CUSTOMERS WELL TO WIN THEIR LOYALTY AND FUTURE BUSINESS

At your service

DURING THE SALES PROCESS, *you devoted a great deal of attention to understanding your prospect's needs, and ideally you have sold a product that meets them. That is not where your prospect's needs end, however. After all, some of your prospect's needs were focused on being provided with product support, advice, education, information, and responsiveness. To build a long-term working relationship with your customer, you need to meet these needs, and this is the point where customer service will play a central role. After all, where do you think the expression "servicing the account" comes from?*

Starting with a commitment

One of the foundations of customer service is to fulfil your commitments. If you made promises about shipping dates, add-ons, training, setup, and the like, they must be kept. It is essential that you literally and figuratively deliver everything you promised.

■ **Rather than wait** *for any questions or problems to arise, it is important to maintain regular contact with your customer right from the start.*

You acted as a partner and colleague during the sales process, and that is exactly how you should act after the sale.

If you have learned that anything is going to be different from what you promised the customer, it is essential that you contact him or her immediately. Let your customer know exactly what is going on and what you are doing about it.

In some of these situations, you may need to do some accommodating to maintain your customer's goodwill. In such a case, you should check with your manager to see if there are adjustments to the product or service that can be made.

As a professional salesperson, it is important for you to deal with your customers on a *proactive* rather than *reactive* basis. Try to keep an eye out for any issues, changes, problems, or developments that may affect your product or overall working relationship, and then contact your customer immediately.

What else can you do?

Be sure that the commitments you make to your customer are reasonable, realistic, and reachable.

> DEFINITION
>
> *A person is operating on a proactive basis when he or she takes steps in advance to either prevent or control a problem. When a person operates on a reactive basis, he or she acts in response to a problem that has already arisen.*

Do not put yourself in the position of basing a sale on a commitment you cannot keep.

You should actually be trying to put yourself in a position where you can deliver more than you have promised. You should always be on the lookout for ways to provide service and support that go beyond any commitments or promises that you have made to your customer.

Keep asking yourself the single most important customer service question: "Is there anything else I should be doing to provide more service to this customer?" If the answer is "yes", then do it.

Let's get together

THERE ARE MANY WAYS TO MAINTAIN *contact with your customers, including by phone, fax, e-mail, teleconferencing, and good old-fashioned post. All of these communication channels play an important role in providing service to your customers and building your relationship with them.*

However, it is easy to let these approaches play too great a role, while allowing one-to-one customer contact to dwindle to the barest minimum. One of the best ways to build customer satisfaction and loyalty, improve sales, provide first-rate service, and develop long-term customer relationships is to spend time with your customers.

When it comes to direct customer contact, the old adage "Absence makes the heart grow fonder" goes right out of the window. A more appropriate adage for those salespeople who minimize this contact is "Out of sight, out of mind".

Regular visits

One important way to maintain a base of consistent contact with your customers is to meet them on a regular basis. The actual frequency of these visits can depend on such factors as current sales revenues, geographical location, and potential sales revenues.

If you are using a Sales Force Automation (SFA) system, there is typically a customer support component to track the key customers and help you establish some service priorities. The system can also track and document the dates for you to be contacting each of your customers, whether through phone calls, e-mail, or meetings. The system can even automatically place the follow-up calls on your call list. And with an SFA system that is linked to the Internet, you can immediately access information regarding key changes and developments in your customer's company, industry, and marketplace, and this can be valuable information to discuss when you and your customer meet.

■ **As a professional salesperson**, *you should always be on the lookout for ways to increase your personal contact with your customers.*

The purpose of regular meetings is more than just a quick check-in to say "hello". This may include updating your customer on product information, providing a compelling demonstration, as well as relaying information regarding new developments in the industry or marketplace.

There should always be a solid business-related purpose for getting together with a customer.

One of the most interesting byproducts of these types of meetings is that the discussion frequently turns towards new or expanded areas in which the customer may need your products. When that occurs, return to your sales mode and try to clarify your customer's needs and the ways that your products can meet them.

Business gatherings

You can also arrange to have additional contact with your customer by including him or her in various business activities. For example, there may be a meeting or lunch that features a big-name speaker, and you can invite your customer to attend with you. If your customer is unable to attend, he or she will still appreciate and remember being invited.

Special events and activities

Another way to increase contact with your customers is to join some of their professional associations, trade organizations, and trade groups.

Beyond the increased opportunities for contact with your customers, your membership and participation in these organizations offer several professional advantages as well. For example, they will help you keep up-to-date on key developments in the industry, help you broaden your network, and present numerous opportunities for you to continue to develop your sales and interpersonal skills.

You should make a point of attending some of the meetings, conferences, and conventions, and seriously consider participating as a panellist in some of the sessions. This is not only excellent experience, it is excellent exposure as well.

On a more subtle basis, it is interesting to recall the point at which people trust people with whom they have a good deal in common. By participating in some of the same organizations and activities as your customers, you are continuing to build the bonds of trust.

Sporting and arts events also provide an opportunity for you to spend time with your customers. For example, if your company has tickets to local professional sporting events, concerts, the theatre, or other special entertainment, you should check with your manager and get your name on any company list that is used to distribute them. When your name comes up, invite your best customer to join you.

Do not forget that some of the best sales and negotiations take place far from the office.

■ **If your customer** *plays tennis and you like playing as well, you could arrange to meet up for a friendly set or two.*

Staying in touch

ALTHOUGH THE IMPORTANCE OF PERSONAL CONTACT
with your customers should never be minimized, the other communication channels mentioned earlier – e-mails, phone calls, faxes, and mailings – should not be overlooked. These types of contact should provide your customers with relevant information, support, and advice, while keeping your name fresh in your customers' minds.

For Your Information (FYI)

There are all sorts of ways for you to stay in contact with your customers by providing them with useful information.

For example, as part of your job, you will come across articles, studies, reports, and analyses about your industry, products, marketplace, and countless other related subjects. As you review them, you will find some that your customers would like to see. When this occurs, be sure to forward these materials to them. And, by the way, you can only gain by sending this type of information to your better prospects as well.

INTERNET

www.businessweek.com
www.ft.com
www.fortune.com
www.digitallook.com
www.wsj.com

Whether you are looking for financial information about a particular company, marketplace trends, industry forecasts, or even key personnel changes, these sites have a search function that can help you find information that may be of interest to your customers.

Your company is also going to have new promotional materials, and many of your customers will want to see them. Send them a copy with a brief greeting indicating that you thought they would be interested in the attached.

In addition to providing information to your customers, you can also maintain contact with them by gathering information from them. When you view your customers as partners, it is important to monitor their feelings and suggestions. You can do this by briefly surveying their attitudes towards your product and company.

Although you could use a brief questionnaire or even a postcard, you can instead use this information-gathering exercise as an opportunity for some two-way communication with the customer if you do it by phone. In such a case, simply tell the customer that you are interested in continually improving the service and support that your company provides, and you would like to ask three brief questions:

(a) What do you like about doing business with us?

(b) What do you dislike about doing business with us?

(c) What are your suggestions?

If you take this approach, be sure to give your customers an overview of the findings, as well as information on the kinds of steps that you and the company will be taking to deal with the issues or problems that have been raised.

DO WE REALLY NEED A NEWSLETTER?

Many companies are finding that a newsletter can help build and reinforce relationships with customers. A newsletter today does not mean a thrown-together rehash of old stories, a batch of irrelevant human-interest tales, or a thinly veiled advertisement for your products.

Contents that count

Today's newsletters can contain simple and readable explanations of your technical products, along with stories about using them. These types of articles are designed to educate, inform, and even entertain readers, rather than induce them to buy. As such, a newsletter is typically regarded as being more credible and unbiased than a flyer, brochure, or general advertisement.

Newsletters also typically include feature stories about your customers, your company, your colleagues, and new products, plus some business-related ideas and suggestions that are actually useful. The newsletter should certainly have contact information, but it should never ask the reader to buy anything. When a newsletter offers a supposedly good buy, the readers are likely to respond with their own goodbye.

Pass it around

Newsletters are not only a way to maintain contact and continuing visibility with your customers, but they are also a good sales tool to send to your prospects. Newsletters tend to be kept for a fairly long time, and, if they are any good, they are passed around among the staff. They usually arrive every month or two, and by their very nature they further differentiate your company from the competition.

Just being friendly

One less obvious aspect of customer service and relationship building is to let your customers know continually that you are thinking about them and appreciate their business. One example at the beginning of the relationship is to send a thank-you note and welcome message from your manager or one of the company's officers.

As the working relationship continues, you can send cards that commemorate an anniversary of the working relationship and holiday greetings. Be sure to send congratulations when your customer has reached a particular milestone, received an award or promotion, or met a particularly significant goal. You can also consider making a donation to your customer's favourite charity or special organization in honour of his or her accomplishment.

If you find a reasonably priced book, videotape, audiotape, or CD-ROM that seems to be perfect for your customer, you should buy it and give it as a present. You can easily post it, but it makes far more sense to call your customer and agree a time to drop it off. This will provide you with an opportunity for some direct contact with your customer, while further demonstrating your professionalism, care, and concern.

Don't waste your time or your customers' time by e-mailing jokes to them.

Most e-mail jokes have already been around the world several times before they get to you, and usually they aren't very funny. On a more serious note, some of them can be offensive, and all of them are an interruption. Most of your customers are dealing with huge numbers of e-mail messages every day, many of which are absolutely useless. You do not want your customers to feel that way about e-mail from you, because these messages are often deleted unread. If that happens to yours, it is no joke at all.

■ **Giving a small present** *to mark a special occasion or as a thank-you is one way of letting your customer know that you are thinking of him or her.*

The finishing touches

PROVIDING CUSTOMER SERVICE *is a never-ending responsibility, and there are always steps that you can take to lift your service to even higher levels. Many of these steps are quite simple to implement, and, as a result, they are often overlooked.*

Problems with the phone

One of the easiest ways to annoy your customers is to be inaccessible. Customers may be able to reach your voicemail, and they need to feel that doing so will trigger a call from you very soon. For some inexplicable reason, many people today take their time returning calls. As a salesperson, this can easily cost you some deals.

To provide first-rate service, you need to be highly accessible and responsive. When your customer leaves you a message, call back as soon as possible.

Speaking of voicemail, try to have a brief outgoing message, a short beep, and then ample space for your customers to leave as long a message as they would like. You may have a basically satisfied customer with a fairly simple message, but if he or she has to fight through your voicemail system, you may encounter one tough customer when you call back.

As part of your commitment to customer service, it is helpful to have a mobile phone. You should obviously turn it off when you are in sales presentations and meetings, as well as in other settings where taking these calls is nothing short of rude. In fact, there is a movement afoot to ban them from restaurants, theatres, and other public venues.

■ **Being accessible** *by mobile phone helps you provide highly responsive service, advice, and support to your customers.*

Nonetheless, there is still plenty of time for you to have the phone on and be available to take calls from your customers. If you spend a good deal of time in your car, you should either have a hands-free system or pull off the road for longer calls.

Oh my words!

In answering questions from customers, there are some phrases that salespeople automatically use that should be permanently deleted. They create an instant barrier between the salesperson and the customer, and they undercut all of the objectives of customer service.

In dealings with your customers, here are some of the key phrases that you never want to utter:

- "It's not my job"
- "It's against policy"
- "Let me transfer you"
- "That can't be done"
- "That's just not how we do it"
- "We've never done it that way"
- "I can't even think about that until next week"
- "I wish I could help you"
- "Read your contract"

There are certainly many more than this, but you get the point. These kinds of comments practically tell the customer, "Get lost." And that's exactly what will happen.

If you want to provide customer service, you should be making constructive, confident, and supportive replies to your customer's questions. Some of the more positive responses are:

- "Let me see what I can do"
- "I've got an idea"
- "If there's a way to do it, I'll get it done"
- "Let me talk to X. He's handled this before"
- "Tell me more"

Trivia...

Try calling yourself on the phone while sitting at your desk. If your phone system goes to an operator before getting to voicemail, he or she will probably indicate that you are on another line, and then ask if you would like to wait on hold or leave a message on voicemail. Tell the operator that you prefer to wait on hold. The obvious issue is how long you will be on hold until the operator comes back to rescue you. More interesting, though, is what you hear when you are on hold. It should be a professionally prepared message about products and developments at your company, but some companies fill the time on hold with radio programmes. The problem is that these programmes can have adverts for your competition, inappropriate language, or messages that you would never want to send.

Dealing with upset customers

ALTHOUGH YOUR COMPANY may have customer service representatives who generally handle customer complaints, many of your customers will want to deal with you. You should be glad to do so, as this can present a real opportunity to demonstrate your dedication, professionalism, commitment, and support. By taking four simple steps, you will find that handling upset customers does not have to be upsetting at all.

The four-step formula

When you hear from an upset customer, the first step is to listen. The customer probably needs to let off steam, so just give him or her the chance to do so. A little empathy also helps. With this approach, you may learn enough about the problem to solve it immediately.

The second step is to voice some understanding and agreement. If you feel that a mistake has been made, you can say, "I agree with you." By taking this approach, your customer is likely to calm down because there is no argument.

The third step is to find out how the customer would like to have the matter resolved. If there are any steps you can take to do so, let the customer know. If you cannot resolve the issue on the spot, tell the customer that you are going to work on the matter and will get back to

■ **Handling upset customers** *is much easier if you find out how they would like the issue resolved and then do your best to accommodate their wishes.*

him or her by an agreed-upon date and time. Do not indicate that any outcomes are impossible until you have exhausted every opportunity to make things work.

The fourth and final step is to take some action to try to resolve the matter, and then contact the customer to discuss what you have been able to do. If you have to bring a higher level person into the process, make sure that this individual calls your customer as well. At this point, you continue the discussion with the objective of reaching a win-win outcome, even if this takes additional time and effort.

If you find it too difficult, tedious, and time-consuming to take care of your customers, always remember that there are plenty of competitors who are trying right now to relieve you of this burden.

The costs involved

There are two compelling business reasons for doing all that you possibly can to keep your customers satisfied. The first is that it costs far more to generate new customers than it does to sell to and service your existing customers.

The second is that when you lose a customer, not only do you lose existing business, you lose future business and a key source of referrals. And worse, this customer is likely to tell other potential customers about the problems of doing business with your company, and you will probably lose them and their referrals as well. When you lose an account, you are losing far more than the revenues it may have been yielding.

You can gain a great deal of insight about your products, service, and productivity by regularly monitoring your *retention rate*. If you are losing a significant number of customers, it is critical to know exactly what is going on and why it is occurring.

DEFINITION

The retention rate *is the percentage of customers that you keep over various specified periods of time, such as 1 year, 2 years, 5 years, and up.*

Trivia...

As important as it is to place tremendous emphasis on customer service, the old adage "the customer is always right" is not right. There will be times when the customer is wrong. Perhaps he or she has completely abused the product that you sold, or perhaps the customer is abusive, hostile, and threatening. You should know in your heart that you have done as much as you possibly can for every customer, but there are some customers whom you will never please. There comes a time in these relationships when the only clear step is out of the door.

Calculating the retention rate is straightforward: you take the number of customers you have as of a given date in the category you select, and then divide it into the number of customers who remain after a specified period of time. For example, if you have 100 customers at the starting date, and a year later 88 of these customers remain, your retention rate is 88/100 or 88 per cent.

It can be particularly useful to look at your retention rate in relation to such factors as the customers' sales revenues, products, company size, geographical location, and other relevant demographics. Your SFA system can continually monitor and update these numbers for you.

The final word

There are salespeople who have lost customers over just a few pounds. When the customer made a request for a replacement item to be shipped overnight, there was a bit of an issue over who would pay the excess freight charges. The result was a lost order, a lost customer, lost revenues, loss of potential business, lost referrals, loss of goodwill, and loss of face.

If you are ever in doubt about going the extra mile or the extra pound for a customer, keep this in mind: it is easy to lose a customer and difficult to get one.

A simple summary

✔ If you want to build a long-term relationship with your customers, you will first need to provide first-rate service and support.

✔ A key to building customer satisfaction and loyalty is to spend time with your customers. This is also an effective way to improve sales, service, and your overall relationship with your customers.

✔ Always look for ways to stay in touch with your customers, such as sending relevant information, articles, and reports, along with holiday cards and congratulations, when they are due.

✔ Providing excellent customer service means that you are accessible, responsive, and orientated towards taking action on issues or questions that your customers raise with you.

✔ When you are dealing with an upset customer, be sure to let him or her talk while you do a great deal of listening. Try to look at the issue from your customer's point of view, and be sure to keep him or her posted on all of the actions you are taking to resolve the matter.

✔ Generating new customers is much more costly than selling to and servicing your existing customers.

PART FIVE

KEEP BUILDING ON SUCCESS AND THE FUTURE IS YOURS

LOOKING FORWARD

YOUR SALES CAREER is a dynamic force, and you can aim it wherever you wish. But to keep building your success, the best step is to keep on *learning*. At the same time, your sales activities are probably going to take you *on the road*. Use the best planning strategies to make your trip  safe, healthy, hassle-free, and successful in all respects.

If you want to be viewed as a great salesperson by your customers, your company, and yourself, one cornerstone has to be your high *ethical standards*. There is nothing difficult about acting in an ethical way, but there can be any number of difficulties for salespeople who don't. Finally, by pulling all of these sales skills together, you are going to find that you are well prepared not only for selling but for *management* and much more.

Chapter 17

Building Your Sales Skills

A S A SALESPERSON, the word "develop" will play a key role throughout your career. For example, you will be expected to develop accounts, goodwill, trust, sales, customer loyalty, and referrals. To do this year after year, there is something else you need to develop: yourself. It's important to take the time to maintain your skills, abilities, and expertise – after all, if your sales skills fall behind, it won't be long before your sales fall behind, too. The best way to stay up-to-date in the rapidly changing field of professional sales is to take advantage of the numerous training and educational opportunities available to you. Some are found in classroom settings, but there are many other attractive educational options.

In this chapter...

✓ Your training needs

✓ Choices aplenty

✓ What to look for

✓ Was it worth it?

COURSES AND LECTURES ARE ONE WAY TO ADVANCE YOUR KNOWLEDGE AND YOUR CAREER

Your training needs

FROM THE SELF-DEVELOPMENT *standpoint,*
one of the most important steps that you can take is
to conduct a needs analysis. *By monitoring and*
understanding your own training needs, you can identify
training resources that can truly help you succeed.

DEFINITION

A needs analysis is the first
step in the training process.
For a company, it typically
entails a study of the
organization, operations, and
employees to determine the
key areas in which training is
needed. For an individual, it
is a review of your entire
performance, with the
objective of finding those
areas where you need
additional training and
development. To enter
training programmes without
this data is strictly a random
approach to employee
development. After all, if you
have terrific prospecting
skills, but a terrible close
ratio, another seminar on
prospecting is a gloomy
prospect indeed.

To determine your training needs, you can do your own mini-
study. By taking a look at yourself, as well as by listening to
significant others with whom you work, you can easily identify
the key areas in which you could do with some training.

Finding it yourself

Your company may make any number of sales training
programmes and seminars available to you. If so, and if they
are the result of a needs analysis, these programmes and
seminars can be informative and productive.

If these programmes are not based on the needs of the
salespeople, however, they still may fit your needs perfectly.
Or they could be a disaster.

Just because your company plays
an active role in sponsoring training
programmes does not mean that
you no longer have to think
about self-development.

Your company may be providing you with
some courses, but you are responsible for
the whole curriculum. After all, it is
called self-development.

■ **To help you** *pinpoint areas for*
improvement, you need to evaluate
every aspect of your sales performance.

One of the best ways to get a handle on your own training needs is to take a careful look at your performance in each step of the *sales cycle*, all the way from prospecting to customer service.

Difficulties at any point in the sales cycle can indicate areas where you need more training.

Perhaps you are losing prospects because you are not handling their objections adequately, or maybe your presentation is nearly perfect until the close, and then the sale is lost. Such outcomes point to a need for additional training in handling objections and closing.

There are a number of other ways to gain insight into your own training needs. For example, you can identify some of these needs by looking back at the self-assessments that you completed after each sale, as discussed in Chapter 13. You can also take a look at such factors as your retention rate and close ratio, along with the various reports that your Sales Force Automation system is providing you with, if you have such a system in place.

■ **Working with your peers** *to solve problems is a useful form of training where both parties can benefit from the other's knowledge and expertise.*

Listen to your peers

Many salespeople go out in teams, and sometimes a key salesperson will accompany a newer salesperson on joint calls. It is important to let your fellow sales professionals know that you are interested in receiving feedback on your sales performance. When they provide it, make sure that you listen without becoming defensive. Rather than trying to defend why you took a particular approach in a given sales situation, you can make this feedback a learning experience by asking your peers how they would have handled the same situation. One of the additional values of making joint sales calls with some key salespeople over time is that they can give you feedback on the way that your sales skills have changed.

In psychology, changes in skills are called "just noticeable differences", or JNDs, and they can tell you a great deal about the path you are on and the emergence of new training needs.

Messages from management

Your sales manager will be monitoring your performance on a regular basis and perhaps going on some joint sales calls with you. Through a combination of conversations, phone calls, memos, and e-mail, he or she will be giving you informal feedback at many points, usually in the form of suggestions, alternative strategies, pointers, and tips.

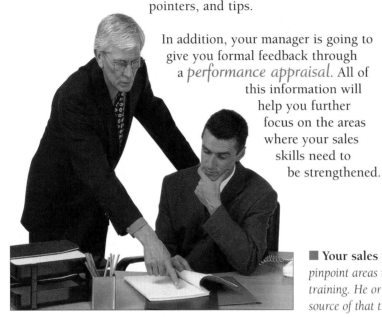

In addition, your manager is going to give you formal feedback through a *performance appraisal*. All of this information will help you further focus on the areas where your sales skills need to be strengthened.

> ### DEFINITION
>
> *A performance appraisal usually occurs annually and consists of a formal meeting with your manager to review your work during the past year. The discussion focuses on the areas where you did well, as well as on those that need improvement. These sessions typically conclude with an agreement between you and your sales manager on the goals and strategies for the next period.*

■ **Your sales manager** *can help you pinpoint areas where you may need more training. He or she can be an excellent source of that training as well.*

Your customers speak

Even your customers can give you valuable insights into your training needs. For the most part, you will not be asking your customers for this type of feedback, but many will provide it spontaneously anyway. Whenever they do, pay careful attention and see if what they are saying fits in with the feedback that you have been receiving from other customers as well as from your peers and manager.

Some customers are going to be direct in providing feedback. Their comments are focused clearly on your behaviour. For example, you may hear "Were you listening to what I said?" or "I don't like being pushed." These types of comments from your customers indicate that you would benefit from more training in such areas as listening, questioning techniques, and building trust.

Other customers may be rather indirect in giving you feedback. Their comments typically focus on the outcomes associated with your behaviour. For example, "Well, I would have paid a lot more for your product than that." This comment indicates that your negotiating skills could do with some sharpening.

Choices aplenty

YOU CAN WAIT FOR YOUR COMPANY to implement a training programme that just happens to meet your needs, but that could take years. Or, since you are taking responsibility for your own development, you can explore the broad range of available training options and select those that will be beneficial to you. This kind of action, in combination with any training that your company provides, will give you a solid foundation of sales knowledge.

Learning while earning

Many studies have found that in spite of the billions of pounds spent on training programmes, the bulk of what an employee learns comes from his or her manager and peers. This means that your colleagues are not only a source of highly useful feedback regarding your training needs, they also play a key training role as well.

Ask the experts

A broad range of training programmes is offered by experts in sales, negotiation, and communication, as well as in product development and marketing for your company. Here is a brief sampling of some of the options available to you:

■ **Small, informal groups** *led by a specialist trainer can be an excellent forum for training. These types of sessions often focus more on the individual learning styles of the participants, and this clearly enhances the learning process.*

(a) **Lectures.** This is one of the more basic training methods, and it can be effective in presenting introductory information. But since it is mostly one-way communication, the trainer does not really know if the trainees have understood the information or can make any use of it. It is not appropriate for most aspects of sales training because there is no opportunity for practice and feedback. Some lectures are also given by motivational speakers in the sales area. Many provide messages that are often interesting, entertaining, uplifting, and informative.

b **Seminars and classes.** Depending upon the trainer, content, teaching methods, and technology, these programmes can be an excellent way to upgrade all of your sales skills.

c **Conventions and conferences.** Many conventions have panel discussions that can be a valuable source of industry, marketplace, and technical information that you can incorporate into your sales presentations.

d **University courses.** A growing number of major universities offer classes in selling, and many are available through their adult education and extension programmes. In fact, students can even specialize in sales at several of these institutions.

e **Product orientation.** As your company introduces new products, you might be trained by a product developer, a product expert, or a senior member of the marketing team. In the light of the rapid changes in most marketplaces, you can plan on plenty of sessions and support materials to familiarize yourself with the newest products and changes.

In addition to the various training programmes, there are vast libraries of books, videotapes, audiotapes, magazines, and CD-ROMs that cover every aspect of selling. Ask any of the best salespeople you know, and they will all tell you that they spend a great deal of time with these types of materials.

INTERNET

www.wilsonlearning .com
www.millerheiman.com
www.tracyint.com
www.tomhopkins.com
www.tsuccess.dircon .co.uk

These are some of the best sites for sales training. They offer programmes on a wide array of sales topics, with some customized online courses as well. Several also offer books, tapes, articles, and opportunities to register for their seminars. These sites are changing all the time, and the services and features they provide are continuing to expand.

■ **Training programmes** *on audio-tapes are effective learning tools for use in the office, home, car, or plane.*

Online training opportunities

DEFINITION

An intranet is a company's own web site that is for the employees only. The general public is unable to access it. It can be used for a broad range of internal company matters, including information on such topics as new products, design changes, and selling strategies. It can be particularly helpful for salespeople who may be spread all over the world but still need to interact regularly with their peers and with management.

A company's *intranet* site can be used for employee training and development programmes, as well as for training-related discussion groups and forums. These can be set up by your sales manager, who e-mails all of the salespeople and lets them know when this online discussion is going to be held. During this discussion, your manager may post information for all of the salespeople to discuss online.

As part of the process, all of the participating salespeople can post their own comments, questions, and answers regarding the manager's messages, and discuss any other issues of importance. This provides another opportunity for the salespeople to learn from each other and from their manager.

Online forums also provide salespeople with a good opportunity to review the effectiveness of the training sessions they have attended.

By joining in an online forum, salespeople can discuss any difficulties they've been having applying the concepts that were presented. This makes the training an ongoing process, which is an essential part of an effective training programme.

In addition to providing the salespeople with sales training and support, product information, and an ongoing forum, these intranet sites generally provide the users with links to other helpful sales training sites on the Web.

■ **Take advantage** *of the wide range of training opportunities available through the Internet and your company's intranet.*

What to look for

WITH THE WIDE VARIETY OF SALES programmes available, be on the lookout for those that have a real likelihood of measurably improving your sales skills and performance. There are a few simple steps that can help you determine if a sales seminar is likely to improve your skills or hardly make a dent.

A matter of tailoring

Sales seminars run the gamut from off-the-shelf presentations that are superficially reformatted from one company to the next, all the way to fully customized programmes that incorporate the company's products, sales materials, sales systems, and typical sales situations.

Although a sale is a sale, there are major differences in the selling process among different industries and among different companies within the same industry.

The closer a sales training programme approximates to the realities of your job, the greater the likelihood of you learning something that can actually help your performance.

> **DEFINITION**
>
> **Experiential learning** *is based on giving trainees the opportunity to learn by doing. When trainees have the opportunity to actually practise hands-on with new material, they generally find that it is much easier to learn, retain, and apply.*

This means that the training programme should include many of the same materials and technology that you use in your sales presentations, and it should place a good deal of emphasis on *experiential learning*. Instead of telling the participants what to do, the programme should give them ample chances to actually do it.

> **DEFINITION**
>
> **Role playing** *is a training technique in which the trainer and trainees act out various parts in order to illustrate key points and facilitate the learning process. For example, in a session on telephone sales, the trainee may play the role of the salesperson, while the trainer plays the role of the prospect.*

Training programmes that utilize experiential learning typically include discussions, questions and answers, case studies, practice exercises, and *role playing*. All of the cases, exercises, and simulations are based on situations that the salespeople actually encounter.

Will you actually learn?

Looking at sales training programmes from a broader perspective, it is important to try to figure out if they are designed to help you learn. People learn in many different ways, and the best programmes try to incorporate at least some of the key elements that actually contribute to learning.

You are most likely to learn something in programmes that include at least some of the following components:

_a_ **Motivation.** People do not learn unless they are motivated to do so. A given programme will be motivational if you sense that it will help you meet some of your needs.

_b_ **A demonstration of effective behaviour.** As a trainee, you need to see the most productive ways to use the new skills in your job. For example, if the session focuses on new approaches to prospecting, the training method would not be just a discussion, but a demonstration of these new prospecting techniques as well.

THE WRONG KIND OF TRAINING

A client company in the financial services industry asked me to review a sales training session that was being presented by an outside firm that specializes in customized sales training for this industry. The leader opened the session with a videotape that instantly placed childish labels on six so-called typical customers, followed by a watered-down set of steps on the ways to deal with each.

When the videotape mercifully ended, the seminar leader handed out a form and asked the group to place some of their individual customers into one of the six personality boxes – presumably this was the customized part of the presentation. At this point, the attendees rebelled. There were comments about customers being more complex, complaints about stereotyping people, and even some questions about the validity of the videotape's premises.

Things only worsened from this point, and the session ended up being little more than a debate. What is not debatable is the fact that there are some real differences in customized training, and the time to find out is not after the training session has begun. That, by the way, was the final point in my review.

c **Practice opportunities.** Once you have been shown the new ways to act, the training session should also provide you with an opportunity to practise them. This further involves you in the process and removes a great deal of the confusion and uncertainty that may be associated with the new skills.

d **Feedback.** As you practise your newly acquired skills, you should be given positive feedback on the areas that you have learned and applied quite well, and coaching on the areas that need some improvement. Without knowing what you are doing correctly or incorrectly, there is no way for you to learn.

e **Relevance to the job.** One of the best ways to facilitate learning is for the programme to provide you with skills, information, and materials that you can easily and productively apply in your job. A training programme may focus heavily on selling by phone, but if most of your sales presentations are to groups, the relevance and learning may be quite low.

f **Variety of training methods.** Since people learn in different ways, it is important for training programmes to incorporate a number of different training techniques. By using a combination of training methods, such as case studies, discussions, and videotapes, a programme is likely to tap into the learning styles of all the participants.

When salespeople take their new skills back to the job and find little managerial interest, enthusiasm, and support, it is just a matter of time before these skills are shelved.

Even if you just completed a perfect training programme, it can be a waste if one key ingredient is missing: commitment from management.

■ **Role playing** *can be a very helpful part of a sales training programme. It provides you with "hands on" experience and guidance that can help build the skills and confidence you need for the real world of selling.*

Was it worth it?

SALES TRAINING PROGRAMMES can consume a good deal of time, energy, and money, so it is always a good idea to review them and try to determine if they were worth the investment. There are a number of ways to do this, but be careful because several of them are traps.

Your instant reaction

One way to get an idea of a programme's effectiveness is to measure your reaction to it. In other words, did you enjoy it and do you think it was worthwhile? The problem is that although your opinion of the programme is valuable, it does not tell you much about the value of the programme. After all, you could greatly enjoy a sales programme, but you might not have learned much of anything.

Do not let your instant reaction to a sales training programme be the sole factor in determining whether the programme was actually worthwhile for you.

What did you learn?

Another way to assess the value of a training programme is to look at what you learned. Some are highly effective in helping you master all sorts of skills and materials. In terms of the programme's worth to you as a salesperson, however, the jury may still be out. After all, you may have attained encyclopedic knowledge about some sales topics, but if this knowledge does not translate into behaviour and skills that you can use when you sell, then there are still questions about its worth.

■ **It is important** *for training programmes to give you a chance to assess their effectiveness, but these evaluations need to measure more than like or dislike of the programme.*

New behaviour

Perhaps you not only enjoyed the programme and learned a great deal from it, but you have been able to make some behavioural changes as a result. The fact that you have been able to make some changes may well be a positive sign, but the worth of the programme is still in doubt unless this behaviour is truly linked to measurable improvements in your sales performance.

The bottom line

A more accurate way to assess the effectiveness of a sales training programme is to compare performance before and after the programme. Prior to the training, you would note such key performance data as your sales revenues, closing ratio, and retention rate. A few months after the training programme has ended, you would look at these performance categories and see if there has been an improvement in any of them. If you find some significant increases, then there appears to be a link between the training and improved sales performance.

Finding some increases after a training programme does not automatically mean that the training actually caused them. The increases in your revenues, closing rate, and retention rate could just as easily be due to other developments, such as some new products that your company introduced or your competition's production problems.

Be careful when drawing sweeping conclusions about the effectiveness of training programmes, and pay extra attention when trainers talk about the ways that their programmes affect the bottom line.

■ **Since training programmes** *are actually investments, they require careful analysis before, during, and after implementation.*

Perhaps the safest conclusion is this: all things being equal, when you enjoy a training programme, learn something from it, change some of your sales behaviour as a result, apply the new behaviour on the job, and then find measurable improvement in your sales performance, it is certainly reasonable to conclude that the training was worthwhile.

A simple summary

✔ Continuously developing your knowledge, sales skills, and ability is essential for long-term sales success; the responsibility for doing so is yours.

✔ One of the key initial steps in the self-development process is to analyze your own sales training needs.

✔ Difficulties at any point in the sales cycle can be a real tip-off as to areas where you may need to upgrade your skills.

✔ There are numerous opportunities to continue your growth and development every day on your job. In addition, there are all sorts of training programmes, materials, and resources available not only through your work, but through the Internet and your company's intranet as well.

✔ The closer a sales training programme approximates to your job, the greater the chance of learning something that can actually help your performance.

✔ If you want to get a better understanding of the worth of a sales training programme, take a look at some of the specific measures of your sales performance before the programme starts, and then look at them again a few months after the programme ends.

Chapter 18

On the Road Again

I N THIS HIGH-TECH AGE, it is easy to think that personal contact with prospects and customers is not all that important. However, consider this: your competition thinks that personal contact is very important. And your competition is right. As a salesperson seeking to build sales, service, and relationships, you will probably be travelling to meet customers beyond your local geographical area. You will be entering the world of aeroplanes, rental cars, and hotels, where a whole new set of dynamics can interfere with the way you operate. To function at your best as a business traveller, there are some simple steps to take before you leave and along the way.

In this chapter...

✓ Before you leave

✓ Gliding through the airport

✓ Playing it safe

✓ To your health

BEING WELL PREPARED WILL HELP MAKE YOUR BUSINESS TRIP SUCCESSFUL IN ALL RESPECTS

Before you leave

THE BEST WAY TO AVOID *a broad range of problems, hassles, and aggravation on your business trip is to do some basic planning and organizing first.*

In terms of organizing the business side of your trip, you simply take many of the same steps as you would for local sales calls. This includes making and confirming appointments, updating yourself on your prospect's or customer's company and needs, organizing your presentation, putting the necessary materials together, and checking maps to make sure that you arrive at your meetings on time.

Just as a Sales Force Automation (SFA) system can help you organize your local calls, appointments, and schedules, it can do the same on a business trip. In fact, it can even locate and highlight additional prospects and customers whom you could meet on your trip.

In addition to getting the business side of the trip into shape, you need to plan and organize the trip itself. While some travel problems are impossible to avoid, many can be easily avoided if you do a little homework.

INTERNET

www.businesstravel
.com
www.expedia.co.uk
www.roomfindersusa
.com
www.businesstraveller
.com
www.priceline.co.uk

These are just a few of the many sites offering online booking services for air travel, car hire, and hotel accommodation. If cost is a factor, www.priceline.co.uk lets you name your own price for these services. It works well, but you may be taking red-eye flights and staying at hotels off the beaten track.

Serious reservations

Before you go on the road, it is essential to have confirmed reservations for your flight, hire car, and hotel accommodation.

You may have an assistant who is responsible for this, or perhaps your company uses a travel agency. If you are expected to make the reservations yourself, you can do so by telephone, or you may have more success using the Internet.

Many travellers find that they can get the best travel prices by going through the Internet. You can go directly to the web sites of the hotels, airlines, or car hire firms that you are considering.

Some people even book their reservations on a company's web site, and then call the company's freephone number to negotiate further discounts and upgrades. The disadvantage is that this approach can take some time.

■ **By booking ahead** *of your trip and ensuring that you have hard copies of any confirmations, you're more likely to avoid last-minute problems or delays.*

Checking your checklist

You should put together a checklist that covers all of your travel needs. Before you go on a business trip, review your list to be sure you have followed it. And after each trip, update the list.

The items on your list can include your preferences in any number of areas, including seating in a plane, flight times, hotel chains and room locations, and car hire companies and makes and models of cars. The list should also cover some of your more detailed needs, such as the preferred size of the desk in the hotel room, the hours of the hotel restaurants, and the floor and location of the room. You can greatly increase the likelihood of a successful trip by making sure that the plans and reservations are in agreement with the items on your checklist. If the list is ignored, you are going to be one troubled traveller.

When travel-related issues bring you down, they are likely to bring your sales down too.

Let's get packing

If you want to reduce a broad range of potential hassles, try to pack lightly so that you only have hand luggage. This disposes of all of the difficulties associated with checking your luggage in and waiting for it to arrive at baggage reclaim, while greatly reducing the risk that it will be lost or stolen.

One of the most important principles in packing for a business trip is to keep it light.

Listed below are ten simple packing tips that can help make business travel go smoothly:

1. Always put your valuables, medicines, prescriptions, and essential sales materials in a briefcase or suitcase that you can carry on the plane. If you are bringing a laptop, plan on carrying it onto the plane. You will want to store it below the seat, since it could get bounced around in the overhead locker.

2. Save space and prevent creases by rolling your clothes into tight logs.

3. Packing your suits in dry cleaner bags can also prevent creases. Nonetheless, when you arrive at your hotel, unpack your bags immediately.

4. Save space and reduce weight by putting any cosmetics in self-sealing plastic bags. Bring shampoo and toothpaste in small travel-size containers.

5. Put your shoes in plastic bags. This can prevent scuffing, and it also keeps them away from clothes.

6. Just in case you have to check in your suitcase, attach a durable luggage label onto the handle. The label should contain either your business card or your name and business phone number. Put your name, address, and phone number inside the suitcase, too, as this can be helpful if the suitcase is lost and the label has fallen off.

7. Use tape or ribbons to make your suitcase look different from the others. This can greatly reduce the likelihood of someone picking it up by accident.

8. Be sure to remove all old baggage reclaim tags from your suitcase. You want to make it as easy as possible for the baggage handlers to know exactly where your luggage is supposed to be going.

9. Don't forget to bring a flashlight and a travel alarm clock.

There are dual-section suitcases that have a larger bottom section on wheels and a removable smaller case on top. Your clothing and larger items can go in the bottom section, and your lighter business materials in the upper section. Separated in this way, the suitcase can be taken onto the plane as hand luggage, with one section placed in the overhead locker and the other under the seat.

Your laptop matters

If you are bringing a laptop on the trip, and that is certainly the case for a growing number of salespeople, you may want to bring such items as a back-up battery, a modem saver/line tester, a modem phone cable, a power adapter, and a security lock. It is also helpful to call the hotel or hotels ahead to see what equipment (such as fax machines, printers, modem lines, and data ports) they have in the guest rooms and whether there is a business centre. If you are travelling to a foreign country, call ahead to determine whether you need to bring additional equipment for Internet access.

BEING PREPARED

As important as it is to pack light, you should still have at least one set of back-up clothing, such as an additional skirt, pair of trousers, shirt, or blouse. This was made abundantly clear at a presentation that I was scheduled to make at a conference centre in Arizona. Because of commitments in California during the day, I had to arrive at the centre quite late at night, and my presentation was fixed for 8 a.m. the next day.

A CHANGE OF APPAREL

As I walked towards the meeting room at 7.30 a.m., I made a startling discovery. All the male staff members in the centre were wearing exactly what I was wearing, right down to the shoes. This actually did not bother me – in fact, it struck me as funny – until a hotel guest asked me for directions. Then I realized that it was probably time to go for the back-up plan.

This could have been a problem, since I typically travel extremely light for an overnight trip. As light as I had packed, however, I had a back-up pair of trousers and a shirt that solved the problem. Back-up clothes are usually for more typical emergencies such as an errant glass of tomato juice. When you go on the road, however, you have to be prepared for anything.

Gliding through the airport

YOU CAN FOLLOW SOME SIMPLE STEPS *to make the most of your time at the airport and avert a broad range of hassles. The first and most obvious step is to arrive early. There is tremendous stress associated with heavy traffic, airport parking, car hire return, security checks, and long queues, any of which can cause you to be so late that your airline seat is released and you are left on the ground. To paraphrase an old adage, "the early bird catches the plane".*

Dealing with delays and cancellations

The easiest way to deal with delays and cancellations is to check with the airline before you head to the airport. You can do this by phone or through the airline's web site.

■ **Keep a close check** *on the boarding time for your flight and allow plenty of time to reach the departure gate. In large airports, the walk from departure lounge to boarding gate can be a long one.*

■ **When dealing with airport staff,** *treat them as you would a prospect. Build a rapport, establish a climate of understanding, and you may be surprised at the good treatment you receive in return.*

Not all is lost if you arrive at the airport only to find that your flight has been cancelled or severely delayed. Ask one of the airline representatives to book you on the next available flight, even if it is on a competing airline. If this is a problem for the agent, you can do it yourself by contacting your travel agent, calling the airline, or going directly to the airline's web site.

In terms of the big picture, if you want to reduce the likelihood of air travel delays in the first place, fly early in the day.

Using your sales skills

You are at a unique advantage in an airport, since your sales skills can help you in all sorts of unforeseen ways. For example, on one coast-to-coast flight I had to deal with a busy, harassed ticket agent. I immediately established a climate of goodwill. "This is a tough crowd today, isn't it?" She looked up, nodded, and said, "It sure is." I then added, "I don't see what the problem is. You're working as hard as you can. The plane's on time." I was practically reading her mind, and as she handed me the boarding pass for my seat in economy, she said, "Thanks for being so patient." A little later as boarding was about to start, I was called to the ticket counter. When I got there, the same agent said, "We've oversold economy. Would you like to fly first class?"

Playing it safe

WHEN YOU GO ON A BUSINESS TRIP, *safety should be on your mind literally every step of the way. It is easy to become casual and nonchalant about safety, and that attitude can put you at considerable risk. In addition to being highly vigilant, here are some specific actions that can help you have a safe trip.*

In the airport

If you put any of your bags down, keep them right next to you. Be on guard for any distractions such as someone bumping into you, spilling something on you, or asking you questions, as they can be diversions to distract you from an accomplice walking off with your belongings.

When you are at an airport, never let any of your belongings out of your sight.

Avoid putting any of your belongings on the security check conveyor belt until your pathway is clear and you can immediately retrieve them when they come out.

At the very least, watch your items as they go through and come out of the security check. One of the most notorious places for theft of luggage and particularly laptop computers is at this checkpoint.

If you are travelling alone, walk with a group when you get off the plane. Always be on the alert for anyone who may be watching you or following you. When planning your trip, it is safer to plan to arrive at your destination during the day.

On the plane

When you get on a plane, the first thing you should do is count the number of rows from your seat to the nearest emergency exit.

■ **If travelling alone,** *try not to look lost or anxious. Walk with an air of confidence, purpose, and direction.*

After locating the nearest emergency exit, look around to see where the other exits are situated in case of emergency.

It is also worthwhile to look around and see what else is happening on the plane. If you see anything that looks suspicious, whether in terms of a possible mechanical problem or some bizarre behaviour by a passenger, you should alert one of the flight attendants.

Because of possible interference with the aeroplane's systems, when asked to turn off electronic devices during take-offs and landings, you should do so immediately. You should also keep your seat belt fastened during the flight, except for brief stretches and visits to the lavatory.

■ **When the flight attendant** *provides the preflight information, stop what you are doing and pay attention. No matter how much flying you do, there can still be some pointers that could make the difference should an emergency arise.*

In the hire car

Aside from all the obvious concerns about driving extra carefully when in a new city, it is also important to take some additional precautions with your hire car. In the first place, you do not want a car that has any markings indicating that it is a hired car. That can be an automatic invitation for you to be followed or for the car to be vandalized after you park it.

You should always bring a mobile phone with you when driving a hired car. If you do not have one, most car hire companies will lease one to you. It can be a real lifesaver.

At the hotel

There is a broad range of safety issues associated with staying in a hotel. Some of these problems can be avoided by the preferences that you placed on your travel checklist, while others will have to be handled when you arrive. Here are some of the major safety precautions:

a   Park in a well-lit area near the foyer if possible, and give the car to a valet if you have any doubts. Either way, do not leave valuables in the car.

b   Insist on a room on an upper level, from the first up to the seventh floor. The problem with the ground floor is that people may be able to break in. And most fire ladders cannot extend beyond the seventh floor.

c It is safer to have a room with a door to the inside of the building, as opposed to a room that has a door opening to the outside. In addition, make sure that there is no easy access to your room from outside, such as an adjacent balcony or access from the roof.

d When registering, give your business address and business phone number. It is often recommended that women provide their initials instead of their first name.

e Take a look around the lobby to see if you are being watched.

f Ask the porter to show you any safety features, and check the wardrobes if you are worried about intruders.

g The room should have an extra lock or bolt on any sliding windows, along with a deadbolt lock, chain lock, and peephole in the door.

h Whenever you leave the room, close the curtains, leave a light on, leave the radio or television on, and put the Do Not Disturb sign on the door.

i Never open the door for anyone you do not know. If there is a maintenance person or other staff member at the door, call the front desk to verify that the person was sent to your room.

j Take the lift and stay out of the stairwells. If you do not like what you see in the lift for any reason at all, wait and take the next one.

■ **If you are unsure** *about parking your car, give it to valet parking.*

k If you are going out for a walk or a jog, ask the front desk person or concierge about safety in the area and where you should or should not go.

l If you have cash in the room, do not keep it in one place. It is advisable to keep your valuables in the hotel safe.

m As you approach your room, have your key out and ready.

n Make sure that you are familiar with the exits and an escape route.

To your health

WHILE IT IS EASY TO FOCUS on your financial condition during these business trips, it is important to pay attention to your physical condition as well. There are several simple steps to make your trip a healthy one in all respects.

Plane food

There are endless stories about airline food, but here is one that has a happy ending.

You can easily order airline food that is healthier, tastier, and fresher than the standard offerings. All you have to do is call the airline ahead and request a special meal.

For example, on many airlines you can order meals that are low fat, kosher, vegetarian, low calorie, low salt, all fruit, raw vegetables, or just about anything else to meet your dietary needs. As a side benefit, these special meals are typically prepared last and served first. Requesting a special meal should be included on your travelling checklist.

If you do not call the airlines ahead with a meal preference, you still have the option of buying healthier food at the airport and bringing it onto the plane. In addition, you may want to buy some high-energy bars and fruit snacks for munching during the flight.

Because of low humidity in the cabin, air travel can be dehydrating. As a result, it is important to drink a good deal of water during the flight. Most airlines are prepared to supply as much bottled water as you would like, and there is often no charge for the service.

Many people drink alcoholic beverages when travelling by air, but alcohol tends to have a dehydrating affect. Drink as little alcohol as possible during a flight.

Staying fit

When on a business trip, it is easy to forget about exercise. At the same time, there are many ways to maintain some fitness when on the road. During your flight, particularly if it is two hours or longer, you should get up briefly and walk the length of the cabin. This can be good for your circulation and for stretching your muscles.

■ **Fit in more exercise** *at the airport by taking the stairs instead of the escalator and walking instead of riding on the moving walkways.*

While in your seat, you can do *isometric exercises* to help tone up your muscles, even with your seat belt on.

There are also many opportunities to get in some exercise at your hotel. For example, if there is a jogging path nearby, you can walk or run on it. And depending upon the safety of the area, you can also take your own walking tour. In addition, many hotels have their own exercise rooms and swimming pools, and some have agreements with local fitness clubs. If you are on an extended trip, it is certainly worth taking advantage of these facilities.

> **DEFINITION**
>
> Isometric exercises *involve contracting your muscles without moving, such as by making a fist, tightening your leg muscles, or tightening your stomach muscles. These exercises are effective in toning your muscles, and they can prevent you from getting stiff during a flight.*

Give it a rest

Another important part of healthy travelling is to get enough sleep. Selecting a quiet room in a quiet hotel can help, but you may want to bring along some earplugs and eye shades as well. It is also helpful to watch your caffeine intake, particularly in the evening.

Since business travel is often tiring and draining, you should also think about taking a brief nap, as it can be good for your physical and mental health. Rather than being regarded as the hallmark of the lazy employee, naps are now increasingly viewed as an effective way to re-energize and recharge yourself. There is even a new phrase for today's naps: they are called power naps. And further, taking a nap puts you in pretty impressive company, including the likes of Thomas Edison and Winston Churchill.

DEFINITION

Jet lag is the disruption to your body clock and your body's rhythms that results from high-speed travel across several time zones.

When you return from a business trip that includes a flight over a good number of time zones, you may find that you have trouble sleeping and may be experiencing fatigue, lack of concentration, and aches in your legs and feet. These are typical symptoms of *jet lag.*

INTERNET

www.tips4trips.com

If you are looking for more travel tips, here is a site with thousands of them, all written by travellers.

There are several treatments for jet lag, yet there is not much of a consensus as to what really works. Some of these remedies are exact opposites, such as eating vs. fasting, or resting vs. exercising, while other remedies include vitamins, sunlight, drinking water, showering and bathing, and homeopathic medicine. These approaches produce varying degrees of success, but there is really not much to worry about since jet lag is a temporary condition. In most cases, given a week or so, you and your clock will be back to normal.

A simple summary

✓ If you want to avoid a wide range of problems on your business trip, the first step is to plan and organize.

✓ One particularly valuable travel tool is a continuously updated checklist that you can use as a guide for each of your trips.

✓ At every point in your business trip, from going to the airport to hiring a car to staying at a hotel, keep safety at the forefront of your mind.

✓ You can use the Internet to make all of your travel arrangements and handle many of the glitches that may arise along the way.

✓ By taking a few extra steps to monitor your diet, exercise, and rest, you can greatly increase your chances of having a healthy trip.

Chapter 19

Sales Ethics

THE SALESPERSON RUSHES into the office, crowing, "They're paying £5,000 more than they should. I added up the numbers wrongly, and they still think they got a good deal!" What is wrong here? The customer seems happy. The salesperson is happy with more commission, and the company is happy with another sale. So, what is the problem? The problem is a matter of right vs. wrong behaviour. The salesperson acted unethically by deceiving and cheating the customer. The customer may be happy now, but won't be when he finds out he has overpaid, and that the salesperson knew. In sales, you will often be faced with ethical questions. This chapter will help you answer them.

In this chapter...

✓ Ethical selling

✓ Ethics within the company

✓ Unethical selling

✓ The bottom line

AN ETHICAL APPROACH TO BUSINESS DEALINGS BRINGS ITS OWN REWARDS

Ethical selling

SOME PEOPLE NAIVELY ASK *if it is possible to be an ethical*
salesperson and a successful salesperson at the same time. The implication
is that to do well in sales, you have to be a little skilful in deceit.
Nothing could be further from the truth. If you want to be a truly
successful salesperson, you have to be ethical.

Let's be honest

Honesty is at the very core of ethical sales behaviour. If you have any interest
in building a lasting relationship with your prospects, this can be accomplished
only if you deal with them in a trustworthy and above-board style.

There can be no shades of grey on this issue. Salespeople are not regarded as being
somewhat, sort of, or generally honest. Either you are an honest salesperson, or you are
not. Therefore any information you provide to your prospects and customers about
your product capabilities, terms of sale, product availability, delivery,
warranty, or anything else having to do with a sale must be truthful.

When salespeople stray from the truth, it is not long before their
customers stray from them.

Do you care?

Ethical salespeople truly care about their prospects and customers, and they
have a real sense of concern and respect for them. The idea of somehow manipulating
their prospects and customers or forcing a product on them is simply out of
the question.

Trying to talk a prospect into buying a product that does not meet his
or her needs shows a total lack of care and concern for that prospect.
It also shows a total lack of ethics.

When you care about a prospect, you have his or her best interests and needs
in mind at all times. If your product can truly meet those interests, then the sales
process continues. If your product falls short, however, you should not be afraid to say,
"I don't think we have the right product for you. I wish I could help you on this one,
but it just doesn't work."

As you reach the end of your presentation, here is a key question to ask yourself: "Knowing what I know now, if I were the prospect, would I want this product?" If the answer is yes, keep working with the prospect; if it is no, wrap up the discussion.

At every point in the sales cycle, ethical salespeople demonstrate a high degree of empathy for their customers. By caring about their customers and understanding their needs, these salespeople are able to put themselves in a prospect's position and then make a decision as to what to do.

In all fairness

Ethical salespeople treat all of their prospects and customers fairly. They do not take advantage of those who may be in dire need of the product, such as by price fixing or forcing the customer to buy expensive add-ons at the same time. In addition, ethical salespeople do not treat prospects or customers differently based on such factors as bias, stereotypes, or other preconceived notions.

Your word is gold

Ethical salespeople are reliable and keep their commitments. If you come back later with changes or excuses as to why some of your commitments have not been met, you undermine not only the sale, but your relationship with the customer as well. In fact, many customers are going to think that your commitments were some sort of ploy to close the sale, and that you never intended to keep them in the first place.

The tendency to break commitments is a classic trademark of the unethical salesperson.

■ **As a salesperson,** *giving your word and shaking hands with a customer should be as good as a signed contract.*

Ethics within the company

IN ADDITION TO MAINTAINING ethical behaviour when dealing *with prospects and customers, it is equally important to maintain your high ethical standards within the company.*

Ethical dealings with your manager

Your company has policies, procedures, and perhaps a *code of ethics* as well. A key part of your job is to adhere to them.

For example, your manager may expect you to make a number of calls in a given time period and keep him or her posted on your progress. Some salespeople may believe that they are expected to make too many calls, or the need to report them is unreasonable. Either way, they then reckon the best way out is just to make up some numbers to get the manager off their backs. They can figure whatever they want, but the fact is that this type of behaviour is highly unethical.

Abusing company practice also falls under the heading of unethical employee behaviour. For example, a salesperson returned from a business trip and decided that she and her husband deserved a nice dinner. They both went out that night for an expensive dinner and she charged it to the company. She felt that she worked hard and they both deserved it. This is a common rationalization for unethical behaviour. This employee needs to take a second look at the code of ethics – hers as well as the company's.

■ **No matter** *how hard you have worked, charging a non-business dinner to the company account is unethical and dishonest.*

> ## DEFINITION
>
> *A code of ethics is a formal statement that spells out a company's standards and expectations regarding employee honesty, integrity, and fairness in carrying out job responsibilities. Even if a company does not have a written code, there can still be strong underlying expectations regarding employee ethics. And independent of any company's code of ethics, you bring your own personal code of ethics to work as well.*

QUESTIONING INCENTIVES

Some companies provide extra cash incentives when salespeople sell specific products that management would like to move out of the door. In one of my college jobs in a clothing shop, slow-moving garments that fell in this category were called "spiffs". Any salesperson who could sell those lime green sports jackets or the checked trousers would get his or her usual commission plus a few extra pounds.

This put the salespeople in a challenging position. On the one hand, they could make more by selling these unappealing garments, or they could act ethically and continue to focus on their customers' needs and sell the spiffs only if they were truly what a customer was seeking.

If a salesperson wanted to act ethically and continue to build a strong relationship with the customer, then he or she would ignore the spiffs. On the other hand, if a salesperson wanted to earn more money, then the spiffs would be the first item that all of their customers tried on.

Some salespeople, who had their customers dressed in checks and lime by the time they took two steps into the shop, would try to rationalize this approach by saying that they were just doing what the company wanted, often adding that most of the salespeople are doing it anyway. This is just another way of saying that they left their personal code of ethics at home.

When you are trying to figure out the most ethical action to take in these types of sales situations, the answer to one simple question will tell you what to do every time. That question is, which action will best meet my customer's needs?

You should never overlook your own personal code of ethics.

If your company expects you to engage in unethical behaviour such as using questionable sales tactics, you should speak your mind. And if that doesn't change anything, you should seriously consider leaving the company. After all, there are always jobs for good and ethical salespeople.

Ethical dealings with your fellow salespeople

You will face any number of situations that call for ethical behaviour when dealing with your fellow sales associates. Sometimes a salesperson will have insight, information, or experience with a particular customer, but wonders if he or she should help the salesperson who currently handles the account.

For example, at a sales meeting, a fellow salesperson may say that he or she will be calling on the XYZ account during the week, and will ask if anyone in the group knows anything about it. If a salesperson withholds information that could help, he or she is not being honest, thoughtful, helpful, or fair. In other words, the salesperson is not being ethical.

To go even a step further in this same case, some salespeople will decide that it is not worth providing any help to their associates if they get nothing in return. The fact is that helping associates generates all sorts of benefits. There is the obvious satisfaction associated with helping others, and there is also something positive about receiving thanks and appreciation for one's efforts. And if the objective is to receive something tangible in return, people who get help from others do not easily forget it, and a favour is usually returned many times over.

■ **Helping your colleagues** *brings enormous satisfaction. Fellow salespeople will always appreciate your efforts and will often show their gratitude by helping you in return.*

Ethics and personal skill-building

Many professional salespeople do not realize that there is an ethical issue associated with pursuing additional product knowledge.

Being a professional automatically implies that a salesperson has a high degree of expertise in his or her chosen field. By failing to stay up-to-date on product functions, changes, and plans, a salesperson is breaching professional ethics.

If you go into the field and sell products without being able to provide the customer with current, accurate, and complete information on them, you are acting unethically. After all, the customer might not have made the purchase if your product knowledge had been complete.

Unethical selling

VARIOUS TYPES OF UNETHICAL BEHAVIOUR are scorned by the public and should be scorned by you. If there is a theme that runs across all of them, it is the tendency to put the salesperson's needs first, and the customer's needs a distant second.

Most likely to deceive

A common type of behaviour found in the unethical salesperson is deceit. This can be seen in salespeople who knowingly mislead their customers to induce them to buy.

Deceitful behaviour typically comes out as gross exaggerations, false claims, and hollow promises. One of the more common unethical phrases is, "If my manager ever found out about this, he'd be furious." This automatically indicates that the salesperson lies. He or she is going to lie either to the manager or to the customer by making the statement in the first place. Besides, if a salesperson is so willing to lie to his or her manager, that certainly indicates that he or she would have no difficulty lying to a customer as well.

Unethical salespeople also demonstrate their deceit when they berate the competition. They have no qualms about understating what the competitors can do, while overstating what they cannot. Customers generally are not fooled by these comparisons, and all that really happens is that the salesperson's credibility is diminished further.

The only time that your competitors should be discussed is when your customer brings them up. When this occurs, all of your comments should be based on fact.

The pressure cooker

Even if the prospect is not ready to buy or does not want to buy at all, the unethical salesperson presses forward aggressively. The salesperson does not listen to what the prospect says, but is merely waiting for the prospect to stop talking. As soon as this occurs, the salesperson starts pushing again. The prospect's needs, desires, wants, or wishes mean nothing. The only thing that has meaning for this salesperson is to close this sale and move on to the next.

These types of salespeople use phrases such as "If you don't act right now…" and "I'm going to write this up now just to show you…" and "This is your last chance."

They wave a pen in the prospect's face, push the contract right in front of the prospect, and then say, "Come on, sign it." For the unethical salesperson, selling is a battle and the prospect must be conquered. The sign of surrender is the signed contract.

The attitude of many of these salespeople is that it is a tough world out there, and a salesperson has to resort to any measures to make a sale. Presumably, that means resorting to a sacrifice of ethics. It may well be a tough world out there, but that just means that a salesperson has to work harder. There is no way in the world a professional salesperson would sacrifice his or her personal ethics to make a sale.

Tricks of the trade

There are all sorts of tricks that unethical salespeople use to convince an unwary prospect to buy. For example, some use a "lowball" technique, which uses a low price to capture the prospect's interest. By the time the prospect has listened to a long presentation, that lowball price is not low anymore. At each step of the presentation, the salesperson has inched it higher and higher. By the end, the weary prospect may overpay for something that he or she was not even looking for in the first place.

Another unethical sales tactic is called "bait and switch". In this case, the salesperson gets the prospect's interest with a seemingly good product at a good price, but the product is not available at all. The prospect may hear "We don't carry it anymore", "We won't get any more for 6 months", or "It wasn't that good anyhow", and then the salesperson tries to push the prospect into buying a higher priced item. The good news from the ethics standpoint is that this kind of tactic tends to run foul of the law.

When unethical salespeople are asked a question that they cannot accurately answer, another trick that they deploy is to confidently make up any response that fits their own needs. When asked a technical question that is far beyond their understanding of the product, they typically respond with something glib, such as "Of course, we do that all the time." When an ethical salesperson does not know the answer to a prospect's question, he or she says so and then gets back to the prospect with an answer as soon as possible.

Unscrupulous salespeople deploy countless sales tricks, including fictional stories to generate sympathy from the prospect, bogus testimonials, and references to customers who are not customers at all. When these salespeople try to book a sale, they use every trick in the book to do so.

INTERNET

www.charactercounts.org

This is an excellent site for articles, books, reports, and seminars on ethics, as well as a forum for discussing ethical issues. You can also access copies of radio commentaries by the noted ethicist Michael Josephson.

AN ETHICAL DEED

When one insurance salesperson closed a sale with a particular association, some of the association's leaders believed that the signed contract was too one-sided in the insurance company's favour. With some trepidation, the association leaders asked the salesperson to come to a follow-up meeting to see if some adjustments could be made to the agreement. The salesperson came to the meeting, sat down at the table, took the contract out of his briefcase, placed it on the table, and then tore it up. "Gentlemen", he said, "let's start again."

People throughout the industry talked about this deed for years, and it led to far more business and referrals. He certainly could have demanded that the signed contract be followed, and for a short period he may have made more money. Over the long term, however, his ethical action was far more profitable in every respect.

Here comes the bribe

One of the most outrageous ploys used by unethical salespeople is to bribe a customer. This can come in many forms, including cash payments, gifts, and even trips.

When companies have sales contests and offer prizes to the salespeople for various levels of sales, some of the more unscrupulous members of the team offer a few of these prizes to their customers for buying additional products during the contest's time period.

On the other hand, the inducement to engage in unethical behaviour can come from a prospect or customer. For example, there are plenty of salespeople who have been advised that if they want to make the sale, they will have to give a *kickback* to the prospect.

Never accept any kind of remuneration as a prospect's condition of a sale. Walk away instead.

> **DEFINITION**
>
> *In sales, a kickback is a percentage or sum of money that a salesperson has agreed to give back to the buyer as a condition of the sale itself. Speaking of percentages, kickbacks are 100 per cent unethical, immoral, and illegal.*

In the trade, buyers who require kickbacks as a condition of sale are often referred to as "being on the take". When they are discovered, they frequently end up being on trial rather than being on the take. And this story tends to have an equally unhappy ending for the salesperson.

The bottom line

BEYOND THE SATISFACTION *associated with treating your prospects and customers in an honest, fair, and caring style, there are some compelling economic reasons for a salesperson to act ethically.*

Good news travels fast

One of your most powerful marketing tools is being known in your industry as an ethical salesperson. Customers talk about the various companies and salespeople with whom they deal, and being described as a salesperson of integrity can be a major source of additional sales and referrals.

Bad news travels faster

When salespeople engage in unethical actions, it is usually just a matter of time before their exploits are discovered. Customers do not regard lies, deceit, misrepresentations, overstatements, and other types of self-serving behaviour too fondly. When they discover that a salesperson has acted unethically, it spells the end of the sale, the end of future business, the end of referrals, and the end of the salesperson's good name.

■ **Customers will talk**... *and you could be the topic of conversation. Protect your good reputation as a salesperson by acting ethically and responsibly at all times.*

Just as customers talk about the ethical actions of the salespeople with whom they deal, they also talk about the questionable actions as well. It does not take long for bad news to travel, and a salesperson's reputation can be irreparably damaged practically overnight.

When the sales manager of a firm in the clothing industry mentioned to the company president that he was thinking about hiring a particular individual who had applied for a sales position, the applicant's name was familiar to the president.

With a little more thought, the president remembered that this salesperson had been deeply involved in a kickback scandal some 10 years before. The president had no interest in hiring this individual all these years later. A salesperson's unethical behaviour clearly has long-term costs.

■ **If in doubt** *about whether a sales action is or is not ethical, ask yourself how you would like to see details of this action in tomorrow's paper.*

A simple summary

✔ To be truly successful in sales, you have to honour your commitments and act ethically.

✔ Ethical salespeople adhere to their company's code of ethics as well as to their own personal code of ethics.

✔ Unethical salespeople put their own needs first, and the prospect's needs a distant second.

✔ Treating your customers ethically is highly rewarding in a personal and economic sense, while treating them unethically has tremendous short-term and long-term costs.

✔ If you wonder about the ethics associated with a particular sales practice, ask yourself how your actions would look on the front page of the newspaper.

Chapter 20

Into the Future

AS YOU EXPERIENCE SUCCESS in sales over the years, you are likely to have the opportunity to move into management. Many people believe, however, that the skills, abilities, and motivation needed for successful selling are different from those needed for success as a manager. This, though, is simply an outdated view. The fact is that good salespeople can make great managers, and many highly successful managers and company leaders continue to come up through sales. This chapter is going to show you some of the key ways that you can use your sales skills to become a highly effective manager.

In this chapter...

✓ Communicating with the troops

✓ The leading edge

✓ Planning for success

✓ It's simply the people

A SALESPERSON'S ABILITY TO COMMUNICATE IS A VALUED SKILL IN MANAGEMENT

Communicating with the troops

NUMEROUS STUDIES SHOW THAT MANAGERS *spend the vast majority of their time communicating with others. Managers who are inexperienced, unskilled, or unconfident in this area are destined to have problems with their staff. The communication skills that you develop in a sales role, however, fit perfectly in a managerial role.*

Are you listening?

One of the most important skills you possess as a salesperson is your ability to listen to what your prospects and customers have to say. This is a skill that you can directly apply to managing. Employees today want to sense that they are being heard. They want to feel that they are being treated like valued resources, and that their ideas, input, and suggestions truly mean something.

■ **Giving your employees** *numerous opportunities to present their ideas, listening carefully to what they have to say, and then applying their input whenever you can, directly parallels what you do with the input your prospects and customers provide.*

One of the most common complaints employees have about their managers is a lack of communication.

Since you are already using a partnering approach in selling, you are conditioned to treat your prospects and customers as valued resources. It is simple to apply this approach to managing, and to let your employees know that you value their input.

To listen to their employees, managers have to be accessible, available, and visible to them. Some managers tend to hide in their offices and hope that the employees' issues, questions, or concerns will just go away.

By nature, managers who have been in sales are not interested in sitting in an office at all. In fact, this was one of the concerns about promoting salespeople into management in the first place. Will they learn to sit in an office? Well, that is exactly what a manager should not be doing today. The best managers genuinely enjoy talking with the team members, asking them questions, and giving them ideas and suggestions. And that is second nature to salespeople.

Effective managers are those who get out of their offices and have plenty of direct contact with their employees.

Respect and trust

These are two of the most important words in management today. In fact, many experts contend that respect and trust are at the very heart of effective management. In your selling experience, this is exactly how you treat your prospects and customers. Respect and trust are the critical building blocks for loyalty, dedication, and commitment from them. The same applies to dealings with your employees.

Many companies today are issuing pronouncements that they want all of their employees to be treated like customers.

Senior-level executives in these companies recognize that many salespeople treat their customers extremely well, and they would like to see this type of treatment extended to everyone who works for the company. This approach is automatically part of the mix for the managers who have a sales background.

■ **For the manager** *who is experienced in sales, presenting information to employees is one of many opportunities to use some of his or her persuasiveness and trust-building skills.*

Power of persuasion

There are going to be times when a manager will need to present information very persuasively to his or her employees. It may be that the announcement of territory changes, new compensation plans, or adjustments in various sales programmes needs a convincing explanation. For a manager who has had no sales experience, speaking persuasively to his or her employees can be a daunting task. Managers who have had sales experience know exactly how to do it.

Their negotiating tools may include pacing, stories and metaphors, emotionally charged words, keeping a climate of goodwill, and letting the employees see the added value associated with the change. In these types of discussions with employees, your ability to ask questions, handle objections, and close a sale can easily turn potentially difficult problems into manageable situations.

Handling meetings

Another concern about the promotion of salespeople into management is that they are not really familiar with group dynamics and what it takes to lead a group. This criticism overlooks the fact that much selling today is to groups. As a salesperson, you developed skills for setting agendas, making presentations, handling questions, and identifying informal leaders, and these are all essential skills for running a meeting.

■ **Convincing groups** *of people that you are worth listening to and that your ideas are worth following are sales skills that directly apply to management.*

The leading edge

YOUR EXPERIENCE IN SALES *can truly build your* leadership *skills as well. Many people do not look at leadership from the sales standpoint, but selling actually plays a critical role when you are leading others.*

Your employees' needs

To effectively lead others, you need to have an understanding of their needs, motivation, and drive. The techniques that you use to learn about your prospects' and customers' needs, particularly those used to observe, ask questions, follow up, and even those used for some trial closes, are the very techniques that you can use as a leader.

If a salesperson has a strong need for recognition, but you believe that he or she is motivated by money, your leadership efforts are doomed to fail. Certainly the salesperson wants to earn more money, but he or she may have additional key motivators as well.

As a leader, you cannot actually motivate an employee at all. Employees motivate themselves. Your job is to understand the employee's individual needs, and then link the fulfilment of these needs to the goals that you would like him or her to meet.

For example, looking back at the salesperson whose needs are focused heavily on recognition, the idea would be to work with him or her to set some sales goals, and then link the achievement of these goals in part to various awards and corporate attention.

Mix and match

When you meet your prospects and customers, you vary your style depending upon their needs, interests, objectives, and general style of interaction. This flexible approach to selling also applies to management, as the most effective managers today vary their leadership styles depending on the individual employee they may be supervising, the nature of the decision being made, and the overall work situation.

■ Managing employees
effectively involves tailoring your approach according to the individual's needs. New staff, in particular, may need close supervision, while more senior members of the team may prefer to work more independently.

When managers ask about the "best" leadership style, the answer is that there isn't just one. And the same answer applies if someone asks about the "best" sales style.

Parallel to what you do in sales, the best approach in management is to try to learn as much as possible about your employees, and then use a style that best fits their needs and the situation at hand.

Following up

One of the most important skills that you develop as a salesperson is your ability to follow up your customers and prospects. For example, if you have finished a sales presentation and the final outcome is that the prospect is going to meet his or her key associates and then get back to you, it will not be long before you want to follow that up. Perhaps you will make a phone call or send an e-mail, but you will have a system, high-tech or not, to let you know that it is time to get in touch.

The same idea applies in the management process. One example is in the area of delegating. Perhaps you delegated a project to one of your employees. That would not be the last time that this person sees or hears of you. You would have various dates where you would get back in touch with him or her to see how things are going. If the employee needs more help, guidance, assistance, or support, you would provide it. In fact, this is one of the ways to treat your employee like a customer.

Solving employee problems

Managers spend considerable time handling difficult employees as well as problems and complaints. This is an area where your sales skills play a particularly important role.

Just as you do when dealing with an upset customer, let an upset employee come up with some proposed solutions to resolve any issues, and then let him or her know what your next step will be. As in sales, keeping the employee informed as to what is going on is essential in this process.

When dealing with interpersonal difficulties between employees, your sales skills can play a problem-solving and mediating role as well.

The first and most important step is to use your listening and observational skills, and then ask plenty of questions to determine the real needs of the parties. Sometimes this approach can be all that is needed for employees themselves to understand the situation better and develop a solution of their own.

■ **You can handle** *an upset employee in just the same way that you handle an upset prospect or customer. Let him or her talk, and then use empathy and pacing to create a climate of goodwill.*

When dealing with difficult employees, your skills as a negotiator can come into play, particularly in terms of your ability to develop win-win solutions.

For example, two employees are in an argument. A manager without a sales background sits down with both of them and dictates a solution, saying "If the two of you keep this up, I'm just going to make a decision and one or both of you will have to go. As it is, I'm putting this whole incident in your files." A manager who came up through sales approaches the situation quite differently, saying "I can see that you are both upset. I want to meet you individually, and then the three of us are going to talk. I know we can resolve this."

Notice the sales techniques laced into the second manager's comments. In the first place, this manager generated instant agreement and a climate of goodwill by saying that he or she could see that both employees were upset. This manager looked at the reality of the situation, and all that the two combatants could do was agree. The manager showed a good deal of respect and trust by saying that he or she wanted to meet both employees individually, and the manager closed the discussion with positive expectations and team orientation by use of the word "we".

Planning for success

IN THE PAST, IT WAS BELIEVED that the large amounts of paperwork, administrative details, and planning and organizing responsibilities of a managerial position were in direct contradiction with the needs, interests, and abilities of most salespeople. Salespeople would much rather deal with people than paper. That is one perception about the suitability of salespeople in management that may have been accurate in the past.

However, that perception is completely nullified because of the growing use of Sales Force Automation (SFA) and the high-tech options now available to salespeople as well as sales managers.

■ **Virtually all** *of the old sales management functions that required countless hours of endless paperwork can now be handled quickly, easily, professionally, and without a single sheet of paper.*

SFA can help salespeople handle all aspects of selling, from prospecting to closing. And SFA can help managers oversee, monitor, and guide staff in each of these areas. The once time-consuming administrative responsibilities for a sales manager can now be handled through an integrated system that includes setting objectives, planning, scheduling, forecasting, managing contacts, sharing information, preparing proposals, preparing reports and calendars, and keeping records.

Managing change

In today's dynamic work environments, one of the more important aspects of management is the ability to help employees handle the numerous changes that can bombard them almost daily. At the same time, effective management implies that you will be creating and introducing any number of new programmes, concepts, and policies to help your team perform more successfully. It also implies that you will be able to do this while generating a minimum of resistance from your staff.

■ **Managers with sales backgrounds** *typically have solid skills and experience when it comes to effectively introducing change and helping people adjust to it.*

RESISTANCE AND THE UNKNOWN

It is widely believed that people resist change. In fact, resistance to change is often described as being part of human nature. The only problem with this belief is that people do not automatically resist change.

For example, let's assume that you are going to face a huge change tomorrow. It is going to change just about everything at work, as well as your home life and relationships with friends. Are you feeling some resistance already? If you are, that's normal. What if this huge change is that you are going to win a £20 million lottery? Presumably this would mean a rather substantial change in your life. Now are you going to resist it? Of course not.

So people do not automatically resist change. The main source of resistance to change is the unknown. When people are given a good deal of information about a planned change, they are far less likely to resist it. And any resistance is reduced further if people have an opportunity to present some of their own ideas and suggestions. This is how salespeople introduce change, and it is a great way for managers to do it too.

As a manager with roots in sales, you will be able to manage change effectively because your sales experience has shown you how to draw out people's concerns, use positively charged words and pacing to help others feel more comfortable, and then listen carefully to their ideas and suggestions.

Salespeople excel at managing change because the sales process is based on introducing a change into a prospect's company. Salespeople who try to force a change on prospects inevitably fail, as do managers who try to force changes on their groups.

INTERNET

www.salesandmarketing
.com
www.salesdoctors.com

You can find a wide range of valuable sales management information, articles, and support resources at these online magazine sites.

You're the coach

Another essential role that managers are playing today is that of coach. Your sales skills provide you with a number of strengths in this area. In the first place, as a successful salesperson, you can demonstrate or model your successful techniques to your team members when you go on joint sales calls. As we discussed in Chapter 17, learning from one's manager is one of the most effective sources of employee training and development.

■ **Going on joint sales calls** *with your team provides them with excellent opportunities to observe, learn, and practise sales techniques that really work.*

Secondly, your ability to ask questions, listen, and understand your employees as individuals will help you coach them. With your insights into their needs and abilities, you can tailor the guidance you provide to meet their particular learning styles and abilities. In sales, an important role with your prospects and customers is that of trainer, and you can directly apply those same skills as a manager to educate and develop your team.

It's simply the people

THE BOTTOM LINE ON BEING SUCCESSFUL *in sales and management comes down to one word: people. Your success as a salesperson can help you develop your ability to deal effectively with just about anyone, and that ability is critical for success in management.*

Never believe the claim sometimes put forward that salespeople do not make good managers.

Professional salespeople possess many enviable characteristics. They are:

● Knowledgeable	● Ethical	● Honest
● Caring	● Excellent listeners	● Reliable
● Fair	● Concerned about others	● Respectful
● Trusting	● Accessible	● Responsive

- Communicative
- Persuasive
- Quality conscious
- Dedicated
- Team players
- Service oriented
- Energetic
- Organized
- Positive
- Persistent
- Goal oriented
- Loyal
- Creative

Armed with all the characteristics of a successful sales professional, you will do well in sales. You will also do well in management. And you will do well in life.

A simple summary

✓ Your skills as a salesperson will contribute directly to your success as a manager.

✓ The most effective managers communicate effectively, listen to their employees, value their employees' input, and treat their staff with respect and trust. Through your experiences with prospects and customers, you already know how to deal with people this way.

✓ Since a growing number of companies want their employees to be treated like customers, your experience with customers gives you the best foundation for doing so.

✓ Your ability to understand your prospects – and to vary your style dependent upon their needs and the work situation – is an essential component of effective leadership.

✓ The paperwork and administrative details associated with managerial responsibilities were once the main reasons for overlooking salespeople for managerial positions. With Sales Force Automation, that concern is all but eliminated.

✓ The essence of successful management is to deal effectively with people, and that is the essence of successful selling, too.

Other resources

Books

Advanced Selling Strategies: The Proven System of Sales Ideas, Methods, and Techniques Used by Top Salespeople Everywhere
Brian Tracy,
Simon & Schuster, 1995

Bottom-Line Selling: The Sales Professional's Guide to Improving Customer Profits
Jack Malcolm,
Contemporary Books, 1999

Close More Sales! Persuasion Skills that Boost Your Selling Power
Mike Stewart,
American Management Association, 1999

Closing Techniques (That Really Work!)
Stephan Schiffman,
Adams Media Corporation, 1999

Cold Calling Techniques (That Really Work!)
Stephan Schiffman,
Adams Media Corporation, 1999

Consultative Selling: The Hanan Formula for High-Margin Sales at High Levels
Mack Hanan,
American Management Association, 1999

The 8 Best Practices of High-Performing Salespeople
Norm Trainor,
Highrise Books, 1998

How to Make Hot Cold Calls: Your Calling Card to Personal Success
Steven J. Schwartz,
Stoddart Pub. Co., 1997

The New Strategic Selling: The Unique Sales System Proved Successful by the World's Best Companies
Stephen S. Heiman, Diane Sanchez, with Tad Tuleja,
Kogan Page, 1998

Power Base Selling: Secrets of an Ivy League Street Fighter
Jim Holden,
John Wiley & Sons, 1999

Prospecting for Gold: 101 Ways to Market Yourself and Strike Gold in Sales
Tom Metcalf,
Oasis Press, 1999

Rethinking the Sales Force: Redefining Selling to Create and Capture Customer Value
Neil Rackham and John R. De Vincentis,
McGraw-Hill, 1999

The Sales Bible: The Ultimate Sales Resource
Jeffrey H. Gitomer,
William Morrow and Company, Inc., 1994

Secrets of Power Negotiating for Sales People: Inside Secrets from a Master Negotiator
Roger Dawson,
Career Press, 1999

Selling to VITO: the Very Important Top Officer
Anthony Parinello,
Adams Media Corporation, 1999

Selling with Integrity: Reinventing Sales Through Collaboration, Respect, and Serving
Sharon Drew Morgen,
Berkley Books, 1999

The Six-Hat Salesperson: A Dynamic Approach to Producing Top Results in Every Selling Situation
David J. Kahle,
AMACOM, 1999

Solution Selling: Creating Buyers in Difficult Selling Markets
Michael T. Bosworth,
McGraw-Hill, 1995

Spin Selling: The Best-Validated Sales Method Available Today. Developed From Research Studies of 35,000 Sales Calls. Used by the Top Sales Forces Across the World.
Neil Rackham,
McGraw-Hill, 1998

Stop Telling, Start Selling: How to Use Customer-Focused Dialogue to Close Sales
Linda Richardson,
McGraw-Hill, 1998

Unlimited Selling Power: How to Master Hypnotic Selling Skills
Donald Moine and Kenneth Lloyd,
Prentice Hall, 1990

Audiobooks

Advanced Selling Strategies: The Proven System Practiced by Top Salespeople
Brian Tracy,
Simon & Schuster (Audio), 1995

5 Steps to Successful Selling
Zig Ziglar,
Simon & Schuster (Audio), 1995

Getting Through: Cold Calling Techniques to Get Your Foot in the Door
Stephan Schiffman,
Simon & Schuster (Audio), 1993

Mastering the Art of Selling
Tom Hopkins,
Harper Audio, 1995

The Psychology of Selling: The Art of Closing the Sale
Brian Tracy,
Simon & Schuster (Audio), 1995

Sell Your Way to the Top
Zig Ziglar,
Simon & Schuster (Audio), 1994

25 Sales Secrets of Highly Successful Salespeople
Stephan Schiffman,
Simon & Schuster (Audio), 1998

Sales web sites

THERE ARE MANY SITES ON THE INTERNET *that deal with selling.*
The following list contains some of the most useful, including some international
pages. Please note, however, that due to the fast-changing nature of the Net,
some of those listed may be defunct by the time you read this. Happy surfing!

www.askjeeves.co.uk
If you are interested in tracking down the answer to a question that could be of interest to your prospect, just ask it here.

www.businessadviceonline.org
www.enterprisezone.org.uk
www.imarketinc.com
www.infospace.com
www.justsell.com
www.salestalk.co.uk
If you are looking for sales leads, be sure to visit these web sites.

www.business-critique.co.uk
www.eurosmartz.co.uk
www.opportunit.co.uk
www.pts.com
www.salestalk.co.uk
These are some of the online business applications for SFA.

www.businesstravel.com
www.businesstraveller.com
www.expedia.co.uk
www.priceline.co.uk
www.roomfindersusa.com
These are just a few of the numerous sites with online booking services for flights, car hire, and hotel accommodation.

www.businessweek.com
www.digitallook.com
www.fortune.com
www.ft.com
www.wsj.com
Here are some web sites that can give you a broad range of corporate financial information, including marketplace trends, industry forecasts, and key personnel changes.

www.charactercounts.org
This is an excellent site for articles, books, reports, and seminars on ethics, as well as a forum for discussing ethical issues.

www.cpa.co.uk
www.dnb.com
These web sites provide information about a company's credit as well as its overall financial picture.

www.crmassist.com
www.onyx.com
www.telemagic.com
These sites offer a broad listing of CRM and SFA software.

www.crmmagazine.com
If you're looking for more information on CRM, this is the site to visit.

www.easy4gifts.co.uk
www.image2000plus.com
These web sites help salespeople select appropriate business gifts.

www.excite.com
www.google.com
www.hotbot.co.uk
www.yahoo.co.uk

Use these search engines to find the web sites of various companies as well as sites that may have additional information on those companies.

www.fool.co.uk
www.ft.com

Check out these sites to see if there are some profits warnings or problematic articles about your hot prospects.

www.gisajob.com
www.stepstone.co.uk
www.totaljobs.com

These are some of the numerous web sites that provide listings of sales positions.

www.mapquest.com

One of the best ways to map out where you are going is to visit this site.

www.millerheiman.com
www.tomhopkins.com
www.tracyint.com
www.tsuccess.dircon.co.uk
www.wilsonlearning.com

These are some of the best sites for sales training, and several offer online courses, along with articles, books, tapes, and opportunities to register for seminars.

www.monster.co.uk

This key site provides an opportunity for salespeople to interact with other sales professionals and with potential employers.

www.oracle.com
www.pivotal.com
www.saleslogix.com
www.siebel.com

These are client server applications, providing the full range of CRM support.

www.presentationsonline.com

This is the site to visit if you need help in putting a sales presentation together.

www.salesandmarketing.com
www.salesdoctors.com

You can find all sorts of valuable information, articles, and support resources for sales and sales management at these online magazine sites.

www.salesdoctors.com

This site has an interactive forum for salespeople to network and discuss sales problems, strategies, and solutions, as well as to share leads.

www.salesproposals.com

If you need some help preparing a sales proposal, you should visit this site for articles, design tips, books, and proposal design software.

www.tips4trips.com

Here is a site with 1,000 travel tips, all written by experienced travellers.

www.toastmasters.org

This is the site to visit if you are looking for tips on public speaking and related educational materials.

www.tsuccess.dircon.co.uk

This site offers a broad range of seminars, books, videotapes, audiotapes, and software programs to help build your negotiating skills.

A simple glossary

Accessories Typically offered when the sale has closed, these are additional items that help the product do what it is actually supposed to do.

Action plan Specific steps that you can follow all the way to your goal.

Action words Words that imply a high level of activity, energy, and enthusiasm.

Add-ons Also offered when the sale has closed, these are additional products that the prospect may want.

Boilerplate A printing term that describes sections from one sales proposal that are dropped in their entirety into another.

Boiler room operation Sales operations that cram a pack of salespeople into a room, hook them up to phone lines that span the globe, and turn them loose with an auto-dialler and a canned speech.

Brainstorm The process of bringing a group of people together to openly discuss a problem or dilemma, and then develop as many strategies as possible to deal with it.

Buyer's remorse A prospect's serious regret at having made a particular purchase, often resulting from a feeling of having been pushed, tricked, or manipulated.

CD-ROM business cards New Age cards that fit right into a standard CD-ROM tray on a computer.

CD-ROM sales presentations All of your charts, slides, and graphics can be downloaded onto your laptop and then plugged into a lightweight projector to make a customized presentation.

Climate of concurrence Using questions, pacing, stories, and power words to generate "yes" responses and an overall feeling of agreement throughout the presentation.

Close ratio A formula that measures the number of sales that you close in relation to the number of prospects that you contact.

Closing a sale A sale is closed when the prospect has agreed to buy what the salesperson is selling.

Closing questions Various types of questions that ask for the order.

Code of ethics A formal statement or set of expectations spells out a company's standards and expectations regarding employee honesty, integrity, and fairness in carrying out job responsibilities. You bring your own personal code of ethics to work too.

Cold calls Phone calls to prospects whom the salesperson does not know and for whom there has been no referral or introduction.

Commission Upon completion of a sale, this is the fee or percentage of the sales price that is paid to a salesperson for the service that he or she provided.

Confirming questions Enquiries that are placed at the end of a statement and change it into a question that automatically generates a "yes" from the prospect.

Conversational hypnosis Persuasive skills used by some salespeople that include pacing, trust building, emotionally charged words, and repetition to create a heightened state of suggestibility in their prospects.

Customer An individual who has bought your product.

Customer Relationship Management (CRM) A set of high-tech tools used to plan, organize, and automate all aspects of marketing, sales, and support.

CV (curriculum vitae) A neat, succinct, accurate, and highly readable summary of your work experience that includes your objectives, qualifications, education, and achievements.

Electronic CV A CV (curriculum vitae) that is prepared specifically for online submission.

Emotionally charged words Expressions and words that can set off an instantly positive reaction or negative reaction from your prospect.

Experiential learning An educational approach based on giving trainees the opportunity to learn by doing.

Extreme it out Taking any sales-related information and presenting it in minimum or maximum terms, such as by breaking down 2,000 cold calls a year to ten cold calls a day.

Flinch factor A subtle movement by a prospect indicating that he or she has an objection.

Formal leader An individual who has the established title, role, and responsibility to provide direction, guidance, and influence over a group.

Goals The specific, prioritized, and measurable outcomes that an individual seeks, supported by action plans, deadlines, and a clear commitment.

Golden rule of selling Sell to others as you would have others sell to you.

Inbound sales call A call that is made from a prospect to a salesperson, often resulting from advertising, promotions, publicity, and referrals.

Informal leader An individual who, by virtue of such factors as his or her own charisma, expertise, or personal relationships, has a high degree of influence over a group.

Intranet A company's own web site that is used only for employees and internal company matters.

Isometric exercises Body conditioning that involves contracting your muscles without moving, such as making a fist or tightening your leg muscles.

Jet lag A disruption to your body clock and your body rhythms that results from high-speed travel across several time zones. Symptoms include fatigue, lack of concentration, and aches in your legs and feet.

Just noticeable differences (JNDs) The subtle changes in your performance that appear over time and tell you a great deal about the path you are on and where you may need additional training.

Kickback A percentage or sum of money that a salesperson has agreed to give back to the buyer as a condition of the sale itself. It is 100 per cent unethical, immoral, and illegal.

Leadership The process of influencing the behaviour of others in order to maximize performance and meet the company's goals.

Leading questions Inquiries that are designed to generate a "yes" or a "no" response.

Metaphor A figure of speech where a word or a phrase that typically means one thing is used to convey another, forming a comparison.

Mission statement A company's expression of its vision, values, and objectives.

Motivation The process that activates and directs your behaviour.

Multilevel listening Using all of your senses in the listening process.

Multitasking The ability to handle more than one work-related responsibility at the same time.

Needs analysis A formal procedure used in the training field to determine the areas in which employees need additional training.

Negotiation A discussion designed to bring about a mutual agreement or settlement.

Network A wide circle of fellow professionals, associates, and friends who form a social base for mutual support, guidance, and referrals.

One-liner A concise sentence that describes the superiority of your product and why your prospect should buy it.

Open-ended questions Enquiries that typically start with "Who", "What", "Where", "When", and "How", and cannot be answered with a "yes" or "no".

Outbound sales call A call that a salesperson makes to a prospect.

Pacing Also called mirroring, this is the trust-building process of matching the verbal and non-verbal behaviour of your prospect, even matching what your prospect is doing and feeling.

Performance appraisal A formal session with your manager to review your work and jointly set goals and plans for the next period.

Pipeline All of your business that is currently in the works, ranging from the earliest preparation steps to sales that are right at the point of closing.

Power An individual's potential to influence others.

Proactive behaviour Taking steps in advance to either prevent or control a problem.

Product benefits The aspects of your product that can meet the prospect's needs.

Product features Every aspect of your product, all the way down to its size, shape, and colour.

Prospect A potential customer.

Prospecting Seeking out potential customers.

Qualifying Determining if the prospect has the needs, wants, authority, and ability to buy the product from you.

Reactive behaviour Action that is taken in response to a problem that has arisen.

Referral An introduction to a prospect that is provided by an individual who is known and presumably respected by the prospect.

Rejection When your prospect refuses to buy what you are selling.

Retention rate The percentage of customers that you keep over a specified period of time.

Role playing A training technique in which the trainer and trainees act out different parts in order to illustrate various points and facilitate learning.

Sales cycle Each of the sequential steps in the selling process, starting with prospecting, and then moving to qualifying, analyzing needs, presenting, handling objections, closing, and then servicing and following up.

Sales Force Automation (SFA) Automating the full range of sales activities, from prospecting all the way through to the close of the sale.

Sales quota A specific amount of production that management expects from you.

Sales script book A line-by-line summary of the actual language that a salesperson can use in every part of the sales process, from the opening line to the close.

Sales storytelling Using compelling stories in your presentation.

Selling Providing needed goods and services to others for a fee.

Serendipity Finding an unexpected positive, fortunate, and pleasurable outcome from a situation that seemed to hold no such outcome in store.

Slump A prolonged period of time in which your sales performance is in a state of decline.

Territory A particular geographical area for which a salesperson is responsible.

Then, Now, and Tomorrow (TNT) questions Enquiries that are designed to help you learn more about your prospect's or customer's needs by focusing on past, present, and future issues, developments, and objectives.

Three "R's" of listening To be a better listener, Repeat, Rephrase, and Remember.

To-do list A written or electronic listing that gives you a clear and prioritized itemization of what you wish to accomplish in a given day.

Trial closing questions Enquiries posed throughout a sales presentation to measure the prospect's opinion and point of view, as well as to identify objections.

Value added The ways that your product will bring additional worth to the prospect in excess of the price, calculated as the sum of the benefits minus the cost.

Verification Validating information from your prospect or customer, while also identifying needs and generating "yes" responses.

Warm leads Prospects that are generated by a company's marketing programmes.

"What-if" game A preparation technique to come up with answers to the most difficult questions that your prospects could possibly ask.

Win-win In negotiations, this is the outcome when both parties feel that their needs have been met.

Index

Acknowledgments

Author's acknowledgments

Of course, there are people who helped make writing this book much simpler for me. The best place to start is with my friend, colleague, and editor Marc Robinson. He was a constant source of excellent advice, support, and humour. Also on the editing front, I offer major thanks to Ruth Strother. I greatly appreciate the help provided by so many people on the DK team, including LaVonne Carlson, Jennifer Williams, David Tombesi-Walton, Simon Murrell, and, at Cooling Brown, Amanda Lebentz and Helen Ridge. Thanks are also due to Diane Mark, Product Manager at salesforce.com, Medo Eldin, Director of Marketing at shotmaker.com, and Jonathan L. Wolff, attorney at law. To Harriet Lloyd, thanks for sharing your insights about dad. A special thanks goes to Jessica, Stacey, and Josh for letting me get my homework done. And, I am grateful in every respect to my personal editor, librarian, and wife, Roberta Winston Lloyd.

Packager's acknowledgments

Cooling Brown would like to thank Alison Bolus, Patsy North, and Fiona Green for their editorial assistance; Hilary Krag and Elly King for their design assistance; and Barry Robson for illustrating the dogs, and bringing them so vividly to life.

Index
Patricia Coward.

Picture credits
Photodisc: 2, 14, 20–21, 22, 24, 26, 28, 31, 33, 36, 39, 42, 52, 54, 56, 61, 63, 66, 68, 72, 73, 74, 81, 86–87, 88, 93, 100, 103, 108, 110, 114, 119, 122, 129, 132, 136, 138, 140, 144, 147, 148, 152, 154–155, 156, 158–159, 160, 167, 172, 177, 178, 182, 186, 194, 197, 200, 202, 208, 216–217, 218, 220, 222, 227, 229, 236, 241, 250, 252, 255, 256, 261, 264, 270, 274–275, 279, 284–285, 286, 289, 291, 293, 300, 303, 306–307, 309, 310, 312, 314, 317, 318, 324, 326, 331, 335, 336, 338.

Additional photography
Andy Crawford, Steve Gorton, Susanna Price, and Tim Ridley.